Origins of the Kurdish Genocide

Kurdish Societies, Politics, and International Relations

Series Editor: Bahar Baser, Coventry University

This series strives to produce high quality academic work on Kurdish society and politics, and the international relations of Kurdish organizations and governments (Kurdistan Region of Iraq) both regionally and globally. The books in this series explore themes of contemporary relevance as well as presenting historical trajectories of the Kurdish populations. The series contributes to the rapidly growing literature on this topic with books that are original and make substantial empirical and theoretical contribution. The series' main focus are the Kurds and the social, cultural and political environment in which Kurdish issues play out. The subjects that we are interested in include but are not limited to: the history of the Kurds, Kurdish politics and policies within Iraq, Iran, Turkey, and Syria, as well as Kurdish politics and their impact on the international relations of the Middle East. This series also publishes books on the policies of the USA, Europe, and other countries towards Kurdish movements and territories, and interdisciplinary research on Kurdish societies, religions, social movements, and the Kurdish diaspora. Lastly, our aim is to contribute to the academic literature on Kurdish culture, arts, cinema and literature. This series speaks to audiences outside academia, and is not limited to area-studies topics. All books in this series will be peer-reviewed and demonstrate academic quality and rigor.

Titles Published

Origins of the Kurdish Genocide: Nation Building and Genocide as a Civilizing and De-Civilizing Process by Ibrahim Sadiq

Kurdish Identity, Islamism, and Ottomanism: The Making of a Nation in Kurdish Journalistic Discourse (1898-1914), by Deniz Ekici

Home and Sense of Belonging among Iraqi Kurds in the UK, by Ali Zalme

The Kurdish Model of Political Community: A Vision of National Liberation Defiant of the Nation-State by Hanifi Baris

Media and Politics in Kurdistan: How Politics and Media Are Locked in an Embrace by Mohammedali Yaseen Taha

Turkey's Mission Impossible: War and Peace with the Kurds by Cengiz Çandar

The Kurds in the Middle East: Enduring Problems and New Dynamics edited by Mehmet Gurses, David Romano, and Michael M. Gunter

Social Media and Democratization in Irai Kurdistan by Munir Hasan Mohammad

Origins of the Kurdish Genocide

Nation Building and Genocide as a Civilizing and De-Civilizing Process

Ibrahim Sadiq

LEXINGTON BOOKS

Lanham • Boulder • New York • London

Published by Lexington Books
An imprint of The Rowman & Littlefield Publishing Group, Inc.
4501 Forbes Boulevard, Suite 200, Lanham, Maryland 20706
www.rowman.com

6 Tinworth Street, London SE11 5AL, United Kingdom

British Library Cataloguing in Publication Information Available

Library of Congress Cataloging-in-Publication Data

Names: Sadiq, Ibrahim, 1966- author.
Title: Origins of the Kurdish genocide : nation building and genocide as a civilizing and de-civilizing process / Ibrahim Sadiq.
Other titles: Kurdish societies, politics, and international relations.
Description: Lanham, Maryland : Lexington Books, 2021. | Series: Kurdish societies, politics, and international relations | Includes bibliographical references and index.
Identifiers: LCCN 2021009335 (print) | LCCN 2021009336 (ebook) | ISBN 9781793636829 (cloth) | ISBN 9781793636836 (epub) | ISBN 9781793636843 (pbk)
Subjects: LCSH: Ḥizb al-Ba'th al-'Arabī al-Ishtirākī (Iraq) | Kurds—Iraq—Politics and government—20th century. | Genocide—Iraq—History—20th century. | Panarabism—Influence. | Nation-building—Iraq—History—20th century. | Iraq—Politics and government—20th century.
Classification: LCC DS70.8.K8 S237 2021 (print) | LCC DS70.8.K8 (ebook) | DDC 956.7/00491597—dc23
LC record available at https://lccn.loc.gov/2021009335
LC ebook record available at https://lccn.loc.gov/2021009336

My mom, Zulekha
My wife, Zakiya

The Day of the Resurrection

It was a peaceful autumn day of 1974, I was resting along the shore of the running water, outside the village where we dwelt. I heard the sound of two airplanes that were storming across the sky of our village. Within seconds, a tremendous force threw me in the water stream with the face down. When I opened my eyes, I saw a massive amount of smoke, dirt, stones, stalks, and leaves raining on me; it reminded me of the horror of doomsday.

At that moment, I was horrified and deeply confused because I did not know what was going on. Later, I learned that the rocket contained napalm (flammable liquid), which was banned internationally. The rocket struck in an agricultural district; therefore, the urban population were located miles away from the blast. It was not long before we moved closer to the Iraq-Iran boarder; we managed to survive the bitter cold weather for two weeks. For the first time in our lives we officially became refugees in Iranian camps, which lacked the basic necessities.

As a result, since those days, my family along with dozens of other Kurdish families have alternated between departure and deportation. The Iraqi authorities blew our village to smithereens as the residents watched—before their very eyes, having no capacity to offer resistance against the authority. I was compelled to switch schools at least fourteen times in eight years until I finished my studies. Finally, our fate brought us to Ramadi, a city of Sunni-Arabs in western Iraq. Here, we faced harsh treatments, constant humiliation, and racial discrimination at school, and at work in the case of my father, and in every encounter.

At that time, I knew we were facing these treatments because we were Kurdish, which was our sin. However, I did not know why we were Kurdish and did not speak Arabic. I could not make sense why I was being attacked.

At home, I had learned that Baathism is immoral, but at school and university I was always under pressure from the Baathists to join them.

Thus, I have been a victim of bitter experiences, as I was deprived of a normal childhood. From those early days, because of my Kurdish background, I have been displaced and expatriate. This personal situation was an important incentive to approach and examine the successive Iraqi regime military campaigns against the people of Kurdistan.

Contents

Contents

Contents

Acknowledgments

I would like to express my very great appreciation to Dr. Peter Wilkin for his valuable and constructive suggestions during my PhD research at Brunel University London. His willingness to give his time so generously has been very much appreciated before and recently. I especially thank Professor Jason Hughes who was always present during the first year of my thesis and encouraged me and helped me even after his move to the University of Leicester. I would like to thank several influential people from Soran University in Kurdistan Region, Dana Salam in London, who spent his valuable time in reviewing the manuscript, and Dr. Bahar Baser at CTPSR, Coventry University, for her support and advice. Most importantly, my sincere thanks go to my family for providing me with timely encouragement and much needed support. I cannot thank my parents enough for their love and prayers. I sincerely thank my wife, Zakiya, for her support and patience. I also want to thank my dear children, Soma, Mashkhal, Hoshang, and Hoshvan for their encouragement and support.

List of Abbreviations

ABSP	The Arab Baath Socialist Party
AC	Anfal Campaigns
BP	Baath Party
BPC	Baath Party Constitutions
CEIP	Carnegie Endowment for International Peace
CPPCG	Convention on the Prevention and Punishment of the Crime of Genocide
CUP	Committee of Union and Progress
HRW	Human Right Watch
ICC	International Criminal Court
KDP	Kurdistan Democratic Party
KR	Kurdistan Region
PUK	Patriotic Union of Kurdistan
UNCG	United Nations Convention of Genocide

Introduction

A major challenge with any study, and the priority for any researcher, is how to resolve a specific problem. The focus of this study is to find the real causes of the Anfal campaigns: Was this a spin-off of the Kurdish conflict with the Iraqi government, or was it due to the structure of the nation state? Here, the book will address two important points to cover the events that the Iraqi state has gone through since its foundation in 1920 to examine any causal relation that might have led to the process of the Kurdish genocide in Iraq. Note that within the Kurdish genocide, the Anfal campaigns in 1988 were one of the most prominent events ever to occur in Iraqi Kurdistan, which I call the "final solution."[1] However, it is not the beginning or the end of the story, as has been stated and shown by many writers and scholars in this discipline. The Anfal campaigns is the name of the military campaigns that took place in 1988, but the whole process of genocide goes back to the early days of the emergence of the Baath Party's ideology in Iraq, specifically, when this party seized power for the first time in 1962. Therefore, this book will investigate the roots of genocide in Iraq and when the process of Kurdish genocide started to be planned, based on two hypotheses:

(1) The process of nation building in Iraq formed the cornerstone for excluding and marginalizing the non-Arabs.
(2) The development of pan-ethno-Arab-centrism led to the emergence of Baath ideology, which formulated a roadmap for the process of the Kurdish genocide.

By approaching the origins of genocide, we will get to know the prevailing ideology in Iraq that was built on ethno-Arab-centrism. This produced different directions of Arab nationalism, the most dangerous of which was

Baathism, which spread, in its early stages, like wildfire. The inspiration of Arab-centrism pushed even the Shiite Arabs to the forefront as vanguards of Baathism. The first person who brought the Baathist doctrine to Iraq was "an Arab Shi'a, Fu'ad al-Rikabi, and Baath member since 1950 assumed the leadership of the Iraqi Baath in 1951 and headed the party for the next eight years" (Cabana, 1993: 26).

However, it did not take long until the Shiites withdrew from the Baath Party with the sectarian excuse of the Baath being Sunni in nature. Thus, to date, Iraq has become a polarized country among three components (Sunni, Shia, and Kurds). When the Baath Party attacked the Kurdish people in its genocide campaigns spanning more than eighteen years, the Sunnis did not openly express condemnation, and the Shiites were suppressed by the Baathists. In addition, when the Shiites and Kurds rose up in the north and the south, the Sunnis did not rise against the regime. After 2003, there was a sectarian civil war between the Shiites and Sunnis, as the polarization became more profound and dangerous, especially when the Kurds had a safe autonomous region, their own parliament, and a regional government; nevertheless, they did not interfere in the conflict between the other two components. Thus, whoever examines the relationship between these components knows that there is a deep polarization that divides the three components.

Consequently, this book examines the civilizing process in relation to nation building as possible grounds for the de-civilizing process and the subsequent genocide of the Kurds in Iraq. The important elements of these two main issues include studying the Arab Baath Socialist Party (ABSP) within the long-term civilizing and de-civilizing process, as well as the factors that have restrained the interrelationship between the Kurds and the Iraqi authority as the representative of the Arab majority, to establish the genocidal relationship.

More specifically, in the context of the micro-level, this book focuses on the long-term development of the genocidal relationship, along with the emergence of the Baath Party and its views, which are pertinent to various elements of the Baath's totalitarian model. This model was imposed with different features, such as a party monopoly over the means of violence instead of the state; transforming the social order into military and paramilitary barracks and intelligence agencies; intervention within the social order in favor of a particular social group; a monopoly over taxes and over the means of production and natural resources; activation of the pan-Arab and Baath ideology through the only legal media machine available; the isolation of groups and individuals from each other through a strong network of spies; a strict, violent policy, in Nazism termed "realpolitik" (Fletcher, 1997: 151), and the prohibition of public freedom—"political restraints." Due to these features, the authoritarian regime can be described as a "Republic of Fear" (Makiya,

1994). Thus, these monopolies, specifically the military and taxation aspects, cannot be separated, as Elias argues: "The financial means thus flowing into this central authority maintain its monopoly over military forces, while this in turn maintains the monopoly of taxation" (Mazzuca, Sebastián, 2010: 6). However, according to Elias's philosophy, he also states:

> The compelling force with which a particular social structure, a particular social interweaving, is pushed through its tensions to specific change and so to other forms of interweaving . . . and only then, therefore, can we understand that the change in habitus characteristic of a civilizing process is subject to a quite specific order and direction. (Elias, 1994: 367)

Through this insight, it is possible to understand the Baath's specific order and direction in its view of power and authority. In addition, the Anfal campaigns as a final security solution, or what Elias calls the breakdown of civilization, are considered to be the summit of action in the genocidal process in Iraq, which took place systematically from 1987 to the end of 1988. This security solution must be researched as part of an understanding of the interweaving social process in order to clarify the reasons that led to the de-civilizing process and facilitated the barbaric behavior against the Kurdish liberation movement. Thus, it is necessary to trace the root causes of the de-civilizing process back to the Baath's accession in 1963 and 1968, as well as the Baath style of state formation and the series of sociopolitical changes that occurred prior to and subsequent to their reign. This is in addition to the failure of nation building, which created the conditions for a new style of interdependence and strict constraints on the social order that led to the breakdown in social relations. These circumstances meant that genocide became one of the strategies used by the Baathists to save some of what, in the Baath's view, needed to be saved.

The Baath, with its new social order, prepared the ground for new interdependence to spur on an ideally pure Arabic society, and this, therefore, made possible the extent of the genocidal events that took place during the 1970s and 1980s. Furthermore, the processes of nation building with its transformation of existing traditional social institutions are central to this account as specific aspects of the social order that led to the action against the Kurdish population, including the genocidal process. Here, in line with Elias's understanding of tribalism, state formation in Iraq faced a contradiction between the traditional and modernity. Throughout his work, Elias points out that "tribal social structures tended to be seen as unchanging constants" (Dunning and Hughes, 2012: 37). This is still an important phenomenon in Iraqi social formation and involves a man with a tribal mindset leading the state; as the Iraqi sociologist Ali Alwardi mentions, it is a "conflict between civilization and tribalism" (Khoury, 2018: 14). This conflict between tribal thinking and modern society in state formation is an important subject that needs to be discussed.

Concerning the emergence of the Baath's ideology, this study will examine how it is linked to the origins of Nazism, along with the Turkish model of Kamalizm or "Grey wolf" (Farrokh, 2005: 7). This includes the possible roots of cultural superiority (Arab centrism) in Arabic-Islamic history in their conduct with non-Arabs and non-Muslims. Thus, the Baath ideology is an extension of these ideologies, which are built on the belief in the superiority of one race or one culture over all others. This view evolved through the long-term socialization process of internalizing the specific norms and values of the nation's predecessors. Regarding the implications of this ideology for the process of Arab nation building as a civilizing process, the start of the genocide process involved a breakdown in civility, as several kinds of procedures were strategically used against the Kurdish residents, because the Baath considered the Kurds to be outcasts and a real threat to its policies in Iraq. Thus, the first action in the implementation of the Baath's nation building was taken against the Faili Kurds—a community of Kurdish people who lived in and around Baghdad in the heart of the country.

Consequently, genocide in Iraq, as a reversal of the earlier civilizing process that had promoted postcolonial nation building, emerged. There are similarities in the causes of several different cases of genocide and politicides after the Second World War, including the Kurds (Harff and Gurr, 1989: 34). Here, close to Harff and Gurr's understanding of the causes of genocide, Elias claims that "during a transition to a new level of integration of a nation state, tensions usually increase between the majority and the minorities within it" (Fletcher, 1997: 161). Elias adds that "assimilation is one answer to this problem, but it is always a long process which may take at least 3-generations" (Fletcher, 1997: 161). However, the dilemma in the Kurdish case is that the tensions between the Kurds and the Iraqi state did not start with the emergence of the Baathist constructed state but can be traced back to the emergence of the formation of the Iraqi state. Similarly, "Elias places the Nazi mass murder of the Jews in the context of inter-state process and the dynamics established-outsider relations" (Fletcher, 1997: 160). Subsequently, the Kurdish genocide could easily be placed in this kind of context of interstate processes (Turkey, Iraq, Iran, and Syria, alongside some Arab ideological regimes that used to support Iraq or Syria) and the dynamics of established-outsider relations.

Hence, this book will examine these different aspects in order to clarify the influence of all of these dimensions. One of the main dimensions is the influence of the Baath's ideology over the Sunni Arabs and their relationship to these events. As we will see, Arab nationalism and its ideology effectively shaped the ground for the Sunni Arab population in terms of seeing the Kurds as traitors, nonbelievers, and followers of Israel. Meanwhile, the Kurdish demands made to the political Arab elites were often seen as obstacles in the way of progress in the nation building process. In this regard, Fletcher has raised a similar question concerning the reasons for the hatred shown by Germans "and why did it express itself in the attempt to exterminate the Jews?" (Fletcher, 1997: 162). Thus, this book aims to discover the factors that caused this long-term process of genocide by examining the objective and subjective factors at play in Iraq's multiethnic society. Therefore, the origins and developments of Iraqi and Arabic nationalism will be traced through the Iraqi civilizing process, which is a new figuration that stems from the formation of the Iraqi nation state as a postcolonial and multiethnic state since the First World War—in particular, how it manifested itself in the form of the Baath's ideology and its aims in the nation building process.

Polarization in the form of Arabism/Sunnism resulted from the emergence of the Iraqi state. Consequently, Arab nationalists through their theorists, including Sati' al-Husri and others, established the hegemony of pan-Arab nationalism in Iraq in its extremist form. The Ba'athists in their ideology developed polarization and established fascism through the Baath's constitution, which considers non-Arabs as guests in the Arab homeland. Elias discusses polarization and emphasizes that "the emotional bonds or valences underline the extent to which people say of themselves 'we' or 'I' in relation to other members of their own group" (Fletcher, 1997: 62). According to the framework of the concept of "identification" (Elias, 2000: 65), the Bath party succeeded in mobilizing the masses based on its revolutionary ideology. One of the most important aspects which will be examined includes the Baath's view and the division between the "we ideal" and the "other"; "nation of civilization" and "enemies of Arabs"; or as explained by the Eliasian concept, "established" and "outsiders." This division, for the Baathists, was necessary to mobilize the Arab people against the "others" who were seen as against Arab unification (ABSP, 1972). In addition, the interrelationship between nationalism and the ideology of the Baathists as a factor in the de-civilizing process, and the consequences of genocide, including the interdependence of the Iraqi Arab community, will be examined. This interrelationship possibly stemmed from religion or an ideological background. The prospect of convergence lies in the "we image" and/or the "civilizing offensive." With regard to credibility, the following are two important aspects of my knowledge in relation to the details of the Iraqi state:

First: My experience during the Baath period in Iraq, particularly when I was living in the Sunni Anbar province, which was one of the regions supporting the Baath regime and its actions, from 1977 to 1981. Consequently, after my return to the Kurdish city of Erbil in 1981, I witnessed the cruelty of the regime in its worst stages: the extermination of the Barzani men and many atrocities against the Kurdish people, including the Anfal campaigns in 1988.

Second: Witnessing some aspects of the Anfals in 1988 prompted me to examine the origins of these campaigns, and consequently, I attempted to discover the essence of genocide. Then, I became active in this field and worked with some organizations to defend the rights of the survivors of the genocide in Kurdistan and Iraq. The gravity of this global crime led me to choose to study for a master's degree and then a doctorate in this field. This book is the result of this personal effort, which took more than seven years.

Hence, I was excited to write about genocide, because I experienced its tragedy directly and indirectly. Because I saw my village destroyed by the perpetrators; they were destroying all the infrastructure of the village, and they did not leave a drop of water even for the animals that were left behind. I saw the people of my nation being led to death in military trucks and we could not utter a word, and I saw the people wounded by chemical weapons who were taken at night to an unknown place, and nobody found a trace of them because the perpetrators did not want to leave any evidence that they used chemical weapons.

This book is one of few academic works on this subject in the context of Iraq. Its value lays in the fact that conflict in Iraq is ongoing, and the issue of the genocide still receives a great deal of attention from the victims, the Kurds, a large number of Iraqis, political parties, and the international community. However, the genocidal process was a direct outcome of two significant elements:

First: The impact of pan-Arab nationalism (the ethno-Arab-centrism), and later on the emergence of the Baath regime's ideology,

Second: As a result of the first reason, the Arab majority attempted to impose a pure Arab nation state on the Iraqi population regardless of its demographic diversity.

This may be considered one of the state's failures in its unwillingness to acknowledge the reality of a multiethnic state. Therefore, the importance of this book lies in the way that it tackles the human, cultural, political, and economic dimensions of the problem. Moreover, discovering the causes of the genocide in Iraq will provide lessons that can be learned, which may help in preventing future ethnic conflict.

The issue of genocide in Iraq relates to the fate of a people whose efforts have been exhausted since the beginning of the formation of the Iraqi state, and therefore, this topic is important for consideration within the current academic discussion. The genocide in Iraq, with its specific dimensions, particularly the Anfal campaigns, is an example of modern genocide. It has become one of the most important subject areas in sociology. It is also "one of the fastest-growing disciplines in the humanities and social sciences" (Moses and Stone, 2008: 1). In addition, the origins of the genocide process still have not received adequate attention, including sociologically. Nation building and the Baath Party's ideology as the other face of fascism in the Middle East[2] are two important background factors to this issue.

An examination of the de-civilizing process and civilizing offensive will reveal important insights, because, as Elias has outlined, there are clear dimensions for both state formation and genocide. It shows the historical processes involved in the interrelationship and interdependencies, inclusive of the consequences, internally and externally, for the Iraqi authority as a representative of Iraqi Arab society and Kurdish society. Elias's theory will be used to conceptualize all aspects of the conflict and the causes of genocide through his sub-concepts of the general framework of the civilizing process.

In the context of this book's argument, the first subject area is the formation of Iraq after the division of the Middle East by the colonial forces as a result of the collapse of the Ottoman Empire. The emergence of the new nation states in the Middle East can be compared to a caesarean birth, unlike the Eliasian civilizing process. In this regard, this caesarean birth of the regional states led to instability and totalitarian regimes, apparent in successive military regimes in Iraq. Moreover, the Kurds paid a heavy price as a result of their division into several different countries and nationalities. This social and geopolitical division led to the de-civilizing process. Thus, the process of division is very clear, and the colonialists did not offer any opportunities for the Kurds, apart from absolute subordination to the dominant nations.

As a result of the formation of Iraq in the post-Ottoman era and annexing the Mosul province to this new, modern state, Iraq has struggled to become a state since its formation. Iraq, as a product of modernity, has attempted to solve its problems using modern means. It has always worked toward power concentration and has used violence against its own population to ensure submissiveness. Thus, there is causality between the "civilizing" of nation building in Iraq and the "de-civilizing" of genocide, as the process of nation building has been pursued unilaterally by one ethnicity against another. From this perspective, the process of building one Arab nation in Iraq in the framework of ethno-Arab-centrism and its attempts to unite with the Arab homeland at the expense of non-Arab communities have produced regional and international confrontations, which led to the conflict and then to genocide.

As a consequence of the process of nation building and the successive failings of its governments, Arabic nationalism spread, and later extreme Arabic nationalism in the form of the ABSP emerged. Here, it will be argued that Baathism at the "micro-level," on the one hand, stems from the same sources as fascism and Nazism; on the other hand, it is a result of the successive fail-ings of the state at the "macro-level," which could have logically resulted in genocide. Here, "because inter-dependence is Elias's central category, he has always been able to bridge the gap between micro and macro sociology with seeming ease" (Mennell, 1990: 369). Thus, it will also be argued that the causes of the genocide are rooted in the ideology of Baathism and the specific socio-historic circumstances that it found itself in during different stages of the process, from 1968 until the main Anfals.

In the context of these arguments, there are major questions which we are attempting to find answers to. The first main question is: Why was the genocide, as a de-civilizing process, carried out against the Kurds in Iraq? Second, to what extent was genocide a result of the state failing or a matter of the illegitimacy of the state? Third, based on the civilizing process, was pan-Arab nationalism, including the Baathist ideology, a consequence of the nation building that led to the process of genocide? Finally, what was the role of religion in its interdependence with state organizations?

Regarding the relevance of the methodological approach, I have carefully attempted to reach satisfying outcomes for this study by choosing figura-tional sociology, which is part of the theory in Elias's work. In this regard, the importance of figurational sociology lies in its mechanisms in relation to social change, unplanned consequences, involvement and detachment, and the power interrelationship between the Iraqi components. This is because humans form chains of "figurations" or "interdependence"; therefore, it pro-vides a clear picture in relation to the conflict between the Kurds and the Iraqi government as representative of the Sunni Arabs.

More specifically, according to Elias, "a figuration is a social structure consisting of a set of individuals who are linked by a set of positions, rules, norms and values" (Segre, 2020: 34). This highlights the need to discover the structure of Iraqi authority led by the ABSP and its ethnocentric policy, which is important as it forms the framework for the nature of the interrelationship between the Kurds and the Arabs, particularly the Sunni Arabs. It involves exploring the process of the genocidal procedure throughout three decades during the age of the Baathists in Iraq and even throughout the previous period of Iraqi state formation.

The research that forms part of this book involved a qualitative approach to examining the causality between the nation state and its institutions, and the process of Kurdish genocide in Iraq, by investigating the interrelationships between various social characters and state agencies throughout the long-term process. In order to realize these objectives, it was decided to conduct interviews as an appropriate method, besides exploring the documentation and the Paath's literature as a reflection of Iraqi policy. Thus, the participants have been divided into four main types: those who are directly involved in the

Baath's authority, those indirectly involved and who were part of the Baath's authority, individuals not involved in any political activities, and those who were directly affected by the genocide process.

Additionally, the documents that have been relied on have been obtained from different sources, despite there being no national archive in the Kurdistan region and the way to the national archive in Bagdad being closed because of the war and Sunni and Shiite terrorist groups. Even so, it was possible to find a substantial archive from people who are working on the cases of genocide and those who have gathered information and written about these issues.

OVERVIEW OF THE CHAPTERS

Chapter 1 sets out the theoretical basis for the analysis in the book. It includes a discussion of the civilizing and de-civilizing process as introduced by Norbert Elias. Additionally, all of the terms and concepts related to the issue of genocide are defined. The aim of this chapter is to present the background in relation to the nation building and genocide process.

Chapter 2 analyses the process of state building in Iraq. It discusses the issue of annexing Mosul Wilayat, which has a Kurdish majority, to the Iraqi state. It examines the conditions created in the new state, from the control of colonialism and bringing in a foreign king to dominate non-Arab elements, as well as the domination of the political elite with a military mentality that was educated by the Ottoman officers, the elite that dominated the reins of the country's administration. These are the factors that marginalized the Kurdish component in Iraq.

Chapter 3 addresses the stages of genocide in more detail. The genocide process in Iraq has different dimensions, and it can be considered one of the longest operations in the history of genocide. In this chapter, the first stage, which is limited to a group of episodes, is discussed, that is, the emergence of the Baath ideology and the preparations for violence (the de-civilization). It highlights the elements of the policy followed by the regime, including the policy of divide and rule and then the disintegration of the Kurdish entities one after the other, starting with the Faili Kurds, throughout the extermination of the Barzanis; the policy of evacuation and forced camps, and the bombing of the city of Halabja with chemical weapons.

Chapter 4 deals with the Anfal campaigns in detail as a genocide process, which was considered to be a final security solution. There were some necessary procedures followed by the regime. These procedures lay within the state's bureaucracy in order to give them legal characteristics in terms of their implementation. These measures included special legislation, and a census and identification. Based on these measures, massive forces were gathered to attack Kurdistan in nine different military campaigns, which were called the Anfal campaigns. Every campaign started by grouping people in closed camps to separate women, men, and children in order to send them to the mass graves. Finally, Anfal has a unique set of characteristics which are discussed in this chapter.

In addition, a connection has been made between these aforementioned three chapters and chapters 4 and 5, which expand on the interviews. These interviews focus on the different aspects of the genocide process, from Arab-centrism through to Arabization and the campaigns of deportation, and ending with the Anfal Campaign, which resulted in the deaths of tens of thousands of Kurdish rural civilians in the Iraqi dessert in the south of the country.

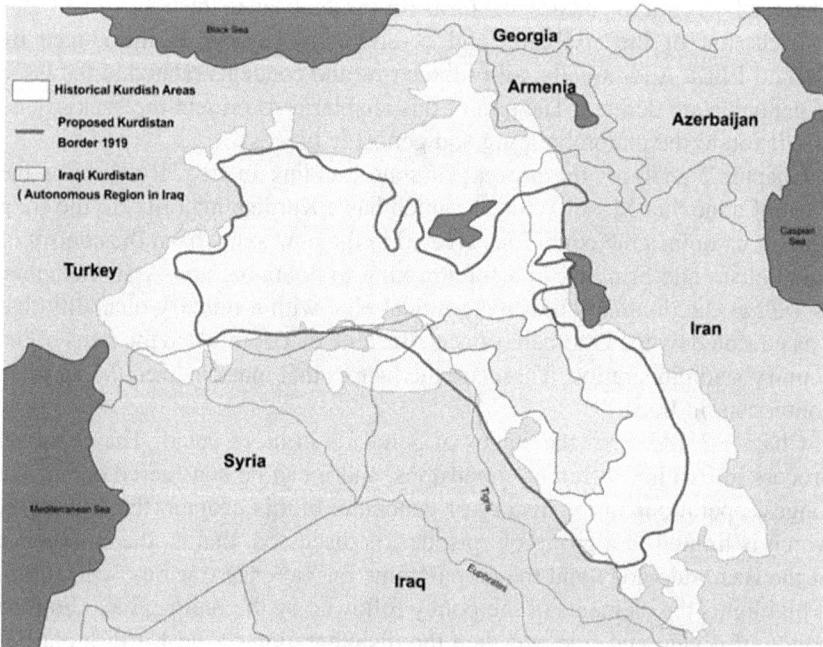

Figure 0.1 Hoshiyar M. Rashid (2021).
The Map of Historical Kurdistan Expresses the Interdependence of the Kurdish Territory as a Strategic Region on All Aides. After the division of this land, the dismemberment of the Kurdish society and its submission to the control of the region's nations, the Kurds were subjected to genocide over and over again, in Turkey, Iran, Syria, and Iraq with the cooperation and supervision of the British and French colonialism after the First World War. What is in front of you is only one part of the genocide of the Kurds, and what you will not hear about is even more horrible. Here begins the story of torment! Hoshiyaar M. R., 2021.

NOTES

1. Final solution: The final solution does not differ much from what the Iraqi Baathist regime called the security solution, because the content does not differ. The final solution was intended to end the Jewish presence in Germany, and the security solution also intended to end the Kurdish presence, not necessarily physically, but in terms of its influence and ending the Kurdish story. Thus, the intention was the final solution, mainly because all other solutions had been exhausted and the security solution remained the ideal solution.

2. "Middle East" is a political term commonly used among intellectuals and politicians around the world, and even among residents of the same region. This term was used for the first time by the American naval strategist Alfred Thayer Mahan in 1902 (Koppes, 1976: 95).

REFERENCES

ABSP. *al-Hizb al-qaid fi al-Nadariyati wa-altatbiq*. Beirut, Lebanon: Arab Institution for Studies and Publishing, 1972.

Cabana, Joel L. *The Ba'th Party in Iraq: From its beginning through today*. Monterey, CA: Naval Postgraduate School, 1993.

Dunning, Eric., Hughes, Jason. *Norbert Elias and Modern Sociology: Knowledge, Interdependence, Power, Process*. India: Bloomsbury Academic, 2013.

Elias, Norbert. *The civilizing process* (revised edition). Trans. Edmund Jephcott. Oxford: Blackwell Publishers, 2000.

Elias, Norbert, and John L. Scotson. *The established and the outsiders* (vol. 32). London: SAGE, 1994.

Farrokh, Kaveh. Pan-Turanianism takes aim at Azerbaijan: A geopolitical agenda. *Rozaneh Magazine*, 2005.

Fletcher, J. *Violence and civilization: An introduction to the work of Norbert Elias*. Cambridge, MA: Polity, 1997.

Harff, B., and T. R. Gurr. Victims of the state: Genocides, politicides and group repression since 1945. *International Review of Victimology* 1, no. 1 (1989): 23–41.

Khoury, Dina Rizk. History and society of Iraq between Hanna Batatu and Ali al-Wardi. *AlMuntaqa* 1, no. 2 (2018): 91–101.

Koppes, Clayton R. Captain Mahan, General Gordon, and the origins of the term 'Middle East'. *Middle Eastern Studies* 12, no. 1 (1976): 95–98.

Makiya, Kanan. *Cruelty and silence: War, tyranny, uprising, and the Arab World*. New York: WW Norton & Company, 1994.

Mazzuca, Sebastián. Macrofoundations of regime change: Democracy, state formation, and capitalist development. *Comparative Politics* 43, no. 1 (2010): 1–19.

Mennell, Stephen. Decivilising processes: Theoretical significance and some lines of research. *International Sociology* 5, no. 2 (1990): 205–223.

Segre, Sandro. *Bauman, Elias and Latour on modernity and its alternatives: Three contemporary sociological theorists on modernity and other options.* London: Anthem Press, 2020.

Chapter 1

Iraq, under the Theoretical Mirror

Nation Building and Genocide

"Iraq, whether it was a failed state" (Baker, 2003: 8; Dodge, 2003: 249) or a "Fragile State," (Calabrese, 2020) is a preliminary description of a country built by Western colonialism after the First World War, and it was designed according to colonial interests (Yaphe, 2003: 383). Consequently, the process of nation building in this country was also initiated as part of the colonial strategy and under its influence. This situation has produced, generally, a pan-Arab centric power, which in turn led to the hegemony of pan-Arab nationalism. Thus, as a result of the abnormal construction process, I attempted to create a causal relationship between ideology, nation building and the process of Kurdish genocide in Iraq. This approach can be compared to what happened after the First World War in Germany with the differences in their structure and nature.

Norbert Elias, the great German sociologist, was one of those scholars who profoundly stood on the German model and the emergence of Nazism, which led to the process of genocide of the Jews. In this regard, Elias produced his prominent theory on the civilizing process, including his essay "The Germans" in order "to use this theory to shed light on the origins and growth of Nazism" (Dunning and Mennell, 1998: 339). According to this theory's framework, the nation building process and the emergence of pan-Arab centrism, as well as the emergence and the growth of the Arab nationalism including Baathizm in Iraq, will be focused on as the two main reasons for the genocide in Iraq.

Iraq, as a new country in the framework of the civilizing process, was built on the remains of provinces of what was once called the Ottoman Empire (Çetinsaya, 2006: 28). It was considered as a strange leap and an anomalous state-building phenomenon if we compare it with the establishment of the nation states on the green continent in comparison to the Westphalia peace agreement. Thus, we can observe a discontinuity between the past of the region when it was under the domination of the Ottoman Empire, with all its Vilayats (Tabbaa and Mervin, 2014: 24), and the history of the formation of several states in the Middle East, including Turkey, Syria and Iraq as a result of the defeat of the Ottomans in the First World War. The important question here is how did the transformation take place in the region in general, as well as the transformation process in building the nation state in Iraq, within the civilization process?

THEORETICAL PERSPECTIVE

In the environment post-First World War, the civilizing process in the Middle East, particularly in Iraq, went through a number of major transitions. In this section, we will focus on three levels of the theoretical framework:

First: The civilizing process in relation to the process of nation building in Iraq.
Second: Ethnocentrism in the frame of Arab centrism since the formation of the state, and how the emergence of nationalism occurred.
Third: The framework of the de-civilizing process and the process of genocide in Iraq.

Thus, the civilizing process is considered to be moving in the right direction toward the legitimacy of the state and creating harmony between the different components of society, with less violence. It is a "forward" direction, and as Elias stated, the civilizing process has two directions—"forward" and "backward." In this case, "the civilizing processes go along with de-civilizing processes" (van Krieken, 1999: 5). In accordance, the turning point is when the de-civilizing process dominates the circumstances of society. This domination of de-civility can emerge due to different variations in the circumstances of the society, or changes in the social system. Thus, the usual trends refer to the moral weakness of the state; for instance, Elias has claimed that "the German state was a weak state that failed at pacifying and civilizing the Germans and therefore allowed a reversal to barbarism to occur" (Lash and Featherstone, 2002: 267). This reversal process, according to Elias, is how the "whole reorganization of human relationships had direct significance for the change in the human habitus" (Elias, 2000: 366). Dependently, this direction does not mean that it is unilinear or inevitable, but it is related to the structure of the society and different circumstances, including ideology. Hence, as Elias maintains, "If we see a particular social structure, a particular form or social interweaving is pushed through its tensions to a specific change and so to other forms of intertwining" (Elias, 2000: 367).

According to this approach, Elias is concerned with the balance between choice and determinism, and that the forward direction could turn into a reversal, as the civilizing process sometimes moves contrary to the current situation. Thus, when the ruling class acts against the national consensus, such as consciously taking unilateral action, including imposing an identity, as a representative and in favor of one entity, the course will move in the opposite direction, and the process of state building in favor of all citizens may head towards ethnic bloodshed. Regarding this opposition to the national consensus, if there is a consensus, the trend is towards a de-civilizing process. From this standpoint, "While the state continues to monopolize violence, promotes and protects civilized modes of behaviour and expression in society, at the same time it perpetrates massive and organized acts of extreme violence towards specific categories of its citizens" (de Swaan, 2001: 265).

In terms of the subject of the fieldwork in Iraq, the main problem has been the Iraqi state, from its formation until the fall of Baghdad in 2003, and it may still be problematic for two main reasons which cannot be avoided. The first is that Iraq was formed by British colonial rule, in support of Sunni Arabs, as Arabcentrism has been the focus. However, the strangest character of this formation is that a foreign family was chosen to become the royal family of Iraq, that is, Faisal's family, who were from Saudi Arabia and supported the British army against the Ottoman Turks when the Western allies invaded the Middle-East region. On the other hand, the British had discovered oil in the Kurdistan city of Kirkuk. This event was an important reason for annexing the Mosul province to the other two provinces of Iraq in 1926 (Rafaat, 2017: 2), without taking into account the wishes of the Kurdish nation within the newly formed country—a country whose main characteristics, including its building against the interests and willingness of one major component in the region, depended on illegal action and nondemocratic procedures.

The formation of the state by "annexing three provinces" inclusive of their territory, nature, and people lasted well into the twentieth century. It was not formed within the principles of a civilizing process, and "it was not a transformation on the level of social structure (sociogenesis) inter-related to changes in the level of personality" (Buschendorf and Franke, 2011: 1). It was not a gradual, dynamic transformation, according to the channels that create change in the habitus of people. It was not a process of civilization that involved a shift from a feudal state through to an absolutist state, ending with the nation state, as happened in Western societies. This form of emergence should be handled more carefully and sensitively; otherwise, it can become an independent form with its own characteristics. The specific form of Iraq emerged with the appearance of colonialism directly after the collapse of the Ottoman Empire and the First World War. In this case, a predicament of political legitimacy is faced, "A system of legality and legitimacy" (Simić, 2008: 190) and, according to this principle, Iraq lacks this kind of legality and legitimacy.

Here, it is essential to distinguish between the social features prior to and subsequent to the development of Iraq, as the social structure faced a certain form of interruption. From the formation of Iraq, there was no longer an interrelationship or interdependence between the past and the future. The new model of life emerged with a special transformation and in new circumstances. This new situation brought about a new figurational process, and a new type of interweaving was formulated. The formation of the historic state in 1920 created a stark contrast between the two separate periods. The first period was when every province, Baghdad, Basra, and Mosul, individually or independently, was administrated by the Ottoman Empire and was subject to their authority. The Baghdad province, in the central and western region of current Iraq, was composed primarily of Sunni Arabs and had maintained a good relationship with the Ottoman Empire. Their relationship with the Ottoman Empire was entwined because of the doctrine of religious uniformity, as opposed to the Shi'a Arabs. However, the Kurdish relationship in the Mosul province with the Ottomans, despite the doctrine of uniformity, underwent periods of instability due to frictional movements of independence, the Soran, Botan, and Baban Emirates before 1800 as examples (Ghalib, 2011).

Concerning the background of the Sunni Arabs, their preparation for the new era was apparent. The Sunni Arabs were affected by both Turkish nationalism and the Arab nationalist thinker "Sati' al-Husri." Al-Husri was a member of the Young Turks but suddenly turned to Arabism and moved to Baghdad. They have been "trained in the best Ottoman government and military academies and they were the last to break with the Ottoman Empire" (Ottaway and Yaphe, 2003: 2). Thus, after the establishment of the Iraqi state, the elite from the Sunni Arabs, militarily and politically and with the help of British forces, were ready to dominate the Iraqi state because they were interdependent and living in central Iraq, specifically in Baghdad. Moreover, the British mandate brought the Saudi Sunni political leader, Faisal, to be king of Iraq. This position gave the Sunni Arabs the ability to gain the concentration of power, but as Bauman has argued, such concentration of power is "not under effective control and can be used for good and evil" (Dunning and Mennel, 1998: 340).

Here, the interrelationship between long-term changes in human conduct and long-term changes in state formation entails two dimensions. On the one hand, the roots of human conduct extend in the long-term to the Arab community before the formation of the state of Iraq in 1920. This means that the Sunni Arabs were living in tribal communities in central and western Iraq.

The tribal social structure and the nature of these communities did not exceed mechanical solidarity. The type of personality did not change under the new interrelated social structure due to the nature of the tribal system. However, as Elias argues, within the state's formation, a huge change began to take place along with the new situation in the main Iraqi city of Baghdad, among certain less important cities. On the other hand, before the state's formation, the elite from the Sunni Arabs were promoted and received special treatment from the Ottoman Empire and were given key jobs in the colonial authority in Baghdad and in Istanbul; specifically, in the military sector. Therefore, Sunni Arabs' relationship with the Ottoman authority is considered to be an integral, continuous, organic relationship and "Istanbul was the Mecca (Kaba) of ambitious Iraqis" (Simon, 2004: 9). For example, "Each year from 1872 to World War 1, thirty to forty Iraqi secondary school graduates went on to Istanbul; in 1903 the Iraqis were 10 present of the total number admitted to the military academy. By 1912 some 1,200 had become Ottoman army officers" (Simon, 2004: 9). From this point, it can be observed that the relationship between the Sunni Arab community and the Ottoman authorities in Istanbul was robust and direct, particularly "for lower-class Iraqis from less prominent families" (Simon, 2004: 9). This sort of interrelationship left its mark on the Sunni population's social composition. However, these Arab officers, accompanied by some intellectuals, chose to return to the new Iraqi state in 1920 to engage in politics and the Iraqi army.

Another important point regarding interactions and consequences around this issue is that these Arab officers communicated with the German officers who were overseeing the training of the Ottoman army. In this case, "Germany was attractive then and remained a model not only for the Ottoman military but also for the Iraqi officers who first encountered the Germans in Istanbul" (Simon, 2004: 9). This contact extended to the German ideology, because "education, therefore, as the means for the transmission of cultural values and political ideas, is the key to analyzing the reasons for the German-Iraqi link in 1941, which, in essence, is the culmination of a process that began before World War I, continued during the turbulence in Iraq in the 1930, and ended with the defeat in May 1941" (Simon, 2004: xii). These officers were not only a normal phenomenon in Iraq, but rather they were controlling the most sensitive and strategic institution of the state, which is the army. Therefore, "in 1941 the British were shocked to find themselves at war with a pan-Arab nationalist Iraq which seemed to yearn for a German victory. The Sharifians had not merely assimilated themselves into the ruling elite, but had, under British noses, provided the new country with an ideology, a focus for loyalty derived from their Ottoman educational experience" (Simon, 2004: 5).

Ideological communication was not limited to the Iraqi officers but extended to the national intellectuals as well, including Sati` al-Husri, who had dominance over the educational sector in Iraq. In doing so, "the ideological underpinnings of what was later to become pan-Arabism was provided by Sati 'al-Husri, who used Germany for his ideological paradigm just as the officers did for their political and military model" (Simon, 2004: 25). These opportunities, which were paved for the Sunni Arabs, were not available to the Shiite Arabs, but they were deliberately marginalized and oppressed (Luizard, 2016: 38). This story was the same for the Kurds, despite the common sectarian identity. Rather, the Ottomans were dealing with the Kurds with the mentality of the occupier and the politics of divide and rule (Yadirgi, 2014: 87 and 136). Thus, it can be seen that the civilizing process among the social units of the Sunni Arabs occurred correlatively over the long-term, with the emergence of modern nation states in the Middle East. These social units, according to Elias, were initially formed primarily through and for war, but the only difference is in the nature of conflict among these units, which was largely dissimilar to what was happening in Western Europe in many aspects.

The new stage of the civilizing process in Iraq, after the formation of the state in 1920, with its monopolization of violence in correlation with the habitus of individuals, took on a new dimension. One of the most important aspects of this new dimension was the annexation of Mosul province in 1926 to the other two provinces—Baghdad and Basra—without any consultation or consensus from the population of the province, who were ethnically and culturally different from the population of Baghdad province. This new political circumstance would affect the individual habitus in the long-term, and in terms of this point, Elias mentions that "if in a particular region, the power of central authority grows, if over a larger or smaller area the people are forced to live in peace with each other, the moulding of their affects and the standard of their drive-economy (Trzebhaushalt) are very gradually changed as well" (Dunning, 1998: 341).

This new position of both the Mosul and Baghdad provinces, according to Elias's argument, occurred within the specific cultural, economic, and political interests of the new dominant force under the mandate of the great and victorious powers of the First World War—Britain and France; however, it was not possible to marginalize the regional conditions involved in the division of the heritage of the Ottoman Empire in the Middle East. This new map led to two dangerous characteristics for the Kurds: first, the Kurds were the collateral damage from the redivision of the region because it was at the expense of the Kurds; second, this re-division led to a "Weberian concern" due to the illegitimate domination of the new nations of Turks, Arabs, and Persians over the land and destiny of the Kurds.

After the redivision of the region, the drivers of a different crisis emerged. The first Iraqi government, under the supervision of the British mandate, was announced. The Kurds rejected this and continued their political and cultural movements against the British mandate as well as the Arab authority in Baghdad during the twentieth century. When Britain attempted to impose the Treaty of June 1930 on Iraq, the Kurdish revolution broke out again. Here, the Iraqi authority, with help of the British mandate, throughout the 1920s and specifically when the Treaty of June 1930 was imposed on Iraq, violently attempted to impose its authority on the South Kurdistan region of "Mosul Province." Thus, if the formation of the Iraqi state is considered a civilizing process, the Kurds during this period can be considered as moving toward an uncharted future or the beginning of the de-civilizing process. Moreover, the first military campaign against the Kurdish area was the first failure of the Iraqi state in being a state for all citizens.

STATE FORMATION

State formation in relation to this fieldwork is discussed for two reasons: first, because of its important position in the theory of the civilizing process or as part of the social structure and how it is influenced and affected; second, because the state is one of the most important aspects to be discussed in this book, as the state is directly involved in the genocide process. Additionally, if "according to Elias" the state is "a violent competitive process through which there emerged successively larger territorial units with more effective monopoly apparatuses" (Mennell, 2007: 15), then it has a larger ability to redesign the society using its own measures and standards. Here, it is worth mentioning that the issue of state formation has taken an important position in the theory of the civilizing process, and at the same time, the exploratory nature of Elias's work mostly refers to the stages of the human struggle in approaching the different successive models of the authorities of the nation state. Thus, the decisive characteristic in this definition is the process of competition in order to control the larger territory through the monopoly apparatuses in Western Europe.

In the same direction, but in more detail, state formation, historically, is a result of "competition between various groups of people, with associated conflict between these groups, culminated in the establishment of a monopoly of one group and the eventual formation of a state" (Hier, 2011: 3). This suggests that the process of state formation in different forms accompanies conflict between national or international groups until one of these groups has dominated and monopolizes the means of violence. The problem here is that the state building, whether in the Middle East in general, or in Iraq in particular, was not the result of this type of conflict between the components, or a result of a general agreement between them, but rather a direct act of colonialism, and the dominant power kept the civil peace at the beginning of the formation of the state.

Accordingly, in the European model, state formation in the civilizing process includes "conflictual affairs which involved 'hegemonic struggle' within the emergent nation states and international struggles between them" (Dunning and Hughes, 2012: 97). Thus, state formation, according to Elias, is a phenomenal social process and an effective part of the civilizing process; it occurred in Western Europe, and this did not pass without violence: "correlatively with the emergence of capitalist—urban—industrial—nation—state" (Dunning and Hughes, 2012: 97) in the European model.

Accordingly, Elias views state formation in the civilizing process as "conflictual affairs, which involved 'hegemonic struggle' within the emergent nation states and international struggles between them" (Dunning and Hughes, 2012: 97). One of the consequences of the continuous conflict was the emergence of the idea of state sovereignty, within its political boundaries, in the sociopolitical concept. This concept was proven at the peace treaties signed in October 1648 in the Westphalian cities of Osnabrück and Münster (Straumann, 2008), through representatives of the new and/ or old entities resulting from the conflict. These state entities continued, within the European house, through a long, bloody, bitter internal struggle throughout its development until the current forms that we are familiar with today.

These huge developments occurred in Europe, from the social structure to the monopoly mechanisms used to cross over to more advanced phases of state domination, yet they did not happen in the colonial model of Iraq. Additionally, the civilizing process "refers to all the fundamental structural changes that, at the same time, result in relatively stable institutions and personality structures" (Kuzmics, 1997: 1). We can see long-term, structural, interactional, and historical changes through international struggle, which has been determined by Elias within the framework of the civilizing process. This process of power transformation, on the one hand, brought with it "changes in the way people were connected with one another, leading eventually to greater integration and greater interdependence between people" (Rohloff, 2011: 3); on the other hand, it launched a shift from different unities such as city states and feudal states, through absolutist states to modern nation states. In this regard, Elias argues, "this change in the form of political rule was a structural change in Western Society as a whole" (Elias, 2000: 188). Here, we realize the transformation of the stages as part of the civilizing process without further discussion about the essence of the state. Additionally, the scope of monopoly is significant in all changes to the state.

MONOPOLY AND STATE BUILDING

The state owns and monopolizes all state institutions, including the means of violence. More specifically, in terms of the nature of the state, according to Elias it is characterized by two important and crucial figures, or in the framework of the historical process of state formation, it has two specific characteristics due to a certain level of monopolization. These two characteristics are as follows: "Free use of military weapons is denied the individual and reserved to a central authority of whatever kind, and likewise the taxation is concentrated in the hands of a central social authority" (Elias, 2000: 268). However, the emergence of this central state authority, according to Elias, involves "grouse and gains increasing monopolisation over the control of violence and taxation, people come to be increasingly integrated and interdependent with one another" (Rohloff, 2011: 3). Thus, during the formation of the state, monopolies of violence and taxation grow gradually, and as Elias argues, they are two sides of the same coin; if one disappears, the other automatically follows (2000: 268). This type of gradual growth in Iraq was not achieved due to the weakness of the state from the beginning, and the other issues that have been mentioned previously.

Accordingly, Elias has focused on the mechanism of state formation and its monopolizing process and developments until this process, through its long-term changes, attains the most modern component, which is the nation state. This mechanism is central to Elias's civilizing process (Van Krieken, 1998: 97). In contrast, Weber's view is different to Elias in a number of aspects. The most prominent difference to Weber is that Elias is more materialistic and examines the state through the interpretation of the development of social processes, and the mutual influence or interrelationships between long-term changes in standards of behavior and long-term changes in state formation. Weber sees the state "as a type of organisation, 'a political organisation' that successfully claims a monopoly over the legitimate physical coercion necessary for the implementation of its laws and decrees" (Weber and Kalberg, 2005: 222). Accordingly, the motivation behind both Elias and Weber's monopolies are different because according to Elias the aim is to dominate the centrality of power in terms of state formation. Moreover, the monopoly according to Weber is to dominate the centrality of power in terms of bureaucratizing the process of legitimate government. On the other hand, Elias is attempting to discover the ways in which the state has been formed, including peaceful cooperation and peaceful competition. In line with these two approaches, "in so far as war results in a victory, it is the subsequent extension of a coordinating authority that spurs people to both peaceful cooperation and peaceful competition" (Loyal and Qually, 2004: 176), whereas

Weber examines the quality of managing the government. Consequently, legitimacy, as an important characteristic in this fieldwork, is essential, and it will strengthen the idea of state formation within Weber's monopoly of legitimate physical coercion.

Here, as long as state formation is part of the civilizing process, with its characteristics of monopolization, the modern state without legitimacy is exposed to several problematic factors. One of which is the "central system," which in Elias's view is considered to be an important factor in the stability of the state. This view goes back to the earlier stages of state formation and feudalism prior to later developments because one of feudalism's traits is its centrifugal character, which according to Elias has "disruptive, dis-unifying, decentralising tendencies" (Dunning and Hughes, 2012: 98). This centrifugal character is considered by Elias to be a kind of de-civilization process that was dominant in Western Europe following the decline of the Western Roman Empire in the fifth century AD. Therefore, the post-feudal state required a centripetal character that had "integrating, unifying, centralising tendencies" (Dunning and Hughes, 2012: 98) in order to form a dominant and strong central state.

This argument about the centrality of the state could be critical to its historical stages in relation to social, geopolitical, and economic factors. In contrast, if we take this view in the current social, economic, and geopolitical reality of the Middle East, it is irrelevant because the central system in itself led to the instability of the state; or, it seems that this rule was unsuccessful when accompanied by weaknesses in the formation of the state, if Iraq has been taken as a centripetal model, which will be discussed in chapter 2. Here, on the one hand, the central systems of some Middle Eastern countries that have authoritarian regimes are a problematic issue, and on the other hand, the division of the ethnic and cultural components, sometimes inside one artificial country, is very deep and controversial. Moreover, the current historical reality is extremely different to the reality of the Middle Ages. Therefore, despite the necessity of this discussion for this research's fieldwork model, it is essential to take into account the real political diversity of the Middle East, including Iraq. Consequently, what are the characteristics of a nation state? How does Elias deal with them? Furthermore, what is it about states that dominate multiethnic and religious components, specifically in terms of the centripetal system? The most problematic point in terms of this fieldwork in Iraq is the unusual caesarean birth of the state, which is an imposed colonial model. This is unlike the state formation process of Europe, which developed historically due to the conditions of the civilizing process, and which has been described by Elias as a "conflict full affair" that led to the emergent "nation state."

In addition, how is it possible to examine the differences between the process of state formation in Western Europe according to the civilizing process and state formation in the Middle East, which only goes back to the First World War? Historically, it is difficult to find similarities between the process of state formation in Western Europe, which involves research into the civilizing process, and those in the Middle East. Here, it could be valuable to indicate a superficial difference between states in Western Europe and Iraq, which have been specified in a special report by the colonial office (1931) itself. It has been noted, "There were two types of state 'the report argued': the 'civilised nations of the modern world,' and those like Iraq" (Dodge, 2003: 40). In this regard, the British mandate clearly indicates the differences between the states of civilized nations and those states that were still in the process of development. Here, according to Sir Francis Humphreys, the high commissioner in 1932, Iraq is not comparable to an advanced state like Britain, but it could be compared to weak states. Consequently, the concept of weak states is very vague, and it can lead to endless weakness and dire consequences, as recognized eighty-eight years after the statement by British high commissioner Sir Francis Humphreys. This type of comparison, if it indicates anything, shows that UK policy makers, who were the designers of the Iraqi state, were convinced that Iraq was not going to be a civilized country. Therefore, Sir Henry Dobbs, the high commissioner in 1927, argued, "An independent Iraq would be no worse off than any of the weak states in the second tier of membership. To ask for anything more from Britain would be highly unrealistic" (Dodge, 2003: 39). This announcement of Britain's mandatory obligations is a kind of evasion of their responsibilities toward the newly created state. The absence of consent between the key component societies was certainly a major factor in its poor performance.

Here, Elias has determined the state formation mechanism in European territories in the framework of conflictual affairs processes from the Middle Ages until the formation of the nation state. In contrast to all of these processes involved in state formation, what has been realized from the fieldwork on the emergence of the new state of Iraq is the unusual introduction of a state that was violently and externally imposed by the colonial power, with the integration of heterogeneous components, and without any clear path toward democratization or any agreement between the territorial components. Moreover, authority was even given to someone from outside the residence of the regions that were incorporated, including the inauguration of the first king of a new state called the Iraqi Kingdom. All of these procedures were processed, and the Kurdish region remained outside the borders of the new state. To highlight this issue, it is sufficient to refer to two important points: "To be sure, Britain and France used these state apparatuses as instruments of economic, political, and military control over the Middle East. Yet by the same token, the newly formed states became the primary vessels within which Arab (and, in Palestine, also Jewish) nationalism took root as a hegemonic political ideology and assumed some of its distinctive typological forms" (Roshwald, 2001: 188).

The first point is that these states were established as instruments of colonialism in order to impose their hegemony, and the second is the absolute marginalization of some important components in these new countries in the interests of pan-Arab nationalism. This indicates that colonialism was not concerned with the issues of freedom or rights of components within these countries. These two different mechanisms or models of state building (Eliasian and colonial model) created a deficiency in the nature of the change between behavior and power, or between the structures of both models of nation building. Here, to approach the process of state formation in terms of Elias's elements of state formation, it is necessary to consider the specific direction of the civilizing process and its consequences in terms of the arguments around the failed state in Iraq, as determining the model of state formation is necessary before delving into the determination of the contribution of power and the levels of legitimacy of the state.

NATION STATE

For a state to be defined as a state, a permanent population is crucial, based on any definition. This population undergoes early selection to determine how to build a nation: "In the nation state generally, everyone, would speak the same language, probably practice the same or similar types of religions and share a set of cultural, national values" (Srivastava, 2010: 128–129). Here, in this definition, four specific characteristics have been determined for a nation. These four characteristics are totally different from those of the state. In contrast to this definition, the characteristics of a nation relate closely to those of a state, and it has been argued that "the basis of every nation is its population, recognizable by certain common characteristics, the most important of which is a sense of belonging to some distinct portion of land" (Deutsch and Foltz, 1966: 33). These basics are substantiated by Elias and Weber's argument concerning state formation, including affiliation, which equates belonging to a particular territory. In the case of a non-nation state or a state within a mosaic type population, the affiliation or belonging of citizens to the state is more sensitive and yet perhaps more balanced. According to a report by the Organization for Economic Cooperation and Development (OECD), the forced affiliation of a suppressed entity inside the state is rejected and not acceptable, as it states that "far more newly independent states, however, had within their new boundaries substantial ethnic, religious, linguistic or cultural minorities, many of whom rejected the identification of the state with a nation to which they did not feel they belonged" (OECD, 2009: 67). Hence, affiliation could be created in a social-historical context over a long-term process and cannot occur without appropriate circumstances or simply through an agreement between the entities. Regarding this issue,

> in many cases, these groups were subject to large-scale, semi-voluntary or forced expulsion (as during the creation of Pakistan) or internal suppression (as in Iraq.) Unsurprisingly, many sub-national groups chose to fight back or to fight to get out. The result in many cases was that independence struggles were followed by civil, separatist or irredentist wars. (OECD, 2008: 67)

Consequently, such belonging or affiliation is not a foregone conclusion, and it could involve different models through a variety of means of competition. This competition in its most extreme form involves emphasizing the affiliation of people to their land and interests. However, the modern nation is "a historical result brought about by a series of convergent facts" (Renan, 1990: 3).

Moreover, in terms of population and its importance, Elias's argument is that "one of the most important motors of change in the structure of human relationships and of the institutions corresponding to them is the increase or decrease of the population" (Elias, 2000: 210). Thus, the discussion about which one comes first in regard to this issue is not useful because Iraq was formed before the creation of an apparent nation. There is still a question mark around the existence of such a nation in Iraq even around 100 years after its creation (Osman, 2013). This is according to those scholars who demand common characteristics in the formation of a nation. One of them is Antony Smith who requires "a distinctive shared culture, a common myth of ancestry (descent) involving a shared history, a strong sense of group sentiment and loyalty, an association with a specific territory, territorial contiguity with free mobility throughout, equal citizenship rights, vertical economic integration and a common language" (Kirmanj, 2013: 14). Considering these characteristics, in order to depolarize the Kurds and Arabs in Iraq, it is difficult to acknowledge the suitability of any of these characteristics, with the exception of the citizenship previously imposed by annexing Kurdistan to the Iraqi state. However, successive Iraqi governments, especially during the period of the Baath regime, did not even adhere to that common characteristic. They followed a policy of exclusion, discrimination, and oppression, as well as genocide. The first Iraqi king (1921–1933) previously described the components within the borders of Iraq as "human imagination," confirming that "the Iraqi nation does not exist but there are blocks of human fantasy, empty of any national loyalty, steeped in the religious traditions and untruths and there is no association to bound them together" (Taheri, 2014). This is without looking for the reasons behind the lack of loyalty to the homeland, or whether there was a nation originally within those borders, instead of complaining about the absence of that nation.

This admission of the first king is the real description of the non-interdependency chains of Iraqi groups. Due to this rooted reality after the domination of Sunni Arabs in Iraq, some Arab nationalists began focusing on Iraqi identity in the form of a "national identity" as a product of the government's policy to unify Iraqis as the first step toward the unification of the Arab Nation. Initially, this means the politics and thinking of the ruling elite, which were not in the interests of the human beings inside Iraq, but rather the goal was ideological. Because "the state is a political and geographical entity; the nation is a cultural and/or ethnic entity" (Srivastava, 2010: 129), the ruling elite wanted and attempted to exploit the state to meet its political and geographical goals; not to invent an Iraqi citizen, but to impose a specific intruder culture that was rejected by the Kurdish people and others inside Iraq. In this context, it can be compared to the transformation that took place in France, when the state exploited its political entity to create the French nation culturally, and not the French nationalism that appeared at the end of the nineteenth century. For example, Hobsbawm explains that at the time of the 1789 French Revolution, only half of the French population spoke some French, and this changed over time; yet the geopolitical situation, and even the mentality of the Iraqi ruling elite, was not in the interests of creating an Iraqi nation. Most importantly, the French state was controlling itself and creating its national policy, but in Iraq, colonialism was controlling the Iraqi state and the Middle East as a whole.

The French model is an indication that the nation state is a consequence of state formation that takes place as part of a long process in a socio-psychogenesis context, which could be viewed as two sides of the same coin. Consequently, the state-driven theories of the origin of nation states such as France mean "these states expanded from core regions and developed a national consciousness and sense of national identity" (Srivastava, 2010: 130). Based on this statement, if the state is a national consciousness and has a sense of national identity, which can exist in any country, no matter how multicultural it is, then what is a nation? Is there a difference between the nation and the state? In this context, the "early conceptions of a nation defined it as a group or race of people who shared history, traditions, culture, and sometimes religion and habit of language" (Stephenson, 2005: 3). This definition of nationhood can apply to several components within a country. They share a sense of a national identity that crosses the circle of the nation, and nationalism is not based on a single characteristic (Walton, 2006: 113). Rather, there must be a set of characteristics that bring together the components to form a nation. These set of characteristics exist in the Kurdish people and also in the Arab people in Iraq. They also exist in the Scottish and the English together. The example of the Scottish and English as being united by one state is similar to the Arabs and the Kurds living in one state, but in the latter case it is based on coercion, and they are not united by a required affiliation, as exists in the British identity.

In other words, the state is the governmental apparatus by which a nation rules itself (Stephenson, 2005: 3). This argument is closer than any other to that of the civilizing process because any population has its own characteristics that make it different from others. However, these nations, according to the civilizing process, were in the primitive stages of transformation until the stage of self-consciousness and the stage of building their own state. Here, according to Elias, "consciousness is an inherent dimension of any society" (Elias, 2000: 115). These two metaphors are different and have parallels at the same time. They interact within the process of civilization, which cannot be separated due to the interrelationship between social structures at the micro-level, and state formation at the macro level. Within this framework, "the building of an integrated national community is important in the building of a state" (Stephenson, 2005: 3).

DE-CIVILIZING PROCESS

By exploring the interrelationship between long-term changes in standards of behavior and long-term changes in state formation and other wider processes, including the de-civilizing process, it may be possible to find some elements that contributed toward the process of building a nation state in Iraq and led to changes in standards of behavior. However, the socio-psycogenesis in Iraq did not facilitate the necessary direction to build a state that would make democracy the dynamic basis for the future of the state. Rather, from its earliest days, Iraq took a convulsive way with itself and its citizens. In other words, the upbringing of the political elite, which was overwhelmingly Sunni Arab, with a polarizing culture, did not prepare the ground for a democratic process, but it prepared the ground to take Iraq toward a nationalist, populist, chauvinist ideology with a single tendency toward the de-civilizing process. In this context, if we consider that there are civilizational features involved in building the nation state in Iraq, at the same time, it was carrying, at its core, some symptoms and features of the de-civilizing process, including the following five factors:

First: The royal family was foreigner who had no social dimension within the Iraqi components, especially considering the tribal depth among the Arabs (Allawi, 2014: P.XViii).

Second: The majority of the political elite came from an Arab, Sunni, Ottoman
   military background and possessed a military mindset (Simon, 1991: 62).
Third: The tribal social dimension was one of the characteristics of Iraqi society. This formation does not change without the ingredients of the state and
   strategies to change this tribal pattern (Nakash, 1994: 444; Hassan, 2007).
Fourth: The geographical division of the main components, except for Baghdad. There is a clear geographical division of areas, which in turn created
   areas of influence as well (Marr, 2018: 12, 13).
Fifth: From the beginning, the Kurds did not have any role in writing the first
   Iraqi constitution, nor did it include any indication of the Kurds. Consequently, there was a regional consensus, including in Iraq, on suppression
   of the Kurdish issue and its curtailment.

These five factors have been set out to identify the breakdown in the civilizing process according to the view that the "de-civilizing processes are what
happens when civilizing processes go into reverse" (Mennell, 1990: 205). Thus,
there should be some auxiliary foundations for this retreat. In this regard, "one
of the distinguished characteristics of the civilizing trend is a rise in the level
of danger and a fall in its calculability" (Salumets, 2001: 38). Consequently,
there could be fixed factors setting the stage for such a regression, as has been
pointed out, or sudden upward factors. It simply means that the crises or the
reversal of instruments of stability could increase the conditions necessary for
the breakdown of the civilizing process; as Elias describes, "the armour of
civilised conduct would crumble very rapidly if, through a change in society,
the degree of insecurity that existed earlier were to break in upon us again, and
if danger became as incalculable as it once was, corresponding fears would
soon burst the limits set to them today" (Elias, 2000: 532). This empirical
description of the de-civilizing process, which has been theorized by Elias,
took place quickly in royal Iraq, with successive coups, where "the state of
political turmoil began early with the crowning of Faisal as king of Iraq in
August 1921 and continued throughout his rule until his death from a heart
attack in 1933" (Hussain, 2006). The pace of coups, political instability, and
the systematic increase in violence became apparent in the history of Iraq.
   Thus, when the crisis takes on dangerous dimensions, security gradually
decreases and feelings of fear automatically increase; it could even crack the
psychogenesis. These kinds of circumstances create change in people's behavior, and therefore a large gash in the social structure is possible. However, it
is impossible to isolate the influence of psychogenesis from sociogenesis, as
has been illustrated by Elias in that "the psychogenesis of the adult make-up in
civilised society cannot, therefore, be understood of considered independently
of the sociogenesis of our 'civilisation'" (Elias, 2000: xi). Therefore, any
level of change will affect people both individually and collectively. In this

context, we return to how Elias uses the concept of the de-civilizing process. There are indications to the term, but there is no specific explanation for the process. The reason could be due to the absence of the need for a dedicated explanation of the process of civilization's decline. It means that "Elias did not develop an explicit theory of de-civilizing processes" (Fletcher, 1997: 83), but based on his empirical study, he points to the Nazis' mass holocaust as a de-civilizing spurt. In addition, the terms "spurt" and "de-civilizing" were used by Elias, "rather loosely to refer to a phase in which the pace of social processes increases, while he uses the term de-civilizing to refer to civilizing processes which go into 'reverse'" (Fletcher, 1997: 83). Thus, depending on this explanation, any researcher in attempting to understand de-civilizing needs to understand the ideational system of the civilizing process. This is because the civilizing process, according to Elias, "has two directions, forwards and backwards. Civilizing processes often go along with the de-civilizing processes" (Fletcher, 1997: 83). Thus, from the signs of the forward indications, it may be easy to recognize any backward movement.

Hence, the notion of crises has often been used to explain the de-civilizing process. This is because, "during times of social crisis military defeats political revolutions, rampant inflation, soaring unemployment, separately or in combination—fears rise because control of social events has declined. Rising fears make it still more difficult to control events. That makes people still more susceptible to wish fantasies about means of alleviating the situation" (Mennell, 1990: 205; see also Rohloff, 2011; Goudsblom et al., 2015).

Thus, the previously mentioned crises measurements depend on the content of the theory of the civilizing process. In the same direction, Thomas Salumets also mentions that "in the Germans, Elias himself wrote about the decline of the state's monopoly of violence under the Weimar republic, and Jonathan Fletcher has argued that it was then, rather than subsequently under the Nazi regime, the civilizing forces were most clearly dominant" (Salumets, 2011: 38). Additionally, the concept of "dominant" here is important to handle the fate of both directions—"forwards and backwards"—of the civilizing process. In this regard, "the relationship between civilizing and de-civilizing processes are here clearly conceived in terms of a balance between dominant and less dominant processes" (Fletcher, 1997: 83), or between the increasing social constraints toward self-constraint, which is central to Elias's conception of a civilizing process.

ETHNOCENTRISM

One of the factors that may accelerate the de-civilizing process is ethnocentrism, which has been studied by Elias differently in his research "Establishment and the Outsiders," as a gradual basis that leads to genocide. Thus, centrism, whether ethnic or religious, can be considered as a preliminary ideology that paves the way for violence as a primary stage to social and political rejection, and then to genocide. Thus, there is a possibility of building on human behavior and its habitus, a rule, which differentiates between the historical stages that are stigmatized as civilized and de-civilized processes. The reason for identifying these characteristics is to distinguish between what is civilized and what is de-civilized to identify the dangerous behavior of ideological groups. Regarding medieval societies as a not civilized, Elias argues, "the pleasure in killing and torturing others was great, and it was a socially permitted pleasure. To a certain extent, the social structure even pushed its members in this direction, making it seem necessary and practically advantageous to behave in this way" (Elias, 2000: 163). For these reasons, many scholars have attempted to discover the roots of genocide and to analyze the origins of the concept. One of these scholars is Graham Kinloch, who has utilized the concept of ethnocentrism as a starting point to the process of genocide.

Kinloch has used this term in a more complex way, as one of the quiet, slow, and effective causes of genocide, because of its social roots and nature. However, this does not mean that Kinloch has been entirely successful in his attempt to utilize the term, because the generalization of the concept has resulted in a very short description and lack of clarity. The main characteristic of social division, depending on Kinloch's view, is ethnocentrism as the central phenomenon within a dominant group and its consequences, such as the dehumanization of the subordinated or less important group. In association with this issue, Kinloch confirms Sumner's definition and believes that "this kind of ubiquitous normative prejudice represents the basis of in-group harmony and out-group hostility and the perception of out-group members as non-human, often expressed in extreme forms of nationalism, patriotism and chauvinism under stressful circumstances" (Kinloch, 2005: 29). He uses the terms "in-group" and "out-group" as two different antagonist entities in the process of a struggle leading to conflict. Thus, ethnocentrism may be one of the most appropriate sub-concepts to use with regard to this research's fieldwork because of the nature of the perpetrator in the Kurdish genocidal process.

Ethnocentrism is central to the sociological approach of William Graham Sumner in his book *Folkways*, which was published in 1906. The nature of this book, to a large extent, is similar to Elias's work on *Establishment and the Outsiders* in their description of social division, except for the differences in the methodology of both studies and their approaches. This similarity lies in raising the subject of the early division between the different components of a society and individuals' behavior towards each other. Despite some similarities between *Folkways* and the *Establishment and the Outsiders*, as two sociological approaches, Elias focuses on "how a group of people can monopolise power chances and use them to exclude and stigmatise members of another very similar group" (Elias, 2000: 12). Moreover, Elias has elaborately described the relationship between both groups, the "establishment and the outsiders," within his specific codes and concepts. Thus, unlike Sumner, Elias does not mention the concept of ethnocentrism and rarely refers to "ethnicity." Perhaps because he is addressing it as a study between two similar working-class groups, but he focuses on in-groups and out-groups, referring to the essence of the Nazis' behavior against the Jews in the Holocaust process.

After all, if the level of negative behavior from an establishment toward an outsider group is so highly aggressive, prejudiced, and explicit, what is the situation between two different entities akin to? Although the basic information in his work is inherently helpful in understanding the concept more accurately and strategically, it is also important to include the concept "ethnocentrism" in the framework of the de-civilizing process, because of ethno-centric tensions and the negative consequences. In addition, both Elias and Sumner have included some books and articles from other scholars, which may be important in enriching the concept of ethnocentrism, along with the study by Kinloch, in order to strengthen the illustration of the genocide process. Here, primarily, the characteristics of ethnocentrism by Sumner as a pioneer of the concept will be defined and illustrated before comparing it with the *Established and the Outsiders* to illustrate the differences and the appropriateness to this research's fieldwork.

Meanwhile, central to Elias's study is determining the roots of the hegemonic position of two similar groups in terms of power chances. Thus, the most prominent concept is the "establishment group" and the "outsider," including some sub-terms like "in-group" and "out-group." These terms form the principle aspect of Elias's strategy for an important reason, which is the interrelationship between in-groups and out-groups. Here, Elias's aim is very specific, and does not want to discover all folkways, but rather the fate of both groups—the establishment and the outsider—in determining their form of power. Concerning the definition of the concept, Sumner argues that ethnocentrism "is the technical name for this view of things in which one's own group is the centre of everything, and all others are scaled and rated with reference to it" (Sumner, 1956: 41).

This view of one's own group's centrality converges with that of Eurocentrism in the frame of civilization, which has been used by Elias to describe the Western expression in terms of explicit self-consciousness. In this regard, Elias argues: "The West believes itself superior to earlier societies" (Elias, 2000: 5). Although there is a lot of debate among scholars about defining the concepts of ethnocentrism, and for some of them this centrality and Eurocentrism are two sides of the same coin, it does have a kind of bias, because such centralization exists among all peoples, ideologies, and religions, but to varying degrees. Even though Eurocentrism is considered a special case of ethnocentrism, the human principles that have been issued by the European democratic system are considered a victory over that centrality, which many failed. With this tendency, however, it triumphed over itself by destroying Nazism and fascism in its backyard. Furthermore, "the tendency to view one's own ethnic group and its social standards as the basis for evaluative judgements concerning the practices of others—with the implication that one views one's own standards as superior" (Joseph et al., 1990: 1). Here, according to this definition, the issue is an ideological dilemma because of consideration of the centrality of ethical social standards.

In this context, it has been considered that "ethnocentrism is a mental habit. It is a predisposition to divide the human world into in-groups and out-groups. It is a readiness to reduce society to us and them. Or rather, it is a readiness to reduce society to 'us' versus them" (Kinder and Cindy, 2010: 8). This attitude makes it possible to include different levels or directions. If we stay focused on the attitude of the in-group, we realize that Elias has approached some unthinkable results. They "think of themselves in human terms as better than the others" (Elias, 1994: 19), because "the established group attributed to its members has superior human characteristics" (Elias, 1994: 22). Based on the foregoing, it is possible to see a kind of polarization and favoritism for one's own group. Such "attitudes include seeing one's own group (the in-group) as virtuous and superior" (Hammond and Axelrod, 2006: 2). When such a sense of a kind of superiority has been crystallized, "each group nourishes its own pride and vanity, boasts itself superior, exalts its own divinities, and looks with contempt on outsiders" (Sumner, 1956: 41). This crystallization "could have religious dimensions" and is based on "anthropocentrism (the belief that humans have the central position on the Earth), but focusing on one's own ethnic group (nation, people)" (Bizumic, 2014: 4). This type of belief by the Baathists played a fundamental role in their racist stance toward the non-Arabs in Iraq. First, non-Arabs have been considered as guests in the Arab homeland. Second, when they combined Islam and Arabism, they twisted the Qur'anic verse "You were the best nation brought out to the people" to form a basic principle in their dealings with the non-Arabs in Iraq.

SUMMARY

This chapter began by focusing on a set of concepts that Norbert Elias developed and investigated, in particular the regression that affects the historical transformation that constitutes the de-civilizing process. This regression is manifested in his essay ("The Germans"), as well as in the framework of the establishment and outsiders, approached in the framework of ethnocentrism. Additionally, this has been followed by an explanation of the essence of violence and state formation as an important part of the civilizing process and its position in this book. Finally, the de-civilizing process as a significant basis for the process of genocide has been considered.

Several characteristics are involved in the process of state formation. The most dynamic character, according to Elias, is the violent competitive process or "conflictual affairs" between various groups of people. The most expected consequence of this competition is a survival unit and successive states, starting with a feudal state, through many other different forms, to reach the nation state. These forms within the state process involve a monopoly over the means of violence and taxation. Thus, Elias has examined the establishment of a monopoly of one group and the eventual formation of a state through his study of European history, specifically, England, France, and Germany, which is called the civilizing process. Moreover, central to the civilizing process is the increasing division of functions. Functions could be one of the central developments of the human structure at both macro and micro levels. Here, the most important function of the state, according to Elias, "is the common defence of its population's own lives; the survival of their own group in the face of attack, and readiness to launch a united attack on other groups" (Fletcher, 1997: 63). If these three general functions formed the content of the modern structure of today's society, in the past, specifically for feudal states, these functions were most prominent in the hierarchy of the state.

Here, the state, as well as the nation state, has a set of characteristics. The most important and prominent characteristics of the state are "a permanent population, a defined territory, government and capacity to enter into relations with other states." However, the state has been defined by Weber as a "human community that (successfully) claims the monopoly of the legitimate use of physical force within a given territory." These primary elements include less important elements, which participate in the process of state formation. This formation, according to Elias, is the long-term conflict engaged in to dominate more territory with the growth of the population. Conversely, the characteristics of the nation state are different from the state, which generally has the same language, perhaps similar types of religions, and shares a set of cultural and national values. At the same time, this difference is relational because both sets of characteristics are related to each other—like a body and soul. In other words, the state can be defined as the governmental apparatus by which a nation rules itself.

In the context of the de-civilizing process, the establishment and outsiders described by Norbert Elias has been approached in the framework of ethnocentrism. This framework is important in order to recognize Arab centrism in Iraq. This kind of centrality shaped the ground for extreme ethno-Arab nationalism.

REFERENCES

Allawi, Ali A. *Faisal I of Iraq*. New Haven, CT: Yale University Press, 2014.
Baker, P. H. *Iraq as a failed state: A six-month progress report*. Washington, DC: The Fund for Peace, 2003.
Bizumic, Boris. *Who coined the concept of ethnocentrism? A brief report*, 2014.
Buschendorf, Christa, and Astrid Franke, eds. *Civilizing and decivilizing processes: Figurational approaches to American culture*. Newcastle upon Tyne, Cambridge Scholars Publishing, 2011.
Calabrese, John. *Iraq's fragile state in the time of Covid-19*. Middle East Institute, November 16, 2020. Accessed December 16, 2020. http://bit.ly/3p0jQeD.
Çetinsaya, Gökhan. *The Ottoman administration of Iraq, 1890–1908*. London and New York, Taylor & Francis, 2006.
De Swaan, Abram. Dyscivilization, mass extermination and the state. *Theory, Culture & Society* 18, no. 2–3 (2001): 265–276.
Dodge, Toby. *Inventing Iraq: The failure of nation building and a history denied*. New York: Columbia University Press, 2003.
Dunning, Eric, and Jason Hughes. *Norbert Elias and modern sociology: Knowledge, interdependence, power, process*. London and New York, A&C Black, 2012.
Dunning, Eric, and Stephen Mennell. Elias on Germany, Nazism and the Holocaust: On the balance between 'civilizing' and 'decivilizing' trends in the social development of Western Europe. *British Journal of Sociology* 49, no. 3 (Sep., 1998): 339–357.
Elias, Norbert. *The civilizing process* (revised edition). Trans. Edmund Jephcott. Oxford: Blackwell Publishers, 2000.
Elias, Norbert, and John L. Scotson. *The established and the outsiders* (vol. 32). London: SAGE, 1994.
Fletcher, J. *Violence and civilization: An introduction to the work of Norbert Elias*. Cambridge: Polity, 1997.
Ghalib, Sabah Abdullah. *The emergence of Kurdism with special reference to the three Kurdish emirates within the Ottoman Empire 1800–1850*, 2011.
Goudsblom, Johan, David M. Jones, and Stephen Mennell. *The course of human history: Civilization and social process*. London and New York, Routledge, 2015.
Hammond, Ross A., and Robert Axelrod. The evolution of ethnocentrism. *Journal of Conflict Resolution* 50, no. 6 (2006): 926–936.
Hier, Sean Patrick, ed. *Moral panic and the politics of anxiety*. New York: Routledge, 2011.
Husein, Karim. Iraq, Tarikh Hafil Bi-Qatil Al-Zuama. *Al Jazeera*, December 30, 2006. Accessed December 17, 2020. http://bit.ly/3oebd0l.
Joseph, George Gheverghese, Vasu Reddy, and Mary Searle-Chatterjee. Eurocentrism in the social sciences. *Race & Class* 31, no. 4 (1990): 1–26.

Kinder, Donald R., and Cindy D. Kam. *Us against them: Ethnocentric foundations of American opinion.* Chicago: University of Chicago Press, 2010.

Kinloch, Graham Charles, and Raj P. Mohan, eds. *Genocide: Approaches, case studies, and responses.* New York: Algora Publishing, 2005.

Kirmanj, Sherko. Anfal-Sirinewei Kurd le Parezgai Kerkuk 18 (2013): 10.

Kuzmics, Helmut. State formation, economic development and civilisation in NorthWestern and Central Europe (1997): 80–91.

Lash, Scott, and Mike Featherstone, eds. *Recognition and difference: Politics, identity, multiculture* (vol. 2). London: SAGE, 2002.

Loyal, Steven, and Stephen Quilley, eds. *The sociology of Norbert Elias.* Cambridge, MA: Cambridge University Press, 2004.

Luizard, Pierre-Jean. Sunnis, Shiites: The second major Fitna. *IEMed: Mediterranean yearbook 2016* (2016): 6.

Marr, Phebe. *The modern history of Iraq.* New York, Routledge, 2018.

Mennell, Stephen. Decivilising processes: Theoretical significance and some lines of research. *International Sociology* 5, no. 2 (1990): 205–223.

Mennell, Stephen. *The American civilizing process.* Cambridge, MA: Polity, 2007.

Nakash, Yitzhak. The conversion of Iraq's tribes to Shi'ism. *International Journal of Middle East Studies* 26, no. 3 (1994): 443–463.

OECD, DAC. Concepts and dilemmas of state building in fragile situations: From fragility to resilience. *OECD Journal on Development* 9, no. 3 (2008).

Osman, Tarek. Why border lines drawn with a ruler in WW1 still rock the Middle East. *BBC News*, December 14, 2013. Accessed October 17, 2020. https://bbc.in /2T61kDn.

Ottaway, Marina., Yaphe, Judith S.. Political Reconstruction in Iraq: A Reality Check. United States: Carnegie Endowment for International Peace, 2003.

Rafaat, Aram. The 1926 annexation of Southern Kurdistan to Iraq: The Kurdish narrative. *American Research Journal of History and Culture* 3, no. 1 (2017).

Renan, Ernest. *What is a nation? Nation and narration.* Edited by Homi Bhabha, 1990.

Rohloff, Amanda. *Shifting the focus? Moral panics as civilizing and decivilizing processes.* London: Routledge, 2011.

Roshwald, Aviel. *Ethnic nationalism and the fall of empires: Central Europe, the Middle East and Russia, 1914–23.* London: Routledge, 2001.

Salumets, Thomas. *Norbert Elias and human interdependencies.* Montreal: McGill-Queen's Press-MQUP, 2001.

Simić, Marina N. The state and modernity as anthropological topics: A very short introduction. *Етноантрополошки проблеми* 3, no. 3 (2008): 189–201.

Simon, Reeva S. *Iraq between the two world wars: The militarist origins of tyranny.* New York: Columbia University Press, 2004.

Srivastava, K. S. *Comparative sociology.* New Delhi: Discovery Pvt. Ltd, 2010.

Stephenson, Carolyn. *Nation building, beyond intractability.* Boulder: Conflict Research Consortium, University of Colorado, January 2005.

Straumann, Benjamin. The peace of Westphalia as a secular constitution. *Constellations* 15, no. 2 (2008): 173–188.

Strayer, Joseph R., Karl W. Deutsch, and William J. Foltz. *Nation-building*, 1966: 17–26.

Sumner, William Graham. *Folkways: A study of the sociological importance of usages, manners, customs, mores and morals*. New York: Read Books Ltd, 1959.

Tabbaa, Yasser, and Sabrina Mervin. *Najaf, the gate of wisdom*. Paris: UNESCO, 2014.

Taheri, Ameer. *Afdzal Za'im fi Tarikh al-Iraq*. London: The Middle East Newspaper, 2014. https://bit.ly/3dhgXzS.

Van Krieken, Robert. Norbert Elias. United Kingdom: Routledge, 1998.

Van Krieken, Robert. The barbarism of civilization: Cultural genocide and the "stolen generations." *The British Journal of Sociology* 50, no. 2 (1999): 297–315.

Walton, Kristen Post. Scottish nationalism before 1789: An ideology, a sentiment, or a creation? *International Social Science Review* 81, no. 3/4 (2006): 111–134.

Weber, Max, and Stephen Kalberg. *Max Weber: Readings and commentary on modernity*, 2005.

Yadirgi, Veli. *The political economy of the Kurdish question in Turkey: De-development in eastern and Southeastern Anatolia*. PhD dissertation, SOAS, University of London, 2014.

Yaphe, Judith S. War and occupation in Iraq: What went right? What could go wrong? *The Middle East Journal* (2003): 381–399.

Chapter 2

Nation Building and Arab-Centrism in Iraq

Understanding genocide in Iraq as a de-civilizing process is impossible without understanding two key aspects: on the one hand, the monopoly of the state institutions by the majority party in its process of nation building in Iraq, and on the other hand, the tendency toward ethnocentrism in the frame of Arab-centrism, which I have divided into Arab nationalism in Iraq, including the ideology of pan-Arabism and the ideology of the Baath Party as a separate version of Arab nationalism. However, understanding the hypothesis of a failed nation state in Iraq remains incomplete in the absence of understanding the desire for Arab-centrism, which primarily consists of the ideology of the Baathists.

The main methods used to understand these elements are the Iraqi regime's documents and the literature showcasing the practical stages of the processes undertaken by successive governments in Iraq, including the imbalance of power, which cannot be separated from the interviews that have been conducted and discussed in this book. This macro/micro analysis throughout the figurational developments shows the civilizing and de-civilizing processes and how the exceeding of elements is apparent and much more steeped in governmental sanctions. Hence, this chapter will establish a causal relationship between the history of the country and the de-civilizing process, the breakdown of the Iraqi state and consequently the genocide process.

IRAQI STATE FORMATION

The Ottoman Sultanate was divided largely due to the insurgence of Ottoman components (Kayali, 1997: 47); the corruption and the skepticism of state institutions (Becker and Hainz, 2014: 24); the new movement of young Turks

37

(Kayali, 1997: 4); the Ottoman Empire partaking in the First World War (Shaw and Shaw, 1977: 310), and its defeat in the war at the hands of the allies (Akçam, 2004: 4). Whatever the causes of the defeat of the Ottoman Empire, the consequences of this dissociation were unplanned (Hopkins, 2008), which led to the establishment of the new states and their formation, and the struggle for monopoly apparatuses in the Middle East. It has been shown that state formation, according to Elias, is "a violent competitive process through which there emerged successively larger territorial units with more effective monopoly apparatuses" (Mennell, 2007: 15). Here, unlike the extension or unity of regions, the legacy of the Ottoman Empire was desecrated as its territory was distributed. It is true that the Ottoman territory was shared amongst several ethnicities and cultures, but it is also true that this division occurred under the surveillance of the victorious allies, also known as colonial powers. This means that the components in the region were divided and reannexed from outside without a significant role themselves or, as Elias describes it, "competition."

This establishment of nation states did not accompany any violence between national groups, but the violence, if it occurred, was against the colonial administration because of the dissatisfaction of these components with the divisions that were imposed on them without their consent, in particular the Kurds. In addition to this process, unlike the process of state formation described in the theory of the civilizing process, the domination of a certain group is impossible via the declaration of a victory, but through the imposing of a majority group as a partner to the colonial powers. Thus, the monopoly apparatuses were transferred to the newly established governments through the colonial administration. Therefore, it is important to examine the effect of the transformation to the newly formed state or the "annexed territory."

The Annexation of Mosul

How did the process of the annexation of the Kurdish Vilayet[1] of Mosul to Arab Iraq, and the transformation of the power relations from the Ottomans to an ethnic minority in Iraq, occur? Were the Iraqis united in this regard? In the process of civilization in terms of the annexation of the Kurdish region to the Arab region in Iraq, two points need to be investigated. The first point is the annexation or the process of the unification of the Kurds in Mosul[2] province (see figure 5.1), with Arabs in Baghdad and Basra province. This is to discover the level of social and political integration between these provinces in relation to the elements of the theory of the civilizing process. The other point is the process of transformation of power from the Ottomans to an ethnic minority in Iraq. This transformation, on the one hand, according to the theory of the civilizing process, is supposed to bring with it "changes in the way people were connected with one another, leading eventually to greater integration and greater inter-dependence between people" (Rohloff, 2011: 3). On the other hand, the transformation from an autonomous city state belonging to an extensive and mighty empire to an isolated and divided region would inevitably lead to a strange and central nation state. In addition to this point, the Kurdish territories were dismembered, and its southern part was annexed to Iraq (see figure 5.2).

The important question here is: What was the position of the Iraqi provinces? Was Iraq united before the annexation of its three provinces? Accordingly, the position of Iraqi structural society with "provinces" before and after the First World War and during the period of its independency, according to Hanna Batatu,[3] constituted something close to "city states," as he notes that "Iraq was composed of plural, relatively isolated, and often virtually autonomous city-states and tribal confederations, urban 'class' ties tended to be in essence local ties rather than ties on the scale of the whole country" (Batatu, 1978: 7, 8). This fragmentation, which is of a drastic mechanical nature, did not terminate with the invention of the state; rather, it extended its dimensions to the present day. Therefore, it has been argued that "Iraq has a deeply fractured polity, with entrenched sectarian and ethnic divides" (Dobbins and Chalk, 2003: 168). This means that this division has two different levels—one is the deeply fractured policy because of the hegemony of one ethnic minority and the other is not just ethnic division but also the sectarian division between Arabs themselves, which was drastically imbalanced. They continue that "in the case of Iraq, the political structures created by the British after World War I did nothing to resolve these questions" (Dobbins and Chalk, 2003: 169).

Therefore, the unilateral Arab-centrism in the administration of the state overwhelmed the state institutions, with a complete absence of non-Arab components. "Instead, politics have always been about authoritarian rule and the settlement of disputes by force" (Dobbins and Chalk, 2003: 169). This is a reflection of the division that has dimensions and consequences that are still considered one of the features of the Iraqi state. Therefore, as it was "at the turn of the century the Iraqis were not one people or one political community" (Batatu, 1978: 39). They are still divided among themselves, even among Arabs themselves, due to sectarian differences, which has been considered as an ethno sectarianism (Rabi and Brandon, 2017).

This situation was not something ambiguous for the British authority in the region after the collapse of the Ottomans. Thus, why did the British power ignore existing ethnic and sectarian division and make them fuel for the establishment of politically and socially unstable states? The history of a hundred years of instability in the Middle East was a reflection of the interests of the colonial powers and the regimes that came to complement

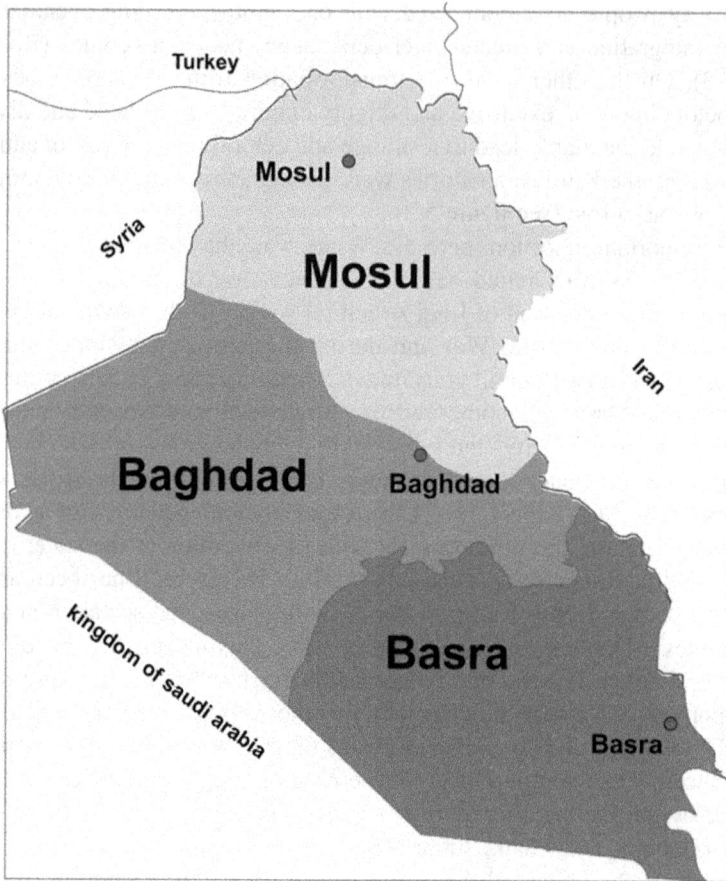

Figure 2.1   Ottoman Provinces. Hoshiyar M. Rashid (2021).

their goals, not the interests of the peoples of the region. The focus was "not upon humanitarian assistance or peacekeeping but rather upon the desire by colonial powers to advance their own interests in the region following the defeat of the Ottoman Empire" (Rear, 2008: 164). In another meaning, the colonial powers separated the region using a unilateral strategy without worrying about the future of the people residing in the region and acted only in the capacity of self-serving interests.

One of those self-interests, which many overlooked in the beginning, was the strategic interests in the region, especially the annexation of southern Kurdistan to Arab Iraq. Many of those who have written about Iraq emphasize that "the decision to make Mosul part of Iraq served several important British strategic interests" (Rear, 2008: 166). One of these strategies was "the presence of oil in the region" (Rear, 2008: 166) of Kirkuk, which belonged to

Mosul Vilayet during that period. Additionally, Hanna Batatu also points out the importance of oil in Mosul Wilayah, as he argues:

> The continued union of the Mosul Wilayah with Iraq, which had, earlier that year, been tied to the granting of oil rights to the nucleus of what came to be known as the Iraq Petroleum Company, was now made also contingent upon the extension of the period of the Anglo-Iraqi Treaty and of its subsidiary Financial and Military Agreements from 4-25 years, or to the date of Iraq's entry into the League of Nations. (Batatu, 1978: 215)

Here, dealing with the fate of Mosul, based on common interests with the Iraqi administration, the views of Batatu are now affirmed. Almost all historians agree that the focal point of the British was on the oil of Mosul Vilayet. Sir Arnold Talbot Wilson, the British civil commissioner in Baghdad in 1918–1920, in his book *Loyalties Mesopotamia 1914-1917*, affirms this key point. In this regard, Sir Arnold is quoted as saying that they "should not encourage any separatist efforts shown by the Kurds living in Iran, as well as those living under Turkish rule, we had to let the Kurds outside the Mosul province with their fate" (Barzani, 2002: 23). However, if this frankness is correct, it should also be borne in mind that the efforts exerted by the Kurdish political elite at that time were weak and did not realize the dangers that were facing them and the generations after them. If the "British attention was attached to the oil of Mosul vilayet" (Barzani, 2002: 23), the Kurdish political elite at that time either did not know what was going on around them, or they failed to convince the colonialists that they are different from Arab Iraq, and they will not accept their joining to Iraq. Indeed, they failed. The other motive behind colonialism strengthening its interests in Iraq is stability based on legitimacy because of the misbalance between the majority Shi'a Arabs and the minority Sunni Arabs, as it has discovered that "the majority of the population within the newly created country were Shi'a Arabs whereas Faisal was a Sunni Arab from the Arabian Peninsula, who had been installed on the throne by the British, the legitimacy of his regime was suspected from its inception" (Rear, 2008: 166). This suspicion led them to create a balance between Sunnis and Shi'a. They knew the roots of the sectarian conflict, and as a result they were suspicious of the success of this state, and they exposed the Kurdish people for the success of their project after they withdrew from the Treaty of Sevres (1920).

Consequently, the colonialists were looking into the temporary legitimacy and balance of the components inside Iraq because both the factors were important for the long-term stability of the power relations. In order to find these two factors, they needed a scapegoat for the balance of the sectarian division, which proved the error of the calculations of the colonizer and the

Sunni political elite that inherited the colonialism and caused the huge damage, with the results that we are still living with. In this context, and in order
to achieve the goal that brought colonialism to the region, "the number of
Sunni Muslims within the mandate would be augmented through the incorporation of the former Ottoman province of Mosul, with its largely Sunni
Kurdish population, within Iraq" (Rear, 2008: 166). As a result, this may be
referred to as a caesarean birth, which lead not only to the enmity of the Sunni
Arabs and Sunni Kurds, but also to further disintegration and fragmentation
of the Arabs themselves. Furthermore, this also led to the continuity of the
lack of interdependence between citizens, which resulted in the backfiring of
the civilizing process. Thus, instead of growing interdependency, the interrelationship was transformed into lasting political tensions and a doubtful
interrelationship between the two sides. These tensions and doubts depend
on the attitude and handling of the political experience and the essence of
the political system. Likewise, "this growing inter-dependency is connected
to increasing functional specialization" (Dolan, 2009: 6) of the political elite.

Based on these different characteristics of the civilizing process, we can
diagnose five main factors that played a major role in the civilization trend
and the structure of the interrelationships between the state of Iraq and
the other components, which in turn have influenced the interrelationship
between the components themselves. As a consequence, the functional specialization, as an element of the civilizing process, changed to promoting a
systematic change in the demography of the Vilayat. This breakdown is based
on the different characteristics of Iraqi state formation, and the following sections set out the five main factors involved.

The Interests of Colonialism

Who gave legitimacy to an international power to start building a state, without the real will of the peoples of the region? Certainly, we can call it the
colonial power that was based on the survival of the strongest. The different
ethnic and sectarian groups were congregated depending on the secluded
interests of colonialist power. The colonial power has utilized the inability
and oblivion of the inhabitants of these provinces to dominate and divide
the region according to their vested strategic interests. One of the reasons
for the collapse of the Ottoman Empire, by virtue of the first global war, was
essentially due to the lacking of legitimacy in controlling the different entities of peoples and its sagging authority. It was also because of the changes
and revolutions that Europe was witnessing; their frequencies reached many
regions in the world, which led to an increase in people's awareness of
controlling their own destiny. The problem was not in the collapse of the
"sick man" (Khoury and Kennedy, 2007) but, rather, the problem was in

"the formation of all these entities (states) over the dismantled legacy of the Ottoman Empire, which did not take into account differentiations between peoples" (Kadar J., PI, June 8, 2015).

In this context, Great Britain "decided to exploit the Arab nationalism for their own interests" (Isa, 2008: 120) and began its first move toward weakening the Ottoman Empire by providing support to the Arabs, and the formation of several Arab states on the ruins of the collapsing empire. Among the Arabs who rose up against the Ottomans, the Sherif of Mecca and his sons, including King Faysal I "because of his family's integral role in the Allied war efforts during the First World War, the British considered Faysal to be the ideal candidate to forge a unified nation out of Iraq's disparate elements" (Bernhardsson, 2013: 20). Nevertheless, it should not be forgotten that Britain acted from a colonial standpoint based on its strategic interests, and among those interests was the support of its Arab allies against the Ottomans, when "Britain did move to compensate the leaders of the Arab Revolt in 1921: it appointed Faysal as the King of Iraq in expanded borders" (Kramer, 1993: 00).

A Foreign King and Pan-Arabism

In addition to the colonial powers' decision to create a country out of contentious groups, the process was not neutral as the leadership of this new state was handed over to the Arab Sunni minority. The Sunnis were the only ones from among the citizens of the three provinces that formed Iraq, citizens who benefited from the capabilities of the Ottoman Empire and the acquisition of sensitive military and intellectual positions, based on sectarian consensus; moreover, they went back to Iraq with pan-Arab nationalism, including al-Husri. Accordingly, "the Hashemite rulers in Baghdad, whose source of legitimacy sprang from their religious ancestry and their prominent role in the Arab Revolt against the Ottoman Empire during 1st World War, regarded themselves as the natural standard-bearers of pan-Arabism" (Podeh, 1995: 2). The establishment of the Hashemite family as the rulers of Baghdad gave a great chance to the rise of pan-Arabism because in King Faisal's view "it was their 'noble mission' to lead the Arab world toward unity, possible with British support" (Podeh, 1995: 2). When they lived with this kind of impression, it led to an attempt to impose one kind of ideology on the rest of the population. This feeling of the Hashemite rulers in Baghdad opened the door wide for the Sunni Arabs to strive for their domination under the tendency of Arab-centrism. This is according to Hanna Battatu, as he argues, "except during a brief period in 1936-1937, the pan-Arab character of the state became more pronounced" (Batatu, 1978: 27).

The king's ambitions were across the Fertile Crescent—a sense of nationalism and an ambition to unify the Arabs in the name of Arab nationalism. He was the one who established the Arabism of the Iraqi state, at least through his Arab ideologue representatives, led by "the general directors of the educational system—Sati 'Al-Husri, Sami Shawkat and Fadel Al-Jamali—who contributed greatly to transforming the Iraqi educational system into a tool for national indoctrination" (Eppel, 1998: 233). With the help of the Ottoman Arab officers and their political and educational experts, Faisal was able to plant the seeds of nationalism in the heart of the new nation (Issa, 2008: 15).

The king's discourse from the beginning was clear, nationally, unitary, and racially, to the point where we can hardly distinguish between what the king said and what Michel Aflaq said. In a speech he gave in Aleppo in June 1919, Faysal said: "Neither minority nor majority among us, nothing to divide us. We are one body, we are Arabs even before the time of Moses, Muhammad, Jesus and Abraham" (Kedourie, 1962: 35). This discourse was converted into reality by King Faisal when he gathered pan-Arab nationalists and began appointing them as the head of the Iraqi educational sector. In this context, when we see Satti al-Hosari, "who was one of the most prominent (perhaps the most prominent) Pan-Arab nationalist ideologists, believed in education as the most efficient means of creating a new Arab society. The central concept in his writing, al-'Uruba (Arabism) is a term of Pan-Arab meaning" (Eppel, 1998: 233).

These strong expressions clearly prioritize Arabism before any other common identity among the Ottoman population. Further, his radical ethnic identity was strongly present when he, as king, seized power in Iraq. Consequently, the Kurds were expected to abandon their ethnic identity. In addition, the king and his politicians turned Iraq into an arena of radical pan-Arab nationalists, whose ambitions and intentions are ostensible, and which include assimilating the non-Arab components. Thus, the king, in addition to educational, military, political, and social institutions "as one body," could not be neutral "for all Iraqis," and "built a Government that was taking its approach from fascism and Nazism. As a consequence, they educated a generation in this way to counter British colonialism" (Issa, 2008: 15).

The Sunni Ottoman Officers

The Ottoman officers were an important element in the post-Ottoman Empire era in the state formation process because of their professional military background and their position in the management of state institutions. The position of these officers has not been hidden even from the Arab and Kurdish people in the region. "The officers, educated in Istanbul and returning to Iraq to play a leading role in the new state, were first and foremost

Sunni pan-Arab nationalists, dreaming of the unity of an Arab nation encompassing the Fertile Crescent and Arabia" (Simon and Tejirian, 2004: vi). In the same direction, "Former Ottoman officers of Iraqi origin had received a high military education at the Ottoman Staff College in Istanbul and had learned Western languages" (Wien, 2008: 16). It is, therefore, clear that these officers had received appropriate education and adequate military training to be part of the Ottoman Sultanate army or political administration. However, they were given more prominent roles when they went back to Iraq to participate in the nation building of the Iraqi kingdom. The officers "who joined Faisal's service in Syria after the end of the war with the Turks in October of 1918" (Batatu, 1978: 319) moved back to Iraq to join the team of administration headed by Faisal. Thus, there is no dispute over the presence of these Ottoman officers, but scholars disagree on the actual number of them. While Batatu limits them to only 300 officers, he states: "They counted about three hundred in all and with few exceptions, were of the Sunni sect and hailed from Baghdad or the northern half of the country" (Batatu, 1978: 319). According to some other sources, this number is double what was announced previously, which means "Iraq's first army was formed, comprising 600 returning Ottoman-trained Iraqi army officers, most from Sunni-Arab families" (Simon and Tejirian, 2004: 32). In addition to these arguments, and regardless of the official Ottoman figures, the background of these officers appears similar to part of the Sunni-based Ottoman Empire, whereas their ethnocentric concentration extended to those sectarian components that shared the same doctrine. Therefore, the Ottomans were able to benefit from the background doctrine on a high level and to take advantage.

These two characteristics of the Ottoman Arab officers were dependent on the social and political consequences of giving the Iraqi authority a particular nature. The families of these officers, "in the last years of the Ottoman Empire, chose a military career as a means to personal advancement" (Eppel, 1998: 236). In this context, "the Sharifians slid more or less unobtrusively into the ranks of the elite notables admittedly with some degree of friction and became part of the ruling class in Iraq" (Eppel, 1998: 236). This military nature became part of the state structure and inseparable from it. This argument is not isolated from Elias's theory of second nature or habitus. It has been discovered that "the level of habitus of thinking, feeling and behaving which are in fact learned from early childhood onwards" (Ritzer, 2004: 105). In addition, this level of habitus "became innate as if we had never had to learn them" (Mennell, 2007: 4). Therefore, the characteristic nature of these officers is threefold, and it is an interesting subject for scholars who are experts in the field of Iraq and could be important for the whole of the Middle East.

Thus, the threefold aspect of these officers has been shown in different lights. Accordingly, linking these important characteristics is to "link their Arab nationalism to militarism and elitism when they took over crucial government posts" (Wien, 2008: 16). Here, the first prominent common characteristic of these officers was their ideology; ideology in the form of pan-Arabism, in accordance with the struggle of Faisal for the unifying of the Arabs, became the main goal of these officers. This reason can be traced back to a pan-Arab nationalism that "developed in Iraq before the creation of the modern state" (Lukitz, 2009: 5). In addition to the entrenchment of the goal of transnational ethno pan-Arab ideology in the mentality of this elite, they also felt a kind of conceitedness that they were the prophets of their time to save the nation that suffered under the rule of the non-Arab Ottomans, without turning to the building of the human being in their new country. If someone fails to build his own house, how can they build houses for others?

This issue created a type of dream of a superior society in their imagination, but they were suspended between the dream of Arab unity with the characteristics of "supremacy in their view" and Iraqi nationalism, which was and still is for the Arab nationalists, part of the great "superior" Arab world. This is what made Iraqi nationalism more "artificial" than that of any other country" (Lukitz, 2009: 6). The second prominent common characteristic of these officers is militarism. According to many scholars, Iraq became an arena of hostility and illegal influence. This aggressiveness has been reflected by the first coup in "the Middle East [which] was in Iraq" (al-Kayssi, 1998: 11), and this "established a military dictatorship coup thinly lined, in the name of national unity" (Kramer, 1993: 181). This resulted in "a massacre against the Assyrian (Nestorian Christianity) minority and was accused of infidelity to the Arab cause, only after a year of its joining the League of Nations in 1932 (Kramer, 1993: 181).

Elitism

The other factor that characterized the Iraqi state's authority was elitism. The political elite, upon the formation of the Iraqi state, faced some problematic issues: "These elites consisted not only of traditional notable families, but also of families newly risen since the Tanzimat reforms in the 19th-century Ottoman Empire" (Eppel, 1998: 227). It could be possible to divide it into two aspects: the civilian elite and the military elite, which have been called "the effendiyya, or Westernized middle stratum" (Eppel, 1998: 227). The first one was the civil elite, who were the minority, to which we can add the term "revolutionary," and they fought the Ottomans under the auspices of colonialism. They include the royal family as a "unifying umbrella to balance the centrifugal powers in the country" (Wien, 2008: 8). There were also some foreign intellectuals who had nothing to do with the three Vilayats that formed Iraq, including Al-Hosri. The second one is the dominant military elite, of Iraqi Sunni-Arab origins, who became the other face of the political elite, as covered by the third point. Inevitably, the conversation here does not include the English officers who were advisers to ministries and state institutions in Iraq.

Elitism carries in its context different forms, including authoritarian elitism, with its different characteristics. Iraq, since its inception, has taken on a form of authoritarian rule, within some artificial democratic aspects. One of its features is that "politics have always been about authoritarian rule and the settlement of disputes by force" (Dobbins, 2003: 169).

Here, in a more specific context, "three possible elite states are described: ideologically unified, consensually unified, and dis-unified" (Cammack, 1989: 2). In Iraq, the authoritarian Sunni elite (exclusively) could be described, not just as ideologically united but also ethnically and sectarian, which is one of the most relevant descriptions; however, limiting these elite to one description could be considered an incomplete approach. These people came from different social backgrounds and formed a new authoritarian elite. They adopted and preached a new doctrine. Hanna Battatu has confirmed this diversity of the Iraqi authoritarian background as follows: "The ex-Sharifian officers were by origin from the middle or humbler walks of life, but by this time many of them had become properties and, though not yet fully accepted socially by the old families, formed part of the political elite" (Battatu, 1978: 28). Here, despite the ideological unification of the Iraqi political elite, they were actually dis-unified. We can trace this back to many reasons, including the Ottoman background and the cultural change that occurred during the years when they were far from the culture of the local community to which they belonged. In other words, these elite "deviated, to whatever extent, from the traditional frame works of thought and society, adopting Western clothing and concepts" (Eppel, 1998: 228). Therefore, it is natural for this cultural gap to form a social dimension between those who preserved their culture, which was characterized by the values of the clan, and Afandiyyah that thinks away from those values.

TOWARD GENOCIDE

This characteristic, in addition to the other four characteristics that preceded it, formed the mentality of the political elite and was the basis for pushing the Sunni-Arabs to defend their domination over the country, the Arabization policies of the land and its people, and the suppression of those considered outcasts, to dismantle them and at least end their moral existence.

This authoritarian approach, within the framework of the nation state, falls within the basic social interconnected functions of despair, which is summed up in their attempt to survive, defend their hegemony, and attack the source that they considered a threat to them. Thus, the Sunni-Arabs collectively attempted to maintain their power under the authority through a united attack on the Kurdish populace and other marginalized groups. The Kurds, on the other hand, have resisted the policy of assimilation through successive political revolutionary movements since the establishment of Iraq. Therefore, the Sunni-Arabs aimed to crush the Kurdish movement, and they were clever enough to utilize the colonial powers to dominate the new state and its components. As a result of this long-term denial of policy, the Kurds acquired the feeling of being outcasts as they were under the threat of a reign of pressure and of assimilation and retreat from their territories. The House of Commons Foreign Affairs Committee reported on this issue and they admitted:

> The Kurdish uprising was crushed, whilst the UK put no pressure on the Iraqi government to implement 1925 League of Nations recommendations on the status of Kurds in the Mosul Vilayet. This has not been forgotten in Iraqi Kurdistan, or the collapse in 1923 of the Treaty of Sevres,[4] which had laid out putative proposals for the creation of an independent Kurdish state, in what is now South-East Turkey or the UK's role in the Sykes-Picot agreement.[5] (HC 564, 2015: 19)

Additionally, marginalization during the domination of the Sunni Arabs in Iraq against the Kurdish component was systematic. The Kurds were considered a threat to the Arab identity of Iraq on the one hand, and an obstacle to the implementation of the Ba'ath Party agenda in Iraq on the other. As a result of this, and the accumulation of the conflict between the Kurdish political movement and the Iraqi state, the Baathists resorted to developing a clear strategy in order to defeat the Kurdish dream of independence either by assimilation (Arabization) in the Arab area of Iraq or by fragmenting and exterminating all who defended its existence completely.

Since their seizure of power in 1963, and then the monopolizing of power in 1968 until the end of their rule, the Baathists, who generally represented the Sunni-Arab component in Iraq, were able to implement their strategy before the British and the international community, disregarding human rights violations, while the Kurdish nation was facing genocide.

THE EMERGENCE OF THE BAATH PARTY

In the framework of the de-civilizing process, under the specific Arabized atmosphere and political circumstances, as well as the Ottoman officers' characteristics discussed earlier, which formed the crux of the state, pan-Arabism became a prominent identity of Iraq (Lukitz, 2009). These factors together facilitated a suitable platform for Arab-ethnocentrism, including a "new version of pan-Arabism by the Baath Party" (Lukitz, 2009: 15). Here, pan-Arabism in Iraq will be examined next as a facilitator of Baath nationalism.

Pan-Arab Nationalism in Iraq

At the beginning of the twentieth century, the whole area of the Middle East was in a process of great transformation, from changing habitus to the division of the Ottoman Empire. In other words, the civilizing process was ongoing after the fragmentation of the Empire's territory to the victor states. One of the sociopolitical movements established that had an effective role in the region was the Committee of Union and Progress (CUP).

As a reaction to the policy of the (CUP), which adopted pan-Turkish nationalism, many Arabs, as well as other ethnic components, rejected the CUP's policy of Turkification. As a result of this process and the awakening of Ottoman ethnic components, the Sunni-Arab elite who were officially part of the Ottoman administration started to diverge from Turkish influence toward pan-Arab nationalism.

After the First World War and the Iraqi state's formation under the surveillance of the colonial powers, the Iraqi identity and pan-Arabism were competing. These two identities attempted to impose their vision on the Iraqi scene. This is reflected in Iraqi political discourse consistently, especially among the Iraqis and the Pan-Arabists. With the passage of time, not only did the Kurds rejected the idea of the Arabist identity, but they also rejected the Iraqi identity due to the bloody history of the Iraqi-Kurdish conflict.

In this regard, there was a struggle between two competing and seemingly diametrically opposed models of political community, one the Iraqis and the other Pan-Arabs, who clashed, and this "was to be the defining feature of Iraqi national identity" (Bernhardsson, 2005: 5). In contrast to this argument, it is true that the two identities were competing. However, at the same time both identities were merging into each other. The supporters of Iraqi national identities disbelieved in pan-Arab nationalism, but they were fewer in number and less powerful; they also disbelieved in a country without an Arab identity. On the other hand, this competition lacked balance and was primarily confined to the Sunni Arabs. In this regard, according to Batatu, "the superior weight of the pan-Arab trend was the consequence, partly, of the monarchy's own initial pan-Arab predilection and, partly, of the fact that a very large number of the younger officers hailed from the northern Arab provinces, which leaned strongly toward pan-Arabism" (Batatu, 1978: 29).

Here, one important remark from the monarchy's own initial pan-Arab pre-dilection was the introduction of certain individuals who played an important role in the pan-Arab ideology, specifically Sati'al-Husri.[6] As we have already confirmed, "Arab nationalism and Pan-Arab ideology became a highly influential factor" (Eppel, 1998: 227) and that the king's exclusive call by King Faisal will bring his ex-minister of education in Damascus and a native of Aleppo, to Iraq, and appoint him as director of the Ministry of Education (Masalha, 1991: 2). This is the best evidence of King Faisal's Arabism tendency and his prior intention to Arabize the culture of the components in Iraq.

Thus, Al-Husri was directly called upon to perform a specific task for a specific strategy, which was to guide education in Iraq. It is worth mentioning that a renowned Ottoman pedagogue, Sati al-Husri, became "an Arab nationalist just before the war and joined Faysal in Damascus" (Jankowski and Gershoni, 1997: 93). This promotion of a spokesman for Arab nationalism (William, 2015: 47) to such an important and sensitive professional position like education raised questions about his stance concerning all components of Iraq. This is because "the outstanding exponent and popularizer of Arab Nationalist doctrine over the past quarter of a century has been Abu Khaldoon Sati' al-Husri" (Kenny, 1963: 231). Here, al-Husri is considered the first missionary of pan-Arabism. In this regard, "it was in the 1920s that Arab nationalism as a clearly enunciated, coherently formed ideology was first propagated by Sati' al-Husri, a Syrian and former Ottoman official who was in charge of education policies in the newly independent kingdom of Iraq" (Dawisha, 2000: 85).

For many scholars, the ideological influence of Al-Husri on the educational sector was significant for many decades of the Iraqi kingdom, and "once Faysal had appointed al-Husri to the Ministry of Education in 1922, al-Husri was quick to incorporate his ideas about the role and content of education in Iraq" (Bernhardsson, 2005: 198). Their goal was clear, as "Al-Husri viewed the curriculum of the schools as a mechanism of social change" (Bernhardsson, 2013: 198). Al-Hosari could not take a single step without consulting the king, and it became apparent that Faisal and Al-Husri rationally understood the sensitivities around education, and there was a strategy for achieving a specific goal. This direction has been confirmed by Al-Husri, as he argued, "I will employ every means to strengthen the feeling of nationalism among the sons of Iraq to spread the belief in the unity of the Arab nation" (Jankowski and Gershoni, 1997: 94). Furthermore, Al-Husri, went further because "to al-Husri, compulsory education and universal military conscription were the two most important mechanisms for the cohesion of the nation, military service being a further stage in the assimilation process of the individual to the nation" (Jankowski and Gershoni, 1997: 94). Thus, for Al-Husri and his most powerful supporter, King Faisal, two sensitive elements in the process of assimilation were essential. Therefore, compulsory education, which comes under the hegemony of Al-Husri, and a universal military, which formed the monopoly of violence, are two unavoidable elements in the success of Arab-centrism. However, it seems that their goal was to build an ideological army, in addition to other security forces. Sati'al-Husri started his activity as a member of the (CUP). This means that the nature of pan-Arab nationalism was an important phenomenon for the new state formation, based on a unilateral ideological education, and the building of a military doctrine based on the same ideology agreed upon between the king, Al-Husri, and others.

Moreover, the attempt of King Faisal to ensure the domination of Sunni-Arabs was unlimited. Here, according to Article 17 of the first Iraqi constitution, the Arabic language is the official language (GJPI, 1925), without specifying any position for non-Arabs in Iraq. This position was proven and explains how "in Iraq, the 1920s–1930s, Pan-Arabism was the command of the day, eventually leading to various interpretations of Iraqi particularities withal a resistance to Pan-Arabism in the 1940s–1960s." All these points were tantamount to declaring war against non-Arabs at the outset, in order to marginalize and assimilate non-Arabs into the melting pot of a state that had started the precursors of the authoritarianism from its earliest days, as well as based on "focusing on the contents of pro-authoritarian, pro-totalitarian, or pro-fascist tendencies among Iraqi intellectuals of the first Iraqi independence period, 1932–1941" (Wien, 2008: 2). It ensured that the ground was created for the emergence and escalation of the Arab Socialist Ba'ath Party (BASP), which was characterized by a violent nature and the foundations of an unprecedented Arab chauvinism.

The Origins of the Arab Baath Socialist Party

The Arab Baath Socialist Party (ABSP), a dangerous part of the history of the Iraqi state, is responsible for the crimes committed under the leadership of the Baathists, from their seizure of power in Iraq in 1968 until their fall in April 2003. Among those crimes is the genocide process against the Kurdish people throughout the 1970s and 1980s of the last century. Here, the important question is, who were the Baathists and what was the essence of their ideology?

The ABSP was established by merging three subsidiary political parties, which were established years before they announced the unification of the three branches in 1947/1952. The most important two points are, first, that the two initial parties are an extension of the crisis that the world went through from an extension of colonialism, the signs of the Second World War, and the emergence of the Nazi and fascist parties. Second is that the establishment was not in Iraq, and there was not a single Iraqi among the establishers. This means that the need was not Iraqi but was built on the illusion of the greatness of the nation from the ocean to the Gulf—an illusion that could not go beyond the backyard of its dreamers.

First: The Arab Baath Movement, led by the two Parisian intellectuals Michel Aflaq (Christian Orthodox) and Salah al-Din al-Bitar (Sunni), "was established in 1940 in Syria." Here two points are important to note: first, the first meeting of 'Aflaq and al-Bitar was at Sorbonne in 1929. "They became in no time intimate friends. They shared experiences, read the same authors Nietzsche, Mazzini, Andre Gide, Romain Rolland, Marx, and Lenin, among others and were caught in the same Marxist wave that swept over the European campuses during the worldwide slump and financial crisis of 1929-1932" (Battatu, 1978: 725). Second, "Zaki al-Arsuzi and Michel Aflaq met intellectually through the conception of the Arab Baath" (al-Charif, 2000: 146).

Second: The Arab Baath, led by Zaki Al-Arsuzi (Alawite), on June 29, 1939, in Alexandria, the disputed city between Syria and Turkey. According to an agreement on June 29, 1939, between Turkey and France, it was handed over to the Turkish Republic (Khadduri, 1945: 424). This was considered a "disaster" (Battatu, 1978: 722). Therefore, "All Arabo-phones—Sunnis, Alawites and Christians—found common ground on at least one issue which was: 'hatred of the Turk'" (Satloff, 1986: 148). As a consequence, the shock of the annexation led Al-Arsuzi to draw his "inspiration from racialism" (Battatu, 1978: 723).

Third: The Arab Socialist Party was founded by Akram Al-Hourani in 1950. Al-Hurani, due to being "big landlords in Hama" (Battatu, 1978: 723), "played a major role in Syrian politics where he was elected as a deputy of Hama and he was involved in 3-military coups in Syria starting with the coup Hosni al-Zaeem on March 30, 1949 and the coup of Sami al-Hinnawi on August 14 of the same year, and the coup of Adib Shishakli in January 19, 1951" (al-Hamdani, 2007: 8). This position of al-Hurani reflects the ideology of the Baathists in believing in violence to seize power.

Crossing the Border to Iraq

A group of factors contributed to the consolidation of the Baathists' position and their ability to spread, according to what was proven by Battatu with regard to the development of the three groups:

1. The French occupation—the colonial hegemony and its dimensions in the region were used by the Ba'athists.
2. The partition of the Arab provinces of the Ottoman Empire and the resultant hindrances to the old trade routes.

3. The decline of the Islamic social order (and the Christian millah structure) and of the old values and loyalties (the collapse of the Ottomans, the wars, and the massive changes in the region, based on the civilizing process, leading to a major change in the psycho/ sociogenesis).
4. The impact of European ideas. This includes Nazi and fascist ideas because the political, social, and security was against colonialism; therefore, people consciously or subconsciously became sympathetic to these ideas.
5. The enfeeblement of the traditional nationalists, that is, the nationalists predominantly drawn from the upper-landed and mercantile classes and loosely organized in the National Bloc (Battatu, 1978: 723).

All these factors combined contributed toward preparing a suitable ground for an extremist pan-Arab nationalist ideology on the one hand, and on the other, the similarity of their ideas and goals led to strengthening of these groups and their unity in the form of the Baath Party.

Thus, that amalgamation paved the way for the party toward the domination of two of the most important countries—Syria and Iraq—in the Middle East. In this regard, the vanguard of the Baath ideology was spurred on in Iraq in 1949, and the first seed was planted in the field of pan-Arab nationalist thoughts. Here, Alexandretta was involved again in the first seed of the Baathists in Iraq, whereby "the first group who planted the seeds of the party in Iraq were three sons of Alexandretta" (al-Hamdani, 2007: 18), but two of them including Fayez Ismail and Wasfi al-Ghanim were 'Alawis" (Battatu, 1978: 724). Here, two points are important to highlight, which are Alexandretta and Alawism. Alexandretta was a sign of the occupation, whereas Alawism was a sign of minority groups. However, a third point is underlined regarding the post-Palestine War era, which "is also an important period for the formation of the Baath in other countries around the Middle East" (Cabana, 1993: 25). Thus, it could be said that the conflict between the Arabs and Israel, in the Middle East until the late twentieth century, was igniting the enthusiasm for pan-Arab nationalism.

Thus, in Iraq since the establishment a kingdom for King Faisal and the return of hundreds of Ottoman officers, merchants, intellectuals, and politicians from Istanbul to Baghdad, the capital of Iraq, the ideology of pan-Arabism in the form of the idea of Arab-centrism, and in the form of different political parties, gradually increased. Hence, in contrast to the class background of the originators of Baathists in Syria, the background of those who were the vanguards of Baath ideology "was made up of predominately lower income groups in Iraq" (Cabana, 1993: 26). On the other side, because Alexandretta group who planted the first seed in Iraq were Alawits or Shi'a groups, the first receiver who embraced the ideology was an Iraqi Shi'a, Fu'ad al-Rikabi.

Baath Ideology

In the framework of pan-Arabism and Arab-centrism, the Baath ideology gradually found suitable ground for spreading everywhere in the Arab areas of Iraq. The spread of nationalism during that period created different challenges for Iraq. As a result of the spread of this unilateral ideology within the framework of the illusion of "uniting the great Arab homeland" and "the struggle to defeat Israel and [achieve] the liberation of Arab territories," all the attention was, therefore, aimed abroad in order to postpone democracy, and under this pretext, "Iraq was ruled by authoritarian regimes of varying degrees of malevolence" (Dawisha, 2005: 15). In addition to these political circumstances, the social conditions and low incomes caused the Baath ideology to spread, as Battatu points out that "25.5-% of the members of the Iraqi commands originated from the classes of low income, 38.3-% from the classes of lower middle-income, and 29.8-% from the classes of middling-income" (Battatu, 1978: 748).

Iraqi society was predominantly tribal, with a mixture of ideology, beliefs, and ethnic backgrounds, as a consequence of the Ottoman Empire and British colonialism. In addition, the humble social status and rampant illiteracy in most parts of the country facilitated the ground for the infestation of a particular thought or ideology, which is typical when there is a kind of political crisis. Here, in the example of Iraq, it could be due to the nature of the society, as its most prominent characteristic was that of a feudalist society with a number of estates, but unlike the Eliasian example of Western society, internal competition was not intensified to expend the land (Elias, 1999: 263); however, the competition was intensified in order to seize power. In other words, Iraqi society was in one of its transformational stages, specifically in terms of power relations, as Elias has emphasized: "In order to properly understand our constraints and opportunities we must understand 'the shifting balances of tensions' or power-ratios" (Kaspersen and Gabriel, 2008: 373). In this regard, the nationalist groups, who had organized within the Baathists, had gained broad experience in various fields. They had experience in terms of political and social mobilization, and also in the political sphere for exploiting opportunities, along with the knowledge of the weaknesses of the existing systems.

Hence, the pan-Arab ideology manifested itself through different platforms, but the priority went to the Baath's constitution of 1947, and Michel Aflaq's discourses and statements, including in some Iraqi newspapers, in addition to Saddam's speeches and announcements. Focusing primarily on Michel Aflaq's statements because of the domination of Aflaq's discourses on the pan-Arab nationalists at that time, it is worth mentioning that we did not find in Iraq a discourse or attention for the founders of the Baath Party, "while . . . Baath Party was founded by Arsuzi, Bitar, and Aflaq, there has only been one ideologue for the party; Michel Aflaq" (Cabana, 1993: 31). If this point is correct for Syria and all Arab countries, for Iraq it is duplicated, because later on Aflaq's ideology gradually became restricted to within the borders of Iraq. In addition to his ideology, he personally lived and died in Iraq, and subsequently left a statement of his conversion to Islam. Thus, this analysis reveals how the Arabs were able to insist that Iraq was officially an integral part of the Arab homeland since ancient times, without paying any attention to the feelings and rights of the non-Arabs in Iraq or in Syria, which will be explained later.

Now, before delving into explaining the Baath's ideology, the Baathists resorted to a variety of means, using the state and its institutions without interference, and the resources of the state to progress the pan-Arab ideology. This fact was reiterated several times by the interviewees that took part in this research. Regarding this issue, the Baathists attempted to transform the state onto the other side of the same coin, where "the preparatory school and the 'cultural' courses of the branches" were also intervened with and that "the Baath Party's dominance in Iraq was much more than simply holding on to power" (Sassoon, 2014: 27). In addition, the Baathists were struggling to have a good quality cadre through the "madrasat al-iʿdad al-hizbi (the party preparatory school)," which, it has been confirmed, was the "cultural institution of the party," and it was connected to Maktab Amanat Sir Al-Qutr (the party secretariat) both financially and administratively through the office of culture and national media" (Sassoon, 2014: 28).

In this case, it seems clear that one of the Iraqi government's ministries like the office of culture and national media was mobilized for the sake of the Baath's ideology. The standpoint of the party's direction was reflected in the state's structure through the transfer of "the good Iraqi is the good Baathist" (Samar Omerr ʿAlī, 2012; Al-Basri, 2006), as they were claiming. This shift was placed on the shoulders of the party cadre through their preparation. It "was achieved through a dual process: on the one hand, by offering an ideologically educated cadre who could represent the regime's interests, and on the other hand, by making sure Iraqi society was exposed to the 'appropriate' cultural material best suited to the party's ideology" (Sassoon, 2014: 27). This dual process is an important sign and highlights the process of Baathification specifically against the Kurds. This strategy "was very similar to those followed in the Soviet Union and Communist China, where education and training played a pivotal role in the efforts of the ruling parties to dominate and control society" (Sassoon, 2014: 27).

The Baath constitution or "internal system" of the Baath reflected the ideological reality of post-colonialism, where most ideas that are mentioned in the constitution reveal a kind of self-image in the form of Arab-centrism.

This self-image is related to the emotional bonds in relation to the feeling of being one of the victims of the Ottoman Era as well as colonialism. It is because "the emotional bonds or valences underlie the extent to which people say to themselves 'we' or 'I' in relation to other members of their own group" (Fletcher, 2013: 62). This means that at the beginning of the twentieth century, and in the second stage after the Second World War, this self-image emerged as a result of consciousness. Here, as a consequence, the BP emerged, along with the content of the Baath institution; the last version of this content was authenticated on April 6, 1947. This version of the content was written by Michel Aflaq himself and was never exposed to any sort of change or amendment even after the unification of al-Hurani's Socialist Party and the formation of the Arab Socialist BP (al-Hamdani, 2007: 12). The Baath Arab Socialist in this constitution has been defined in its preface by the slogan: "One Arab nation with an eternal message." This announcement was established on the basis of the three pillars of unity, freedom, and socialism. These three pillars were restricted to the Arab nation. The fact that they were not changed means that these principles were very important for all kinds of participants, and as a remarkable definition of the BP. The preface of the constitution states: "One Arab Nation with an eternal message, the Arab Resurrection Socialist Party, a popular national revolutionary movement striving for Arab unity, freedom and socialism" (ABSP, 1947).

Much has been written about this motto of "One Arab Nation with an eternal message." In terms of the second part of the "eternal message," the idea has been derived from German philosophy and "Aflaq's historical studies and his acquaintanceship with 19th-century German philosophy are brought out in the program's section on the "immortal mission" of the Arab Nation" (G. Torrey, 1969: 447). It means that Baath's ideology had been influenced by German philosophy, "although 'Aflaq and Bitar emphasize the 'uniqueness' of the Baathist message, the influence of Western concepts is found throughout their teaching" (Torrey, 1969: 447). The ostensible influence of the Germans has been shown previously in the army fieldwork and other fields, especially when German officers were training the Ottoman army, which was to include many Arabs from Iraq and other countries. Furthermore, regarding the one Arab nation, the constitution in its seventh article determines the homeland of Arabs as "the Arab national homeland is that part of the earth inhabited by the Arab people and which lies between the Taurus mountains, the Zagros mountains, the Persian Gulf, the Arabian Sea, the mountains of Ethiopia, the Sahara Desert, the Atlas range and the Mediterranean Sea" (ABSP, 1947: 197).

As a consequence of this article, the possession of this homeland has been confined among the Arab habitants as confirmed by the following: "The Arab homeland belongs to the Arabs, they alone have the right to utilize its resources, its wealth, and to control its potentialities" (ABSP, 1947: 196). The dilemma of these two articles is varied. On the one hand, the areas inside the Taurus and the Zagros mountain borders include half of the Kurdish inhabitants and are known as South and West Kurdistan or (Iraqi and Syrian Kurdistan), yet in this constitution, it is considered part of the Arab homeland. In addition, Saddam Hussein made a speech to the Kurdish people on Kurdish National Day "Nawroz" on March 21, 1979, and this speech is considered a historical document from the 11th National Conference and was also issued under the name "The Humanitarian Track of Baath." It was an attempt to prove that the Kurds are living in the land of the Arabs, and they are not different from the Arabs, as he claimed: "The land, which these nationalities are inhabiting were part of the Arab countries, originating thousands of years ago, the latest of which was the great Abbasid state . . . and any separatism whatever forms, contents, appearances, grades and motivation is a perverted tendency and contrary to the reality of history, and harmful to the Arab nation, and these nationalities" (Saddam Hussein, 1979: 30).

This position is very clear in that the Baathists did not accept any kind of autonomy; it is not the matter of degree, but it is the matter of principle contentment. In addition, the non-Arab citizens that inhabited the Arab countries were told they must serve the Arab interests. Therefore, the demands of autonomy have been accused of being driven by colonialism, and any incitement from colonialism leads to perdition.

On the other hand, the Baathists and the Arab political elite, since the establishment of the Iraqi state, had given Iraq the Arab identity, and there was no appreciation for the feelings of non-Arabs living in Iraq or in other countries that were given the Arab identity. In this context, the preview religious cleric and the Iraqi vice minister of the 'Ministry of Endowments and Religious Affairs' and later Iraqi MP Dr. Muhammad Sharif, in a lengthy interview with him, emphasized: "The difference between Kurds and Arabs is very deep because of the difference of the language, the origin, history and the background. We are in humanity similar and also sharing the same religion but because they did not respect the religion, they have emptied it of its content. It became zero" (June 2, 2015).

Thus, on the basis of this hypothesis of the Baath constitution, the Kurds did not have a right to live in this area and to utilize its resources. The reason is contained in its eleventh article, which concludes, "Whoever agitates on behalf of or is connected with a racial group opposed to the Arabs, or whoever immigrates into the Arab homeland, for the purposes of colonization, will be expelled from the Arab homeland" (ABSP, 1947: 196).

The motive behind this article or the detour around it comes out of a chauvinistic spirit and a preexisting accusation to accuse the Kurdish opposition or any other non-Arab opposition of being loyal to foreign powers such as

Israel and Iran. The Ba'ath Party did this systematically, leaving space for the Kurds to be accused as a pocket or an agent of Israel on all occasions. Similar accusations have made the Kurds suffer. For example, this is what was implemented by the Ba'athists against the Faili Kurdish citizens, and their only crime was their Kurdish affiliation. This Ba'athist behavior was also witnessed by the former Kurdish MP, Aso Karim, as one of the interviewees, and he stated that "the Kurds by the Baath Party were considered as traitors" (Karim A., PI, June 7, 2015). In contrast, the Baath constitution also described who is an Arab, as it is explained in Article 10: "An Arab is anyone whose language is Arabic, who lives in the Arab homeland or aspires to live herein, and who believes in his connection with the Arab people" (ABSP, 1947: 196). In this case, no preference is given to compatriots, but to the race of Arab, and it is assumed that belief in affiliation to this race is a precondition for living in that location. This shows that patriotism or citizenship is not included, but, rather, it is about the language and loyalty to the owners of this language. The Baathists also determined its policy toward the outsider or the non-Arabs, as explained in Article 15: "The national tie will be the sole (social) bond existing in the Arab state. It will guarantee harmony among the citizens and it will guarantee their fusion in the crucible of a single nationality. It will combat all other denominational, factional, tribal, parochial, or regional loyalties" (ABSP, 1947: 198).

Thus, the Baath party's domestic policy regarding interrelationships between the social components in terms of national ties is the assimilation of all different entities in the Arab body. Therefore, according to the previous Iraqi MP, Dr. Muhammad Sharif,

> The BP was following the theory of impossibility. They were always repeating, that the Kurds have two rights, first as Kurd, and the second as Iraqi but if they become a threat, either to becoming an Arab, or being deported from their own region, this means displacement, or if they commit any action against the law or against the Baath's policy, in this case they will exterminate them, as they did in Anfal campaigns. (June 2, 2015)

Culture in Baath Ideology

In addition to the Baath slogan, there is another important area of Baath ideology where the discourse is oriented toward outsiders. Baathists, primarily supporters of Michel Aflaq, were distinguishing Arab nationalism from European nationalism, claiming that Arab nationalism is not racist but rather cultural. Here, before delving into Aflaq's discourse, Saddam's speech, which is oriented toward the Kurds, will be highlighted. It was issued under the name "the humanitarian Track of Baath." Saddam claimed: "Those who are

hostile to our party are attempting to provoke confusion and saying; how can the Kurds (for example) be a member of the BASP?"

> The proper principle answer is that the adjective of "Arab" for the party is not an ethnicity, but it is described as a nationalist civilized humanity. . . . Politically, the party has been able to find a peaceful balanced solution to the issue of the Kurdish tendency towards the cultural and social development, in the context of one country, the branch[7] of Iraq, through the general Arab identity in a sense of nationalist, human and civilization which I have referred to. (Hussein, 1979: 30)

Saddam in these sentences is either deceiving his own soul, or his cultural level does not rise to an understanding of the essence of the issue of identity. Once he gives the characteristics of Arabism an identity, there is a description of a certain race and a certain culture. In understanding Saddam Hussein, the country is Arab, and the adjective is Arabic, as is the adjective of the Baath Party—Arab, and it is known that the adjective indicates a description. When a person is told that he is Kurdish, for example, we can recognize a certain definition, and also when someone is told that he is an Arab, we recognize certain cultural and intellectual characteristics. For these reasons, a Kurd cannot carry the adjective Arab, just as the English cannot carry the adjective German. An Englishman can live in Germany, but he doesn't say "I'm German." Likewise, the Turkish state bears the name of the Turkish race, and as long as this name is not modified, it is difficult for a non-Turkish person to say "I am Turkish," even if the name indicates the state as well. Thus, a Kurdish person may be forced to say "I am Turkish" as an indication to the state, but at the same time the constitution states that all citizens in Turkey are Turks. Therefore, the purpose of carrying the name of the race for the state is evidence of non-recognition of the existence of non-Turks in the country. The name of the state itself is racist, and so is the Arab adjective.

Additionally, the Baath constitution was a common document for Baathists, and Sati' al-Husri as a father of pan-Arab nationalism, along with many Arab nationalist writers or even some Arab Islamists, has also affirmed this aspect of pan-Arab ideology. It can be understood from the statement of Saddam Hussein, and the second point of the first fundamental principle of the Baath's constitution, that "the Arab nation is a cultural unit. All of the differences among its members are artificial accidents, which will cease to exist as a consequence of the awakening of Arab consciousness" (Hanna and Gardner, 1969: 305). The dilemma in the ideas propagated by Aflaq is the existence of superficial ideas, which are widely scattered in the folds of five books called "On the Way of Resurrection" or "Fi Sabil al- Baath." I have attempted to find out the exact keywords or a definition in association with this cultural nationalism, but there is very little explained or highlighted elsewhere. However, the content apparently focuses on human nationalism in connection with other keywords, and introducing pan-Arab nationalism as a necessary resource for all humanity, as Aflaq argued: "Our nationalism is guaranteed from the past because it is combined with a humanity message, and this is something that is only unique in the case of Arabs" (Aflaq, 1975: 155).

This means that Arab nationalism has its own roots in the past, and that past is Islam, because "the Arab consciousness is accompanied by a religious message" (Aflaq, 1975: 145). In addition, the Baathists claim to believe in "humanity and the Arab nation has a humanity message" (Aflaq, 1975: 62). Additionally, this Arab message "as they are claiming" about humanity is unique and it is different when comparing it to European humanity. It is because when Europeans were "calling for the humanity, the ambitions of colonialism are behind it as a purpose of expansion. French humanitarian thinking that have been emerged during the revolution was the preparation for expansion" (Aflaq, 1975: 155). Here, the problem with Aflaq's view is his attempt to Arabize every single concept through an imaginative description of Arab intellectual and historical values. In other words, there is an attempt to reestablish Arabism as a resource for every social scientific concept, without offering a logical interpretation of these concepts. In this regard, it has been explained by al-Hamdani that "Michel Aflaq's ideas and writings contain a collection of scattered speeches which were written when he was following the events in Syria, and his ideas are not homogeneous or coherent without careful analysis and development of the facts" (al-Hamdani, 2007: 9). Moreover, Aflaq's cultural pan-Arabism is dependent on the past—a past made up of different stages, but the most important stage for Aflaq is the emergence of Islam. Therefore, constantly, "Islam is renewing Arabism and its perfection" (Aflaq, 1975: 144). This is because "Islam is a vital shake, which is moving the latent powers in the Arab nation" (Aflaq, 1975: 142). Here, Aflaq has pursued this path to secure two aims.

The first one is to Arabize Islam and to create a social consciousness within Arabs that they are the owners of Islam and others have deviated from its tracks. As a result, Aflaq is attempting to create a sense that the Arabs are the best and they are at the heart of Islam—if the Arabs disappear, Islam will disappear too. The first aim leads to the second one, which is to change and improve the non-Muslim's circumstances, specifically Christians, under the domination of the Arab Islamic society. It is because the Christians suffered a lot "according to Aflaq" in the absence of the Arab leadership of Islam, and the aggressive Ottoman behavior toward non-Muslims at the period of Ottoman rule. Thus, Aflaq in his most extreme position, to show Islam as an Arabic culture, announced that "the Arab Christians must know, when nationalism is waking up in themselves completely and they retrieve their natural character, they should know that Islam is their nationalist culture, they must work to understand it and love it and to be careful about Islam, as their eagerness is the most precious thing in their Arabism" (Aflaq, 1975: v148). This is one of the principles that "Islam cannot be represented except by the Arab nation" (Aflaq, 1975: 146). However, this argument is not only Aflaq's demand but in one form or another, it has been reiterated by the Arab elite, particularly by Arab Islamist leaders. Here, it can be understood that Aflaq aimed to withdraw the legitimacy of the representation of Islam from non-Arabs to anchor it with the Arabs only. This was to create the idea of Arab-centrism because in Aflaq's view "the epic of Islam is inseparable from its natural Arab homeland, which is the land of Arabs, its heroes and its employees all of them also were Arabs. Thus, He chose for it the Arab nation and its hero the Arab Apostle" (Aflaq, 1975: 144, 145). All this concentration on the Arabs, according to Aflaq's allegation, did not come from vacuity but "the selection of Arabs to convey the message of Islam was due to the advantages and essential virtues in the Arabs" (Aflaq, 1975: 145). Here, the bottom line is that they have the ability and employability to become the center of the world because they are a key resource in Islam; in addition to that, they are carrying the essential virtues that distinguish them from others. Thus, they are the center of humanity and Islam in the form of ethnocentrism.

This narcissistic view of the Arab-self from a nationalist standpoint created a state of blindness in its owners that does not see the peculiarity of the other—the non-Arab. The non-Arab was created in Aflaq and other Baathists leaders view to serve Arab issues as long as they live on the land of the Arabs, meaning that they must consider themselves as Arab because their culture is "Arab Islam," and the land on which they live is Arab homeland; therefore, they must be assimilated into Arabism. Any attempt to break out from the Ba'ath strategy and demanding a kind of sovereignty, within the framework of self-determination, is considered treason.

Non-Arabs in the Baath's View

There was problematic relationship between the Kurds and the Iraqi Arabs in power from the early days of the formation of Iraq until the end of Baath's rule. The central point of disagreement between the Arab authority in Baghdad and the tendency of the Kurdish demands has always been denial and nonrecognition of even the basic rights. On the other hand, the Kurds have continuously attempted to prove their existence and their influence, but the demands have always been met with denial, maneuver, and a policy of divide and rule, as a fixed policy for dealing with the Kurdish question. Substantiated by the interviews and documents of the Baath, it is abundantly clear that they always attempted to marginalize and exile the Kurds from their places, both physically and morally. This denial appeared in different views and actions, starting from theorizing it and ending with its practical implementation on different levels. From this point, the vision of the Baathists took several detours around the issue of non-Arab components in terms of their existence within the nation state.

The constitution of the Baathists gives rise to friction and creates problems from its inception, starting from the classifying non-Arabs with foreigners, neglecting of historical facts about the existence of non-Arabs, and ending by not recognizing the Kurdish component. Thus, according to the Baath's constitution, the only tie in the Arab country is Arabism, as it states in Article 15 that "the nationalist tie 'Arabism' will be the sole (social) bond existing in the Arab state" (Hanna and Gardner, 1969: 308). The "assimilation" of other components according to the only tie of Arabism is unavoidable and "it will guarantee their fusion in the crucible of a single nationality" (Hanna and Gardner, 1969: 308). Hence, it appears that a single nationality is a long-term goal to "guarantee harmony among the citizens" (Hanna and Gardner, 1969: 308). In addition to this clear assimilation policy, "it will combat all sectarian, tribal, ethnic and regional fanaticism" (Hanna and Gardner, 1969: 198). This is the general and forcible principle of the policy of the Baathist, with no recognition of the social or political differences.

In the shadow of the constitution's articles, Aflaq in one of his speeches described the Kurdish existence in Iraq as a racial minority, as he said, "Let us take racial minorities such as the Kurds, for example; we ask why the Kurds or some of them are afraid of the Arabizm 'Urouba?'" (Aflaq, 1972: 181). According to Aflaq's ideology, the Kurds should not be afraid because, as he argued, "this fear mostly is due to the modern colonial propaganda extending to five decades before" (Aflaq, 1972: 181). In a very short journey into the literature of Aflaq, his party appears to show that colonialism is the source of all problems and setbacks. According to Aflaq, if there was no colonialism, no problems would have occurred between the Kurds and Arabs. Based on Aflaq's historical theory, "The Kurds have remained for hundreds of years living with Arabs and fighting valiantly defending the Arab territories" (Aflaq, 1972: 181). From these statements, we know the gullibility of Aflaq's thought, who confuses Islam and Arabism. Initially, the Kurds lived on their land, and during the period of the Ottoman Empire, there were pure Kurdish principalities, and they lived in completely different geographies. It is true that there were great Kurdish scholars who served Islam. Likewise, we may find those who served the Arabic language as part of their service to Islam, and even the wars of Salah al-Din al-Ayyubi were in defense of Islam, not Arabism, as stated by Aflaq, on the one hand, and on the other hand, if we accept the argument that the wars of Salah al-Din ultimately served the Arabs, should the Kurds remain under the hegemony of the Arab authority? Are they not entitled to live as the fourth biggest component in the Middle East, to enjoy their freedom and choose their own destiny? In the perception of Aflaq and the Baathists, not only must the Kurds remain defenders of the Arab state under the Baath rule because "in 1969, Aflaq's struggle in Baghdad was not just a rejection of the legitimate rights of the Kurdish people but also by some superficial conversations, wanting to link the Kurdish race to the Arab race and blaming colonialism for separating the Kurds from the Arabs" (Issa, 2004: 171). Aflaq does not only stand within the limits of describing the Kurds as servants to the Arabs; rather, he also goes with a naive imagination beyond what can be imagined, as it asserts that "for a couple of centuries, when the Arabs were forming one country, the Kurds were Arab Muslim citizens" (Issa, 2004: 171). This naivety is not only historical but also an ignorance of intellectual ethno-social realities.

It is worth mentioning that there is a certain compatibility and similarity between Michel Aflaq and Saddam Hussein's stances toward non-Arabs. Here, in his speech on the Kurdish national day of Nowruz,[8] Saddam Hussein highlighted the issue of the land, as he repeatedly emphasized the "Arab identity of the land that was inhabited by non-Arabs and it did not come through oppression or colonialism or alienation" (Hussein, 1979: 30). Thus, the presence of the Kurds on this land is in the vision of Saddam Hussein, and the speech here is oriented toward the Kurds on the Nowruz festival day; he claimed that the situation did not come about through oppression or colonialism, or alienation. According to him, this means that the non-Arabs are immigrants, and live on these lands as a result of successive migrations. Baathists are going even further as they stated in one of their propaganda books called *The Kurdish Question and the Autonomy*, which was published by Baath's "committee in the Labor Culture foundation." It is emphasized that "the Mosul case is considered a serious problem, created by colonialism, feudalism and wanting to cut out a part of the Arab homeland to annex it to Turkey" (CLCF, 1975: 13).

Thus, in the case of the non-success of the policy of assimilation, aggression or hostility will be the second "option to combat all sectarian, tribal, ethnic and regional fanaticism" (ABSP, 1947: 198). This is what the Baathists practiced in Iraq and Syria with the Kurdish people. In Syria, there are settlements planted in the heart of the Kurdish region, as part of the Arabization policy that, in addition to the Arabization of the land, "they deprived approximately 300,000 Kurdish people from Syrian nationality" (McGee, 2014: 174). In Iraq, the process of Arabization since the formation of the State of Iraq did not stop one day, whether it was spontaneous or systematic, and at the period of Ba'ath's rule, Arabization became a systematic part of the genocide process. This policy constitutes a basic principle in the Ba'athist constitution, which stipulates that "whoever called or joined a racial group opposed to the Arabs or whoever immigrated to the Arab homeland for the purpose of colonialism will be expelled from the Arab homeland" (ABSP, 1947: 197). Here, the common link between Aflaq and the Baath constitution is the "racial group," and in front of the obedience to the assimilation policy is the opposition or rebellion against the authority of the Baathists. In practice, this policy has been aggressively implemented as a key principle in the Baath ideology, primarily against the Faili Kurds who were expelled from the capital city of Baghdad and taken to the borders of Iran with their properties/ assets confiscated.

THE PHENOMENON OF MILITIAS

The developments of state formation in the modern age of the West, according to Elias, meant the "free use of the military weapons is denied to the individual and reserved to a central authority" (Elias, 2000: 268). In addition, the monopoly of taxation included the means of violence because, according to Elias, "they are two sides of the same monopoly" (Elias, 2000: 268). What is not understood, according to Elias, is the questions: "Who are to control it, from whom they are to be recruited and how the burdens and benefits of the monopoly are to be distributed?" (Elias, 2000: 268). What is important to mention here is that every nation state has gone through a unique experience and has implemented its own particular process in building a state and its formation. This is what we can understand from the detailed interpretation of Elias regarding the history of a long process of nation building in the case of Western societies, specifically when he points to separate models of European countries and illustrates the differences in the processes of development. In addition to the process of nation building, these issues concern scholars and political elites of modern societies with regard to finding out how to prevent totalitarian authority within the nation state. Concerning this matter in Iraq, throughout the century after its establishment in 1920, the state with its means of violence was suffering from the monopoly of a single party with a singular leader. Its people were suffering from the arrogance of the state as a large prison for the majority of its citizens. Its jailer of that big prison was the ideology of pan-Arabism that brought havoc and destruction not only to the Kurdish people but to all those who lived within that geography, which was weaker than the spider's house. Its architecture was tenuous when the Americans invaded it in 2003. The ideology failed to unify the Arabs of Iraq, let alone the unification of the Arab nation, with its deceptive slogan, one Arab nation, with an eternal message. The message was the genocide of the non-Arab peoples within the geographical area that now contains hundreds of mass graves. Thus, "Nation building in Iraq faces a number of challenges. Iraq has no tradition of pluralist democracy; politics has always been about authoritarian rule and the settlement of disputes by force" (Dobbins, 2003: 169). This shows that the Middle East is a "unstable and undemocratic region" (Dobbins, 2003: 168).

Thus, in addition to the violent aspects of ideology proposed by the Baath, which also emanates from the same society, it is clear that there must have been something wrong with the state structure or the culture of the state administration and the society. Here, I will focus on some aspects specific to the creation of the culture of the Baathists and its experiences.

Violence in Iraq has erupted in multiple forms, and one of these forms is the armed militia that accompanied pan-Arab nationalism. The first militia to emerge in modern Iraqi history was after Rashid Ali's Movement in 1941 to form the Futwa—organizations under the command of Dr. Sami Shawkat—which is considered a national militia with major similarities to the Nazi youth (Achcar, 2010: 122). This being influenced by Nazi ideology, or perhaps by one of its principles, the goal is to create an ability to accept those principles in society, albeit reluctantly.

Accordingly, the British and liberal democratic values have been rejected and "turned instead to a militaristic Germany, whose political ideology stood at the extreme edge of Romantic nationalism" (Simon, 2004: XI). Thus, using the Eliasian process of figurational sociology to understand this phenomenon, we must be attentive to the past and its procedural dimensions as sympathy with Nazism did not come out of the blue or without reasons. Perhaps the purpose was to create a specific capacity for the passage of policies that the political elite wanted. On the other hand, these officers were part of the society restricted to interdependent chains, specifically at the level of the political elite. In this regard and as ratification of Eliasian figuration, "by 1939, Syria and Iraq had become hot-beds of Arab nationalist sentiment" (Barrett, 2015: 31).

After the so-called revolution of July 1958, which was a military coup, a ministerial order was issued to form a militia of Popular Resistance, and it was considered to be a military arm of the Iraqi Communist Party (Ismael, 2008: 79), but after less than a year, it was canceled by ministerial decree. In contrast, secret militias formed in order to confront the militia of Popular Resistance, and the conflict escalated through assassinations and military clashes in the streets, especially in the case of Baghdad, Kirkuk, and Anbar. Then, Law No. (35) in the year 1963 formed the militia of the Nationalist Guard, belonging to the "Baath Party" (DeFronzo, 2009: 59); however, after nine months, it was also abolished by presidential order. Besides the Nationalist Guard, and in the situation of a conflict of doctrines between Sunni and Shi'a Muslims, a limited number from another armed militia emerged, known as Khalisi's group. This was headed by the command of

Sheikh Muhammad Mahdi al-Khalisi in Kadhimiya, but it was terminated when the militia of the Nationalist Guard was officially abolished.

Iraq's furtive construct brought with it several other mysterious and problematic issues. These issues are accompanied by the challenges of the identity of the state, legitimation, affiliation, unity, and diversity. Despite Iraqi politicians portraying that they have put a great deal of effort in building a prosperous nation state, its repercussions have been counterproductive in respect to creating harmony with the other components that are generally considered to be outsiders. However, according to the historical documents and interviews, the politicians involved could not distribute their authority and power on the grounds of democratic principles. This fact was the most problematic issue during the process of the Iraqi nation building.

With the rise of the Baathists to power in 1968, a new phase of militarizing society began. The Baathists were working constantly on different levels to fortify their authority. Thus, the party "re-emerged successfully in 1968. Reconstituting the pan-Arab ideology" (Simon, 1986: 157). With their return, they infiltrated all aspects of the state and society. That is, the Baathist rulers of Iraq "created a political narrative that drew upon the Sunni, pan-Arab history of Iraq instituted from 1921 on and implemented it via military and academic institutions" (Simon, 1986: 157). From the perspective of the military, it is essential to highlight the philosophy of the Baathists, which entailed violence in the form of a coup (upheaval). Michel Aflaq, in his writings, constantly emphasizes one concept, which is al-inqilab or upheaval (coup). Aflaq questions, "How can the party be the owner of its message and able to carry this message? It is to be the nation of upheaval before achieving the upheaval of the nation" (Aflaq, 1975: 74). The strategy of the Baath in achieving power is al-inqilab. However, Aflaq only reserved a single interpretation of al-inqilab as he concluded, "The coup has only a clear frank meaning, it is a conflict and reflex of mentality, character and prevailing interests. The Baath ideology is born from this conflict" (Aflaq, 1975: 76). Al-inqilab for Aflaq is the synonym of war, as he argues, "The stage of a coup is similar to a state of permanent war, whatever war means of vigilance, caution and doubling the effort" (Aflaq, 1975: 79). Thus, his view is that the only road to achieving all the Arabs' targets and hopes is war, nothing other than war, according to his statement: "The Arab revolution in this day and age is war, because it is the broader and fuller field and safest way to open up all their talents and outbursts their skills and heroism. Civilization, which it seeks to build, will not be built only through the struggle at the top of its ranks and forms of any armed popular struggle. Arab civilization is a war, a revolution" (Aflaq, 1975: 81).

When we investigate Aflaq's literature, we see a world empty of decency. In his vision, Arabs are weak because colonialism did not leave any chance for them, and everyone who opposes the conduct of the Baathists must be a humiliated follower of colonialism and Israel. In a similar direction, regarding the Kurdish areas that were outside the control of the Iraqi authority in 1974, and the refusal of the return of the Iraqi army after the collapse of negotiations and the rejection of the Kurdish proposed autonomy project, Saddam Hussein announced: "We are determined to keep the areas that are not under our sovereignty to a cruel siege. This issue is part of the process of the war, which we explain our perceptions on and its aspects of economic, social, psychological, and its principles include its political and military aspects" (Hussein, 1987: 129). Thus, according to the theoretical interpretations and practical behavior of the Baathists, violence was inherently rooted in their ideology. They believed in using violence absolutely without any humane or religious deterrent. This ideology is reflected in the Baath's behavior in establishing several militias in different forms after July 17, 1968.

Baathist Militias after July 17, 1968

Resorting to the formation of the militias in Iraq has been one of the phenomena of the policies of successive Iraqi authorities, as well as its political parties. However, when the Iraqi Regional branch of the Baathists seized power, this phenomenon reached its highest level in terms of number and aggressiveness. "The primary goal of a militia is population control" because they are "capable of using violence as a means of influence" (Hodgson and Thomas, 2007: 8). In addition, "The Baath has also sought to control society through the use of its paramilitary force" (Cabana, 1993: 68). Here, these paramilitaries and governmental militias will be highlighted, specifically because all their paramilitaries participated in the Anfal Campaigns.

Youth and Vanguards

The ideology adopted by the Baathists in terms of social control within its power deserves to be examined in more detail. There have been different methods of controlling not only the youth but also adolescents. This quote by Saddam Hussein was written everywhere in Iraq: "Let us win the young to safeguard the future" (Hussein, 2009: 58). This control over youth and adolescents by the Ba'athist institutions reached such an extent that parents did not trust their children when talking about politics due to the fear of the leakage of their views through their children at school, which would expose them to interrogation and possible arrest. This was a common phenomenon in Iraq, and many parents were arrested for this reason. The following example illustrates the extent of the issue: there was one occasion where Saddam rewarded a father who killed his own son for leaving the military services. This militia phenomenon was part of the ideological principles and provided a road map for the totalitarian regime that dominated even the people's breath.

As a consequence, two Pro-Government Militias (PGMs) of youth and students were organized on the order of the Revolutionary Command Council (RCC) under the name "youth and vanguard brigades No. 162 of 1975" (IRCC, 1975). In addition, in one of Saddam Hussein's books *Social and Foreign Affairs in Iraq* (Routledge Revivals), he states, "In the Iraqi Youth organization the first group are the vanguards (Tala'i) aged from 10-15 years, then the Youth (Futuwwa), from 15-20 years" (Hussein, 2009: 58). Moreover, recruiting people to the ranks of the party involved going through very advanced stages according to the age of these youths and students, calling them Al-Ansar, which means "partisans." It has been stated that "the first grade in the Baath Party is the supporters (Mu'ayiddin), then the partisans and finally the members" (Hussein, 2009: 59).

In the same direction, the book of "cultural curriculum," as part of the educational approach, was prepared specifically for the third phase of youth, the "Futuwwa" students, in the first, second, and third years of secondary school. This book highlights the dangerous ideological characteristic of brainwashing the children of Iraq. Thus, under the title of "who are the enemies of the homeland and the Arab nation?" in the third section of the book, it says that "experience has shown that the Zionist entity and the Persian regime, including the traitors of the nation who are supporting those enemies and renegades from the Arab traditions, are not only hostile to Iraq, but fighting in secret and in public all kinds of rebirth and progress in the whole Arab World" (General Federation of Iraqi Youth, 1983: 27). Here, Saddam Hussein has also been described as "father militant leader Saddam Hussein, President and Commander of the Armed Forces." This book also stirred up many issues in order to prepare these young people from an early age to blindly obey and sow hatred in their hearts.

Additionally, it is worth mentioning that there is a great similarity between these Baath governmental militias and the former Iraqi Futuwwa organization under the command of Dr. Sami Shawkat in 1941 and the Nazi youth (Achcar, 2010: 122), even in their militant clothes.

The People's Army "Militia" (al-Jaish al-Sha'bi)

Attempts to militarize society were continuous by the Baath leaders. Remarkably, they were not sure if they could stay, therefore, "after the coup of July 30 1968, the fear of Baathists from the army in attempting to overthrow their rule, the mind of Saddam Hussein may taper in the creation of a partisan army, dubbed as People's Army, instead of the notorious National Guard" (Al-Hamdani, 2007: 76). As an extension of the Nationalist Guard formed under Law No. (35), during the year 1963 (DeFronzo, 2009: 59), and as the Baathists returned to power in 1968, they did not give up reviving the new paramilitary guard. In this respect, the People's Army militia "is basically the same organization that was responsible for the campaign of terror when the Baath took control of the government in 1963" (Cabana, 1993: 68). Additionally, the RCC formed this nationalist paramilitary in 1970, as a quasi-military organization, including members of the Arab Socialist Party in Iraq. In addition, it was the Iraqi Baath Party Militia, "officially," and it "included a special youth section. Formed in 1970, the People's Army grew rapidly, and by 1977 it was estimated to have 50,000 active members" (Metz, 2004: 224). However, just before the Anfal Campaigns, this paramilitary force increased to a force of over 650,000 in 1987 (Cabana, 1993). It came to the point where there was no family in Iraq that did not have one or two members organized in one of the armed wings. The Popular Army was an effective participant in controlling the security situation, sending "units to Iraqi Kurdistan before 1980 and to Lebanon to fight with Palestinian guerrillas during the 1975-76 Civil War" (Metz, 2004: 225). Additionally, this militia was harassing people in order to recruit them into their ranks, and nobody had the ability to reject cooperating.

Government Security Organizations

Beside the Iraqi army, with its miscellaneous and large size, which was considered one of the biggest armies in the region, as well as the People's Army militia, there were a large number of irregular forces, militias, and security units, including

- Public security
- External intelligence
- Internal intelligence
- Private security
- Emergency Baghdad
- Military security
- National security
- Presidential guard
- Regiments of National Defense or al-Juhush—little jackass

SUMMARY

What is the purpose of understanding the process of nation building in Iraq as a civilizing process? Through many documents and the historical literature on Iraq, an attempt has been made to evaluate the ways used to create Iraq as part of a nation building process. This has included examining whether this process led to a deep cleavage between the Sunni-Arabs as the dominant ruling elite and the Kurds who were exposed to genocide. It has been found that attempts were made to nationalize the state as a single ethnic minority under a monopoly rule. In this context, "The ruling elites of the 'nationalizing state' often accuse the national minorities of 'disloyalty'" (Kuzio, 2001: 137); in fact, the Kurds have regularly been accused of disloyalty. However, as in the case of many instances of nation building, the process of state formation is often a violent emergent process, or as Elias describes it, a competition between the components. The establishment of nation states in the region did not initially accompany any violence between national groups, but the only violence that happened was against the colonial administration. This is because the Ottoman Sultanate was divided, and some new state models were forcedly imposed in the interests of the colonial powers. Internally, the Iraqi nation's state model was formed from three provinces, including Mosul province, without a regular legal referendum in the region. Thus, the interests of one ethnic group were taken into consideration at the expense of other groups in the new nation state. There started the process of suffering and persecution of other groups, particularly the Kurds, by the Sunni-Arab minority. Additionally, the violent approach that was taken by the Sunni-Arab elite, particularly through the policy of the BP in dealing with outcast groups, led to a big change, according to Elias, in the way people were connected to one another. This led to greater disintegration and greater independence between the different components, resulting in the de-civilizing process at the end.

Accordingly, this breakdown is based on different characteristics of Iraqi state formation, including the interests of colonialism, fetching a foreign king along with their push for pan-Arabism, the hegemony of the Sunni-Arab Ottoman officers, a kind of ethno-pan-Arab elitism, and marginalizing or persecuting the rest of the elements. Hence, as a consequence of these characteristics, pan-Arab nationalism in Iraq dominated the state institutions and all public/private sectors of society at the expense of the non-Arabs in Iraq. In this regard, Hanna Batatu has argued, "the superior weight of the pan-Arab trend was the consequence, partly, of the monarchy's own initial pan-Arab predilection and, partly, of the fact that a very large number of the younger officers hailed from the northern Arab provinces, who leaned strongly towards pan-Arabism" (Batatu, 1978: 29). However, these exceptional disintegrated circumstances led to the emergence of the ASBP (the insurgence of Al-Umma), with its aggressive chauvinistic ideology, in order to build one Arab nation according to a specific form of religion, as the culturally best nation. Finally, to attain these goals, the ASBP resorted to militarizing the society depending on the formation of several forms of militias and paramilitaries beside the National Army. This process was a systematic way of building one Arab nation in Iraq, and other non-Arab outcast groups had to be wiped out or at least assimilated.

NOTES

1. Vilayet (linguistically) has Arabic origins and, administratively, was a form of management that was pursued by the Ottoman Empire. Vilayet, according to Franck Salameh, is considered "a (state) by the same name, ruled by an Ottoman Vali (governor)" (Salameh, 2015: 148).

2. The demography of Mosul vilayat (province) throughout twentieth century has been changed to five provinces, including Mosul, Erbil, Kirkuk, Sulemani, Duhok, and Halabja.

3. Hanna Batatu (1926, Jerusalem–June 24, 2000, Winsted, Connecticut) is a Palestinian Marxist historian, who specialized in the history of Iraq and the modern Arab East.

4. "The Treaty of Sevres, signed in August 1920 by the delegates of the Allies and of the Sultan, incorporated the Covenant of the League of Nations and, among other stipulations, provided for the recognition or creation not only of the Arab states of Hijaz, Syria, and Iraq, but also of an Armenia, and of a Kurdistan which might include the Eastern vilayets of Turkey south of the line fixed for Armenia, together with the Mosul vilayet then under British occupation" (Edmonds, 1971: 90).

5. Sykes–Picot agreement: a secret bargain negotiated by British diplomat Mark Sykes and his French counterpart François Georges-Picot in May 1916 (Dodge, 2014). Under this agreement, the Middle Eastern region was divided and several nation states, on the ruins of the Ottoman Empire, were established. Additionally, the division of the Kurdish homeland into four parts took place.

6. Sati' al-Husri (1882–1968) was born in Sana from Syrian parents. He "modified his name to Abu Khaldun Sati' al-Husri in order to connote his conversion to Arabism. Husri graduated from the Mulkiya Mektebi in Istanbul—the school for Ottoman bureaucrat" (Simon, 2004: 28). According to Reeva S. Simon, "Al-Husri could not accept the French nationalist concept that the existence of a nation was predicated upon the existence of a special state, for the Arabs had no state of their own. Nevertheless, to al-Husri, they were a nation. Therefore, German nationalism with its differentiation between the nation and the state, the cultural being distinct from the legal or the mechanical entity became the model, the lack of a state now being irrelevant" (Simon, 2004: 28). This is an important point in understanding the belonging of Arab nationalism to the German nationalist school.

7. ABSP has considered these states as part of the Arab homeland; therefore, these states are just a branch of the United Arab Republic, which does not exist.

8. Nowruz, linguistically, means "the new year" idiomatically is a Kurdish national day and its roots date back to the time of the Medes the Kurdish ancestors.

REFERENCES

ABSP. al-Taqrir al-Siyasi al-Sadir An al-Mu'tamar al-Qutri al-Thamin, Baghdad, January 1974.

Achcar, Gilbert. *The Arabs and the Holocaust: The Arab-Israeli war of narratives.* United States: Picador, 2010.

Akçam, Taner. *From empire to republic: Turkish nationalism and the Armenian genocide.* London, Zed Books, 2004.

Al-Basri, Dawud. Al-Iraqi Aljayid..Huwa al-Baathi al-jayid?, Baghdad, February 4, 2006. Accessed April 15, 2020. https://bit.ly/2z1Lpzf.

al-Charif, Maher. Zakī al-Arsūzī and his contribution to the Arab nationalist ideology, Damascus, March 2000.

al-Hamdani, Hamid. *Sanawat al-jahim, Arbauna Ama min Hukm al-Baath fi Al-Iraq 1963–2003.* Vaxjo: Veshun Media Sweden, 2007.

al-Kayssi, Rakiah Dawud. *Iraq under Saddam Husayn and the Ba'th Party.* PhD dissertation, University of Glasgow, 1998.

Barrett, Roby C. *The collapse of Iraq and Syria: The end of the colonial construct in the greater Levant.* Joint Special Operations University MacDill AFB United States, 2015.

Barzani, Ayub. *The kurdish resistance to Occupation 1914–1958, Vol. 2, al-Muqawama al-Kurdiya lil-ihtilal' 1914–1958.* Genève: Genève: Ed. Orient Réalités, 2002.

Bernhardsson, Magnus T. *Reclaiming a plundered past: Archaeology and nation building in modern Iraq.* University of Texas Press, 2005.

Cabana, Joel L. *The Ba'th Party in Iraq: From its beginning through today.* Monterey, CA: Naval Postgraduate School, 1993.

Cammack, Paul Anthony. *The new elite paradigm: A critical assessment No. 89.* Institute of Latin American Studies, University of Texas at Austin, 1989.

CLCF. *al-Qaziya al_kurdiya wa al-Hukm al-Thati.* Baghdad: Committee in the Labour Culture Foundation, 1975.

Dawisha, Adeed. Arab nationalism and Islamism: Competitive past, uncertain future. Published by Blackwell Publishers, USA and Oxford, *International Studies Review* 2, no. 3 (2000): 79–90.

Dawisha, Adeed. Democratic attitudes and practices in Iraq, 1921–1958. *The Middle East Journal* 59, no. 1 (2005): 11–30. Accessed March 24, 2021. http://www.jstor.org/stable/4330094.

DeFronzo, James. The Iraq war: Origins and consequences United States: Taylor & Francis, 2009.

Dobbins, James F. America's role in nation-building: From Germany to Iraq. *Survival* 45, no. 4 (2003): 87–110.

Dodge, Toby. Can Iraq be saved? *Survival* 56, no. 5 (2014): 7–20.

Dolan, Paddy. Using documents: A figurational approach. *Approaches to Qualitative Research: Theory and Its Practical Application* (2009): 185–208.

Edmonds, Cecil John. Kurdish nationalism. *Journal of Contemporary History* 6, no. 1 (1971): 87–107.

Elias, Norbert. *The civilising process: Sociogenetic and psychogenetic investigations.* London: Wiley Blackwell, 2000.

Eppel, Michael. The elite, the Effendiyya, and the growth of nationalism and pan-Arabism in Hashemite Iraq, 1921–1958. *International Journal of Middle East Studies* 30, no. 2 (1998): 227–250.

Fletcher, Jonathan. *Violence and civilization: An introduction to the work of Norbert Elias.* John Germany: Wiley & Sons, 2013.

GJPI. Constitution of the kingdom of Iraq, 1925. Accessed December 10, 2020. https://bit.ly/3a0BVVC.

Hanna, Batatu. The old social classes and the revolutionary movements of Iraq: A study of Iraq's old landed and commercial classes and its communists, baathists and free officers, Princeton: Princeton University Press,1978.

Hanna, Sami Ayad, and George H. Gardner, eds. *Arab socialism. [al-Ishtirakīyah Al-'Arabīyah]: A documentary survey.* Brill Archive, 1969.

Hodgson, Terry L., and Glenn R. Thomas. *Rethinking militias: Recognizing the potential role of militia groups in nation-building.* Monterey, CA: Naval Postgraduate School, 2007.

Hopkins, Gareth. A sociological investigation in to the dynamic power balance between the Football League and Football Association: Using the Football League Cup as a window for exploration. University of Chester, UK, (2008).

House of Commons Foreign Affairs Committee. *UK Government Policy on the Kurdistan region of Iraq.* London: The Stationery Office Limited, 2015.

Husain, Saddam. *About writing history 2.* Baghdad: Dar Al-thawra, 1978.

Hussein, Saddam. al-masar al-insani lil-Baath, Baghdad: The General Secretariat of the Culture and Youth, Cultural Directorate. Baghdad, (1979).

Hussein, Saddam. *About the northern issues.* General Meeting Baghdad: Baghdad TV, 1987.

Hussein, Saddam. *Social and foreign affairs in Iraq (Routledge revivals).* United Kingdom, Routledge, 2009.

Ismael, Tareq Y. *The rise and fall of the Communist Party of Iraq.* Cambridge University Press, 2008.

Issaᵗ Albert. *Xiwêdnewei Be's bo Fašîsmî Mêjuyî.* Silemani: Office of Thought and Vigilance (PUK), Sulaimaniya, KRI, 2004.

Issaᵗ Albert. *Nasionalismî Erebî le Împiratoryetî Usmaniyewe bo Iraqi Serdemî Fašîzim.* Silemani: Office of Thought and Vigilance (PUK), Sulaimaniya, KRI, 2008.

Jankowski, James P., and Israel Gershoni. *Rethinking nationalism in the Arab Middle East.* Columbia University Press, 1997.

Kaspersen, Lars Bo, and Norman Gabriel. The importance of survival units for Norbert Elias's figurational perspective. *The Sociological Review* 56, no. 3 (2008): 370–387.

Kayali, Hasan. *Arabs and Young Turks: Ottomanism, Arabism, and Islamism in the Ottoman Empire, 1908–1918.* University of California Press, 1997.

Kedourie, Sylvia. *Arab nationalism: An anthology.* University of California Press, 1962.

Kenny, Lorne M. Sāṭi'Al-Ḥuṣrī's views on Arab nationalism. *The Middle East Journal* (1963): 231–256.

Khadduri, Majid. The Alexandretta dispute. *American Journal of International Law* 39, no. 3 (1945): 406–425.

Khoury, Dina Rizk, and Dane Keith Kennedy. Comparing empires: The Ottoman domains and the British Raj in the long nineteenth century. *Comparative Studies of South Asia, Africa and the Middle East* 27, no. 2 (2007): 233–244.

Kramer, Martin. Arab nationalism: Mistaken identity. *Daedalus* 122, no. 3 (1993): 171–206.

Kuzio, Taras. 'Nationalising states' or nation-building? a critical review of the theoretical literature and empirical evidence. York University, *Nations and Nationalism* 7, no. 2 (2001): 135–154.

Lukitz, Liora. Nationalism in post-imperial Iraq: The complexities of collective identity. *Critical Review* 21, no. 1 (2009): 5–20.

Masalha, Nur. Faisal's Pan-Arabism, 1921–33. *Middle Eastern Studies* 27, no. 4 (1991): 679–693.

McGee, Thomas. The stateless Kurds of Syria: Ethnic identity and national ID. *Tilburg Law Review* 19, no. 1–2 (2014): 171–181.

Mennell, Stephen. *The American civilizing process.* Germany, Polity, 2007.

Metz, Helen Chapin. *Iraq, a country study.* Whitefish: Kessinger Publishing, 2004.

Michel, Aflaq. *Fi Sabeel al-Baath.* al-Tali'a Publisher, Beirut, Lebanon: (V.1), 1972.

Michel, Aflaq. *Mukhtarat min aqwal Muessis al-Baath'.* Beirut, Lebanon: Arab Institution for Studies and Publishing, 1975.

Podeh, Elie. *The quest for hegemony in the Arab world: The struggle over the Baghdad Pact* (vol. 52). Brill, 1995.

Rabi, Uzi, and Brandon Friedman. Weaponizing sectarianism in Iraq and Syria. *Orbis* 61, no. 3 (2017): 423–438.

Rear, Michael. *Intervention, ethnic conflict and state-building in Iraq: A paradigm for the post-colonial state.* New York, London: Routledge, 2008.

Ritzer, George, ed. *Encyclopedia of social theory.* United Kingdom: SAGE Publications, 2004.

Rohloff, Amanda. *Shifting the focus? Moral panics as civilizing and decivilizing processes.* London: Routledge, 2011.

Salameh, Franck. *Charles Corm: An intellectual biography of a twentieth-century Lebanese "Young Phoenician."* Lexington Books, 2015.

Samar, Omer, Alī. *Shamal al-Iraq, 1958–1975: Dirasah siyasiyah.* Bayrut: al-Markaz al-'Arabi lil-Abḥath wa-alDirasat al-Siyasat, 2012.

Sassoon, Joseph. The Iraqi Ba 'th party preparatory school and the 'cultural'courses of the branches. *Middle Eastern Studies* 50, no. 1 (2014): 27–42.

Satloff, Robert B. Prelude to conflict: Communal interdependence in the Sanjak of Alexandretta 1920–1936. *Middle Eastern Studies* 22, no. 2 (1986): 147–180.

Shaw, Stanford J., and Ezel Kural Shaw. *History of the Ottoman Empire and Modern Turkey: Volume 2, reform, revolution, and republic: The rise of modern Turkey 1808–1975* (vol. 11). Cambridge University Press, 1977.

Simon, Reeva Spector, Eleanor H. Tejirian, Gary Sick, and Gary G. Sick. *The creation of Iraq, 1914–1921.* Columbia University Press, 2004.

The Iraqi Revolutionary Command Council (IRCC). *Qanun al-Futuwa wa Kataib al-Shabab, Raqam 62 lisanat 1975.* Baghdad: Iraqi Laws and Legislation, 1975.

Torrey, Gordon H. The Ba'th: Ideology and practice. *Middle East Journal* 23, no. 4 (1969): 445–470.

Wien, Peter. *Iraqi Arab nationalism: Authoritarian, totalitarian and pro-fascist inclinations, 1932–1941.* New York, London: Routledge, 2008.

Chapter 3

Genocide and the De-Civilizing Process in Iraq

There are studies and examination linking the Nazi national ideal with the principles that generated the decade's long establishment of ethnic-Arab centrism, that is, a conscious or an unconscious belief in the ideology of the national ideal (Scholtyseck, 2012: 261). This belief is presented in the policy of "the country is part of the Arab homeland," which is included in the Iraqi constitution, and that Iraq has a responsibility to participate in the Arab issue and resist Israeli expansion, along with the threat to the eastern gate, and the imposing of an ethnic totalitarian rule, which negatively affected the non-Arabs in Iraq. The ideology of the national ideal is similar to the Nazi national ideal, as Arab nationalists "generated an implicit requirement for national ideals, beliefs, principles and standards that could be obeyed absolutely" (Fletcher, 1997: 148/149). This led to the internal and external creation of the illusion of enemies. As a consequence of the national ideal, particularly reiterated by Baathists, the internal enemies who were threatening the state's national front needed to be eliminated and destroyed. Thus, dependent on this belief, the stage for genocide was set.

The previous chapter investigated how the process of the annexation of Mosul province to the Iraqi kingdom was established as part of state formation in the frame of the civilizing process. Additionally, the role of British colonialism as a major player, and its lack of neutrality toward the new state's components, has been considered. However, the interdependencies between Sunni-Arabs and the colonial power concerned the Kurds in relation to the domination of pan-Arabism and later on the emergence of the Baathists. In this chapter, we now turn to exploring the developments of the genocide process through its stages, including the genocide of the Faili Kurds, the evacuation and deportation from Kurdish rural areas, and the Barzani Kurds' gendercide. Hence, the Anfal Campaigns will be addressed separately in a later chapter. These campaigns of destruction of the Kurds in Iraq have been considered to be the result of the unilateral domination of one ethnic group within its totalitarian rule as part of the de-civilizing process. Here, an attempt has been made to combine the concept of genocide with the notion of the de-civilizing process, including civilizing offensives.

To expand on the ideology of the national ideal and to reach the level of the purity of Arabization of the country, the series of violence and the genocide process in Iraq started with a policy on three levels: Arabization, Baathization, and deportation. The Baathists started their rule, targeting the Faili Kurds in Baghdad, while at the same time they pursued the policy of awaiting dialogue with the Kurdish movement as a method to gain more time and power. This policy was implemented as part of the March 11 agreement. Additionally, after the Gulan war in 1975 between the Kurdish movement and the Iraqi authority, the evacuation of thousands of villages and towns, and the gathering of the inhabitants in forced camps, took place.

ADOPTING VIOLENCE

As previously mentioned in chapter 2, the establishment of a number of militias outside the state institutions occurred throughout the process of seizing power. The Baathist's belief in violence, in order to defeat their opponents, took on different dimensions, including atrocities and ethnic cleansing against Kurdish civilians in the disputed areas, particularly the city of Kirkuk (Curtis, 2008: 89), Khanaqin, and Shangal. Thus, while strengthening the idea of the purity of the Arabization of Iraq, the Baathists started the process of genocide from the time they assumed power in 1963. This attempt by the Baathists was subject to international objection, specifically by the Soviet Union and Mongolia, as it had been "urging one of its satellites—outer Mongolia—to level charges of genocide against the Iraqi regime at the UN" (Gibson, 2016: 67). In addition, Law No. (35) of the year 1963 highlights the real face of the Baathists and the Iraqi political system, besides the aggressive ideology, through the formation of the Militia of Nationalist Guard (Al-Haras Al-qawmi) (Al-Ali and Pratt, 2010: 30). Here, according to Article (2) of the Act, "the National Guard is an organized popular force, have been trained on the use of arms and its pillar are the believer people in their rights to a free and dignified life" (Waqa'i Al-Iraq, 1963: No. 35).

Consequently, in this preface to Article (2) of the Act, paragraph A states that the National Guard (NG) is "to protect the Arab breakthrough in Iraq and established a progressive revolutionary way" (Waqa'i Al-Iraq, 1963: No. 35). From these contexts, it is clear that the NG was an instrument for Arabization in the form of protecting the Arabs' existence in Iraq (Curtis,

2008: 89); nevertheless, as they were the biggest majority, there were no threats to their existence. In addition to this explanation, the "National Guard (Al-Haras Al-qawmi)" is considered one of the Baath's pillars (Karol, 2009: 20). Here, if the process of state formation means "the development of the monopoly over the means of violence by a centralised state authority" (Fletcher, 1997: 32), albeit including taxation (Elias, 2000: 268), and resorting to creating a militia beside the state army institution, it would of course be problematic. The prominent issue here is the question of legitimacy, because the administrative staff of the state "upholds the claim to the monopoly of the legitimate use of physical force in the enforcement of its order" (Fletcher, 1997: 32).

Here, we are facing a state institution that did not have the power to overcome the multipolar tensions or multi-central physical forces. This means that the state was still on its way toward formation. However, "tensions within a shifting balance of power always exist between the 'state,' its representatives and those who have little or no access to control of state power monopolies" (Fletcher, 1997: 35). This is a consequence of the conflicting process among the different social, political, and ethnic components, which makes matters more complex, and gradually heads toward the de-civilizing process. On the other hand, in terms of Arab-centric connotations, the Baathists' resorting to using their militia against those considered as outsiders could be more prestate than civilization, which is in contrast to Elias: "With a 'barbaric' or 'primitive' state of human existence and is used as a substantive in polar opposition to these two terms: it has obvious ethnocentric connotations" (Fletcher, 1997: 45).

Likewise, before the coup, the Baathists had a goal. In order to implement their goals outside the military establishment, they set an early plan with regard to the future of the country, including the formation of the NG militia. This was before the eyes of the Iraqi population, as they wanted "to achieve their hopes and goals after having been dependent on the forces of the fascist 'nationalist guards,' which were prepared before the coup and expended and legalised after the success of the coup" (Al-Hamdani, 2007: 26).

In addition to the NG, various outlaw groups "acted as though it were the highest authority" (Batatu, 1978: 1012) in the country. The Baathists knew the challenges they were facing with regard to other political forces that presented a major challenge to their existence, including the communist party and the Kurdish political movement in the north. Thus, the "National Guard was formed to check the strength of the Communists and other opponents of the Ba'ath Party in the streets" (Karol, 2009: 20). This meant that these militias were operating freely without the permission of the central ruler, in order to impose their hegemony and spread terror in the souls of the people, even if this was considered a crime against the country and its citizens, because

"committing acts of physical force within the limits of a certain central authority becomes a crime" (Fletcher, 1997: 35). Accordingly, Hamid Al-Hamdani,
an eyewitness, has described Baath's attitude and behavior towards its opponents when they seized power as follows: "Gangs have started the investigation with the detainees, whether military and civilians," and he continues,
"The coup supporters began conducting the screening of the detainees. Thus,
whoever was a communist or a Kurdistan Democratic Party (KDP) member,
would immediately be shot without any trial" (Al-Hamdani, 2007: 26/32).

In addition to Al-Hamdani, senior fighter Ibrahim Jalal, a participant in the
Kurdish movement, is another eyewitness of the events and those involved.
He describes the Baath's campaigns against Kurdistan, including the Syrian
Baath's army of "Yarmouk Forces," which interred Iraqi Kurdistan to support
the troops of the Iraqi Baath Party's campaign, as creating a disaster. Jalal
concludes:

> In addition to the Iraqi army and the Syrian Yarmouk forces, thousands of Arab
> mercenaries (National guard) were involving the campaign to attack Kurdistan,
> and they have been told; this is the Kurdish war against the Arabs, if you do not
> destruct and annihilate them, the Kurds will attack to occupy Arab villages and
> cities to wipe them out. On the other hand, they were promised if they occupied
> any Kurdish area, they have right to loot everything. In conclusion, this attack
> was so brutal; the media of some socialist countries have described it as geno-
> cide. (Jalal, 1999: 115)

In addition to this important statement, Al-Hamdani as an Arab communist
during that period confirms Jalal's admission and concludes: "It was less
than four months after the Baathist coup, the leaders of the coup took the
initiative even without warning to launch a large-scale military campaign
against Kurdistan. They used the destruction weapons and aircraft, harassed
the Kurdish people, the destruction of their villages and killing thousands of
their children" (2007: 32).

This claim has also been confirmed by the interviewees in the current
research who were also eyewitnesses. One of them is a senior lawyer and previous KRG MP; Tariq Jambaz stated, "In 1963 unfortunately the Nationalist
guards arrested many people. At that time, I was in Erbil and I was around
14 years old" (Jambaz T., PI, June 1, 2015). The interviewee Muhammad
Sharif, also an eyewitness, affirmed the behavior of the Nationalist Guards
and stated: "In 1963, when Arabs came to our area, they took all the Kurds'
properties. Those people were belonging to the Nationalist Guards, wearing
civilian clothes, and taking all the animals of the Kurds" (Sharif M, PI. June
2, 2015). What the witnesses narrate proves the intention of the Ba'athist
authority to terminate the Kurdish presence at least in some important and

arable areas and to expel Kurdish peasants from the larger areas. This excessive violence, which Baathists resorted to, is consistent with what has been reported "with respect to humans would include actions which infringe physical integrity, such as torture, wounding, killing and rape or destruction by impact or arson" (Fletcher, 1997: 47, see Van Benthem van den Bergh, 1980a: 15).

Another crucial point regarding violence described by Elias is the number of people involved (Fletcher, 1997: 48). For Elias, the image of violence is related to the different kinds of levels of violence, from individual criminal acts to political violence, and ending with larger scale intergroup violence. Here, "the larger scale inter-group violence (war and the threat of war) is more intertwined with identities centered on a particular state or nation" (Fletcher, 1997: 48, in cf. Van Benthem van den Bergh, 1980a: 7–8). Therefore, we can note two kinds of characteristics: the numbers of people involved and the identity of those people, which was the main issue for the Baathist Nationalist Guards. Consequently, the increase in the number of participants in this militia is evidence of the Ba'athists' insistence on implementing an aggressive agenda against the components that may become a stumbling block to their rule, and therefore, they were working on the militarization of society by increasing the number of participants of the NG, formed of Arab Bedouin men—the majority of whom were uneducated: "On the day of the coup, in February, this force counted no more than 5,000 men, but by May it had grown to 21,000 and by August to 34,000" (Battatu, 1978: 1012).

This huge increase in the numbers of Nationalist Guards over just a few months is in itself considered a reflection of Arab-centrism in the form of pan-Arabism, and the desire of the people to join a violent organization. On the other hand, according to Elias's we-image in the form of I-identification, the Baathists were, from the beginning, planning a specific procedure against the non-Arabs in order to monopolize the identity of Iraq in the form of pan-Arab nationalism, and this is clearly reflected in the Baath's political literature. On the other hand, in association with the figures involved and the identification of violence, they cooperated with the other Baathist party in Syria to collaborate against the Kurdish political armed movement—as Munif al-Razaz called it "Arabized fighting" (Al-Musilli, 2000: 155). As a consequence, "The Syrian Yarmuk forces entered in early October 1963 under the command of Colonel Fahd al-Shair. These forces have been incorporated under the command of the first unit commander of the Iraqi army and then have took the initiative to participate in the fighting immediately after it centered in the regions of Zakho and Dohuk" (al-Alrazaz, 1986: 154; Kunji, 2018). Al-Hamdani explains it as "the liquidation of the Kurdish movement" (Al-Hamdani, 2007: 32).

THE SECOND BAATH REGIME AND VIOLENCE

The previous section has shown that the aim of the Baathist campaign was to eliminate the Kurdish presence in large areas, with the aim of Arabizing them and expelling the citizens by terrorizing them through extreme violence. However, after a bloody ten-month rule in 1963, against the various Iraqi components, nationalist military officers carried out a countercoup against them. However, the Baathists did not give up and did not despair but, rather, began preparing and organizing their affairs in order to return to power. Throughout the period of the 1960s, the violence in Iraq continuously increased and "the Baathists returned to power by pulling off two coups, one on July 17 and the other on July 30, 1968" (Battatu, 1978: 1074). This kind of return could have been the inevitable result of changes in the interdependency of human relations due to the internal and external conditions.

Here, in Iraq's example, we face the similarity of two or more groups who are resorting to violence under the "we-image" in relation to Arab-centrism and attempting to seize power using the army and paramilitaries. Thus, after the collapse of its first coup in 1963, the BP attempted to return stronger, both ideologically and militarily. This sort of return was possible due to many factors, including the weakness (Al-Hamdani, 2007: 64) of major general "Abd-ur-Rahman Aref," who seized power on April 16, 1966 (Battatu, 1978: 1070). These successive coups raised many questions around Iraq as a model of a nation state, which is supposed to have a "stable government, for a stable popularity, in a certain part of the earth" (Alheims, 2013: 224). However, the majority of researchers in their analysis of nation states in the Middle East do not approach the legitimacy of power when a political party seizes power illegally. Therefore, "when the rulers are perceived to be working for themselves and their kin, and not the state, their legitimacy, and the state's legitimacy, plummets" (Rotberg, 2010: 9) and remains the legitimacy of the force only. This statement is an exact description of the Baath Party's authority, which was monopolized by Saddam Hussein and his family (Nalepka and Manoukian, 2014: 5; Post and Baram, 2002: 10). In other words, in a more accurate statement, "Decision making in the 1980s and 1990s become centralized in the presidential domain, but in both decades the party was deeply involved in micromanaging the country" (Sassoon, 2011: 5).

This distance from legitimacy as a decisive issue was constantly ignored under the hegemony of the streams of pan-Arab nationalism and throughout the chaotic process of authoritarian rule. Likewise, the will of the various components and their political and cultural aspirations within state institutions was ignored. Thus, "the culture of violence, weapons, power and what is carrying of synonyms and derivatives that were the recipe's membership in both structure, its general strategy of the Baath Party and a condition of belonging to him. They considered it as part of the virility of the party and the masculinity of its sons in conquering enmity and rooting them out when it is necessary" (Al-Saadi, 2007: 26).

This nature of violence led the Baath Party to militarize Iraqi society to a large degree. The Baath's legitimization of violence was fed by revolutionary legitimacy and pan-Arab centrism. The common features between Iraqi Baathism and Nazi Germany include militarizing the society: "Both Fascist Italy and Nazi Germany pursued the militarization of their own countries domestically through the establishment of mass movements devoted to the creation of alert, physically fit, warlike population" (Blamires, 2006: 422). This ideology is "based on a social Darwinist belief in the endemic nature of struggle in the world and on the glorification of war as a means of building heroic character" (Blamires, 2006: 422).

In this regard, the Baathist ideology can be discussed as if it is based on social Darwinism. Thus, Ba'athism is "very distinct from cultural forms of Arab nationalism, including the brand advocated by Sati' al-Husri, this nationalism approached to be social Darwinist in ideology as well as in practice" (Tejel et al., 2012: 146/147). Hence, it seems that the Ba'athists were utilizing elements of social Darwinism in terms of shaping their vision towards the outcast or the outsider. The primary goal of establishing these militias was "militarization of Iraqi society, suppressed any popular movement and the distraction of large numbers of Iraqi people" (Ahmed, 2016).

Genocide and the Partition of the Kurds

The process of genocide in Iraq against the Kurds is complicated because of the intricate Baathist strategy. The Baathists and the political system in Iraq pursued different levels in order to implement their policy of genocide. The most prominent Baath project was the division of the Kurds, depending on the Machiavellian principle of "divide and rule," in order to dominate Kurdish society. In other words, the Baathists did not see the Kurds as an independent society but as some untamed or unmanageable group that they had to civilize through the policy of Arabization. In order to implement this policy, "the Iraqi leader split the two groups (Shiites and Kurds), pursuing policies of divide and rule as well as the carrot and the stick" (Nakash, 2003: 278).

However, this policy was not limited to subgroups, but it was very specifically aimed at the Kurds in terms of absolute domination. In this context, "Saddam was probably not surprised by Kurdish desire for self-rule, his violent response to the Shi'i insurrection suggests that he perhaps felt betrayed by the Iraqi Shi'i, particularly after many had demonstrated their loyalty to the Iraqi state in fighting their Iranian coreligionists in the course of the Iran-Iraq war" (Nakash, 2003: 278). The purpose supposed by the policy of the

Baath, as a secular nationalist party, toward Shi'a Arabs was totally different in comparison to the Kurds, because the conflict with the Shi'a Arabs in the beginning was inherently integrative. Later, after the uprising of 1991, the interrelations gained some apparent sectarian dimensions. Additionally, the Baath's policy toward the Kurds was built upon ethnic background in order to Arabize the Kurds.

As a consequence of the Baath's vision of the Kurds, a specific procedure was initiated. Additionally, as previously discussed, the policy of the Baath Party concerning the Kurds had different levels depending on the principle of "divide and rule." Therefore, every Kurdish component and area probably gained its own specific genocidal policy and particular genocidal stages in order to conceal the process.

FAILI KURDS: THE WEAKEST CHAIN

Faili Kurds, initially, were selected because of their membership of a collective group, as well as their background as an out-group. The Iraqi authority, depending on the genocide model, intentionally created a plan within the administrative procedure or through issuing specific legislation (Hilberg, 1985). In this regard, specific legislation, including deliberate identification, was considered. Thus, "The political report of the eighth region Conference for Baath Arab Socialist Party, 1974," purposefully explains all the justifications for expelling the Faili Kurds from Iraq. The most reiterated justification is the "appropriate treatment of the dangerous foreigners" (BASP, 1974). This justification could be handled through the Eliasian principle of "attack and defence" as a social formation process. Thus, pursuing this principle is not because of the real threat from the Faili Kurds but because of the Faili's background. In addition, Baathists consistently highlighted the dangers and the existence of the plots to harm the Arabs from external enemies and internal traitors (BASP, 1982: 62). Therefore, the Baath Party launched a specific policy involving a long-term process against this important Iraqi Kurdish component.

The first action against the Faili Kurds took place in 1963 when Abd al-Karim Qasim was overthrown from power by the Baath Party and its allies. Here, as an initial base, "under the Baath regime, they (Faili Kurds) were specifically targeted and killed, or stripped of their Iraqi citizenship, under suspicion of having links with Iran, traditionally considered an enemy by Iraq" (Taneja, 2011: 8). The Baathists attempted to unsettle the social, economic, and political position of the Faili Kurds through a process of changing the citizenship law, and they issued multiple directives against them. The first stage appeared with the issuing of the new Iraqi citizenship Law No. (43) in the year 1963, after the Baathist's coup. According to Article 19 of the law, "The Minister may withdraw the Iraqi citizenship from a foreigner who has acquired it or if he attempted to do anything is considered as a threat to state security or its safety" (Iraqi citizenship Law No. (43) for the year 1963). According to this article, the Faili Kurds fell under category (B)—those who acquired Iraqi citizenship. Moreover, the Faili community was involved in active participation in the resistance against the coup of the Baathists in 1963; therefore, their fate after the issue of this nationality act was in the hands of the minister.

Consequently, after the Baathist's second coup in 1968, the security campaigns against the Faili Kurds intensified, and they were targeted everywhere; however, in 1970 these security campaigns become more extreme and more intense. Thus, the security campaigns were reliant on some legal official documents. One of these documents is the Iraqi Temporary Nationality Act No. (21) of 1968. According to Article 20 of this act,

> An Iraqi nationality is determined by the law and shall not be dropped from Iraq who belongs to the Iraqi families and was living in Iraq before 6 August 1924 and have been enjoying the Ottoman nationality and chose the Iraqi pastoral.
>
>   B. It is possible to withdraw the citizenship from naturalized citizens in cases specified by the nationality act. (IR-SJC, 2010)

This means that the person's nationality could be dropped from the previous non-Ottoman nationality. It justified the withdrawal of nationality from the Faili Kurds, considering them as foreigners or Iranian dependents. This justification made their expulsion to outside of the country easier, under any pretext, and at the time, everything was taking place with extreme secrecy and the media was completely under the control of the regime. In addition, "The Faili Kurds were thus one specific element of the Iraqi policy of Arabization that sought to reduce Kurdish numbers, and thus influence, in Iraq in favor of the Arabs" (Gunter, 2009: 51). From this argument, we can understand that the issue is the social, economic, and political influence of the Faili Kurds in the Kurdish or other Iraqi political movements. However, the hatred against the Faili Kurds reached a very dangerous level when the Iraqi government under the leadership of the Baathists during the time of the March Manifesto of 1970 "refused to approve the Kurdistan Democratic Party (KDP) nominee, Habib Karim, (the Faili Kurd) as vice president of Iraq under terms of Article 12 of the Manifesto" (Gunter, 2009: 51). Nevertheless, "any hope of implementing the manifesto soon evaporated, as shortly after the signing, the regime expelled thousands of Faili-Kurds from Iraq and launched a policy of Arabization" (Kirmanj, 2013: 151). Here, Arabization appeared at the core of pan-Arab- centrism and as a consistent Baath policy. However, the existence

of Faili Kurds in the capital Baghdad and around it, as the home base of the
majority of them and their active social, political, and economic participation,
was totally in contrast with Baath policy. Therefore, the practical steps taken
by the Baathists, in terms of eliminating the Faili Kurds, found their way.

The position of the Faili Kurds, according to the Baath Party, in comparison to the rest of the Kurdish nation, was more dominant and more sensitive.
This is because of four main issues, which are ethnic, economic, political, and
religious factors (Al-Fazil, 2002), as set out later in the chapter.

Ethnicity

The Faili Kurds, according to many Kurdish or other historians, are an
authentic Kurdish community from both sides of the Kurdish area at the
Iraq-Iran border, and they lived in this area for a very long time. The defense
of the existence of Faili Kurds in these areas, and acknowledgment of their
presence, is crucial because of the Baath's argument for the process of Failis'
deportation and extermination. The prominent Arab author Abbas al-Azzawi,
in his examination of the history of the Iraqi city of Amara, declared that "this
city was formed in 1860 and was inhabited by the clan (Dozawah) of Allure
Faili's, include some of nomadic tribes" (Abbud, 2007). Many Faili Kurds,
"in the nineteenth and early twentieth century, began migrating westwards to
Iraqi cities, primarily Baghdad, where they took on key commercial, social,
and cultural roles" (Fawcett and Tanner, 2002: 15). Many Western writers
have fallen into the trap of the great changes that have taken place in the
region, starting with a change in the history and ending with a huge change
in the demographics of the region, as a result of the mass migrations and the
process of Arabization of the region. Therefore, the majority of these writers
did not understand the geography of the region or recognize it as the homeland of the Kurds. Among these writers is Michel Gunther, who reported
that a "group of some 150,000 Kurds originally from the Kirmanshah region
in Iran who had lived in Iraq (many in Baghdad) since Ottoman times, but
without Iraqi citizenship" (Gunter, 2009: 51). This argument, including its
simplification of the history of this important entity, is different to the geographical reality of the Kurdish inhabited region, which was divided before
the formation of Iraq.

In contrast to the previous argument, the Faili Kurds are "a group of
Kurds from a region of the Zagros Mountains straddling the Iran-Iraq border. Due to the geography of their homeland, the Faili Kurds have family
members on both sides of the border" (Fawcett and Tanner, 2002: 15). This
argument is closer to the majority of historians regarding the existence of
Faili families living on both sides of the border, and it primarily refers to
the division of the Kurdish homeland since the "Chalderan" war between the

Ottoman Empire and the "Safawit" state. The Faili Kurds, as with the rest of the Kurdish people, had their homeland divided by the Ottoman Empire and the Safavid state. In this context, they have been divided between the two sides of the border. The existence of the Faili Kurds on the side of Ottoman Empire extended from the Iranian border to Baghdad, across a large area of Diyala province. This was done "after several treaties and protocols concluded between the two sides, they ratified a final agreement on 15 July 1929 without consulting the Faili Kurds living in the border areas" (al-Faili al-Alawi, 2008: 17). "As a result of this agreement it remained Faili land located between Kirkuk in the north and Basra in the south of the modern Iraqi state" (2008: 17). In relation to the origins of the Faili Kurds, "they are native to Mesopotamia population (Mesopotamia) and that the current population in the south and central Iraq are descendants of Faili and do not belong to the Arabs or remember any link" (Abbud, 2007: 29). In this regard, "the fragmentation of the homeland of Faili Kurds between the two countries without taking their opinion and even took the Arabization policy of compulsory taking place against the residents in these areas" (al-Faili al-Alawi, 2008: 17).

Thus, "Iraq, when it was invented, inherited its political system of democratic governance of Representatives from the State mandate similar to Western democratic systems. Though, after the independence in 1932, this system was emptied from its content" (Al-Faili, 2005: 13). However, the pursuance of this Western model by the British mandate was holistically imposed and its influence spread. Thus, the Iraqi constitution has a direct relationship with the formation of Iraqi institutions and a particular model of constitution based on the will of the colonial powers. Additionally, "one of the first who challenged the Kurdishness and also the Iraqiness of Faili Kurds was the representative of the British administration in Iraq 'Cecil John Edmond' at the period of the occupation of Iraq" (Abbud, 2007: 24). However, the shadow of the long conflict and the sectarian ideology between the pan Sunni Ottoman Empire and pan Shi'a Iranian Safawit imposed its influence on all stages of the formation of the Iraqi nation state, including its institutions. This influence of the Sunni pan-Arab Ottoman officers included the pan-Arab king Faisal, as has been explained previously. In this regard, "the survival of the regime under the hegemony of a minority whether a clan, sectarian minority, a political party or racial minority, making the resort to tyranny objectively a reality, because the adoption of a correct parliamentary representation enable the power's transfer to the majority owners" (Al-Faili, 2005: 14).

Preventing Faili Kurds from the Ottoman identity may have been due to the rejection of joining the Ottoman army, specifically through the forced recruitment methods. In this regard, "the Ottoman Empire was in dire need of soldiers in the wars with the Balkans, the Caucasus and northern Iran and Tripoli countries, and if the soldier went to war, he does not return unscathed" (al-Faili al-Alawi, 2008: 25). However, the difference in the sectarian religious faith could be the most important reason for the Faili and some Shi'a Arabs rejection of Ottoman army service. Additionally, "there was an easy way to get rid of the impasse forced recruitment. Many people of Faili Kurds and Arabs took the initiative to buy Iranian citizenship for a sum of money. On the other hand, the Ottoman staff that were part of the administrative rampant corruption were ready to accept bribes to delete the names of recruits" (Al-Faili, 2005: 14). As a consequence of the absence of the Faili registration in the Ottoman records, and as a result of the existence of the sectarian atmosphere, the tendency of discrimination and pan-Arab-centrism, the Faili Kurds had their Iraqi nationality removed based on their Iranian dependency. This has actually been reiterated by many authors, one of whom is Shahrough Akhavi, who declared that Faili Kurds "could not receive full Iraqi citizenship, their ancestors having declined Ottoman citizenship in an attempt to avoid military conscription" (Akhavi, 2004: 25). For this reason, many Faili Kurds preferred to gain Iranian nationality to avoid joining the Ottoman army. Therefore, they have been considered "Iranian dependency cases" (BASP, 1974).

Thus, under Iraqi citizenship Law No. (42) for the year 1924, "the Iraqi established citizenship has been imposed in two cases; the imposition of the Iraqi established citizenship and this citizenship has been imposed on two principals which are usually Ottoman residence in Iraq, and to be an Ottoman employee in the Ottoman government even if they are not normally resident in Iraq" (Al-Iraq, 1963). An important question here is who is the Ottoman? In this regard, according the Ottoman Law "No. (42) defined the characters of Ottoman citizen as: who is living in any part of the Ottoman Empire" (Al-Faili, 2005: 14). Dependent on this definition, any foreigner from any part of the Ottoman area deserves Iraqi citizenship, except Faili Kurds due to their dependency as "taba'yya," which means the followers of Iran, and they confirm that "two specific groups stand out, the Faili Kurds and the taba`iyya who are mostly Shi'i Arabs" (Fawcett and Tanner, 2002: 14). Hence, this citizenship law was considered as a judgment or as majeure for Iraqiness. In addition, the Faili Kurds who had not served in the Ottoman army and had registered for Iranian dependency "became an Iraqi citizen of second class" (al-Faili, 2007), which involves the acquisition of citizenship in place of an established citizenship. This kind of distinction between the two types of citizenship exists in the British legal system, as there is the title "naturalized subjects" (NWE, 2008). In addition, "there had always been a distinction in English law between the subjects of the monarch and aliens" (Dunham, 1951: 43).

Religion

"Contrary to the majority of their Kurdish brethren, they are Shi'a" (Fawcett and Tanner, 2002: 15). This factor, along with the other factors, highlights the position of the Faili Kurds. Thus, the issue of religion could be another dilemma for the Faili Kurds' citizenship and later the process of genocide. In this context, the important question is: Why the Faili Kurds people were exposed to the worst ethnic disposition operation in Iraq? Here, more than one factor has affected the position of the Faili Kurds, including geographical position, ethnicity, political activity, economy, and religion. However, ethnicity and religion are perhaps the most important issues highlighted by successive Iraqi authorities, from the kingdom to the republic of the Baathists. In this regard, according to the report "Iraq's Minorities: Participation in Public Life" by Preti Taneja and published by "minority rights group international," "the Faili Kurds are Shi'a Muslims by religion (Kurds are predominantly Sunni) and have lived in Iraq since the days of the Ottoman Empire" (Taneja, 2011: 8). In addition, the difficult interrelationship between Sunni and Shi'a Muslims, as has previously been explained, meant the Shi'a were generally marginalized by the authority of the pan-Arab Sunni king, and later all successive Sunni ethno-Arab authorities. The ethnic factor is the basis that shed light on them, because the authorities know that the majority of Arabs in Iraq are Shiite Arabs and have not been dealt with in this form of barbarism, but "the ethnic factor as they are belonging to the Kurdish nation, the sectarian factor is the other reason to double the persecution because they are from the Shi'a doctrine" (Al-Faili, 2005: 15). Many researchers have affirmed this view that the identity of the Faili Kurds is characterized by a complex ramification, and it has made them targeted by "the chauvinists who have ruled over power in Iraq, have committed against the Faili Kurds three crimes that cannot exempt them from punishment."

The first crime is disbelieving that Faili Kurds are an integral part of the Kurdish nation. Second, they are followers of the Ahl al-Bayt[1] and specifically followers of the doctrine of (Shi'a) Ja'vari. This sect was followed by the Faili's in Iraq before the conversion of Iranians to this doctrine.

Third, the Faili Kurds engaged in the Iraqi national political movement from early on, especially within the left-wing circles, "because of the injustice they suffered" (Abbud, 2007: 7). This means that the multiple dimensions of their identity always led to accusations and have been viewed as a dilemma for Iraqi Sunni-ethno-Arab-authorities. This dilemma includes political and economic factors, which are explained in the next section.

Politics and Economics

Politics and commercial activity transferred the Failis to the stage of direct targeting. This targeting was planned, not only behind the scenes but also in the media and circles of power, especially when the Ba'athists seized power. It is possible to compare this Faili situation to the situation of the Jews in Germany during the Second World War, and the highlighting of the commercial side of their lives, to identify them as a threat to the future of the country. The political role of the Failis, not just in Iraqi national politics but also in support of the Kurdish political movement, physically, financially and morally, doubled and hastened the targeting of them.

We conclude from the foregoing that the political role of the Faili Kurds, as "the financial resources to support the Kurdish revolution" (al-Faili, 2005: 18), gave them a high capacity for cultural influence in Baghdad, as "many Faili Kurds began migrating westwards to Iraqi cities, primarily Baghdad, where they took on key commercial, social, and cultural roles" (Fawcett and Tanner, 2002: 15). Likewise, their role in establishing the "Baghdad Chamber of Commerce in the 1960s" (Taneja, 2011: 16). In addition, their formation of an influential human bloc, which can be considered a Kurdish pressure group (lobbying), had a direct impact on the political elite in Baghdad, the capital, as well as their influence on the political and economic developments there.

As a consequence of these arguments, the influence of the Faili Kurds on political, economic, and social activity became a critical obstacle to the totalitarian policy of the Baathists. The targeting was based on systematic stages to complete the process of genocide.

THE EXPULSION

Since the Baath's takeover of the authority in 1968, the policy of expulsion took on dangerous dimensions, as it had several serious levels. Hiding behind national security, the Arabization of the country moved toward advanced stages against the mixed areas and the Faili Kurds.

First: the general motive according to the Baathists was the Iranian occupation of the three United Arab Emirate islands in the Strait of Hormuz. Here, the pan-Arab centrism in the Baath discourses was activated in practice. This policy is reflected in the media of the Baath authority and its literature. In addition, it is stated in the "central report of the 9th regional Conference of the Baath Party":

> When Shah Iran (Iran's Kind) terminated the Convention of 1937 in April 1969 and became a threat to the sovereignty of Iraq, he was threating the Iraqi sovereignty on the Shatt al-Arab and conspiring against the revolutionary regime and supporting the gangster Barzani, the Iranian residents in Iraq and some of those with acquired naturalized Iraqi nationality, forming the (fifth column) within Iraqi society. They were behind most of the propaganda and the tensions

in Iraqi society, they were providing information to the Iranian and international Zionism intelligence on the Iraqi economy, the strategic locations, the armed forces positions and all other necessary information, which the Iranian intelligence and its co-operator intelligence needed. (BASP, 1982: 61)

If we look closely at this paragraph, in linking Barzani as a symbol of the Kurdish movement with Iraq, and Zionism, we can see the extent of the hatred that was controlling the Baathist political elite in Baghdad, considering the Kurds upwardly as part of the external conspiracy, especially the Faili Kurds from Baghdad, the capital. This announcement in the Baath annual report forms the most believable evidence and reveals the Baath's policy on Faili Kurds. This text includes further preparation for the campaigns through pan-Arab-nationalistic ideology. It structuralizes the idea of conspiracy in order to influence public opinion. Additionally, this report claims:

When the dispute intensified with the Shah of Iran's regime, this (fifth column) attempted to repeal the revolution openly and its conspiratorial activity has escalated against the homeland. Here, as a precaution, the revolution has deported a few thousand residents in Iraq to Iran, as a redeem from their evil and their plotting, as a punishment for those who are traitors to the land which has sheltered many generations of them, and this happened at the end of 1971 and continuously to later periods. (BASP, 1982: 62)

Here, the report is admitting that a few thousand "fifth columns" had been expelled and their properties captured. Thus, as with all genocidal processes, the targets should be dehumanized and demonized in order to dilute the issue and spread support for the process, along with the participation of the public. This is what the Ba'athists did to prepare for the next phase of genocide. The Baathists did not stop their activities for the genocide but, rather, started other measures to expel the remainder, at a time when arrests and executions were in full swing. In relation to the first step, the Baath authority announced: "Any citizen who wants Iraqi ID documents, has to prove their Iranian dependency. However, who wants the Iraqi nationality certificate they have to visit the residency and citizenship office" (Al-Faili, 2008: 26).

In addition to this declaration, "whilst Baathists were hunting those people, they were also preparing lists for their displacement, which affected a lot of Iraqi merchantsincluding non-Faili Kurds, because for a period of time they were their neighbors " (Al-Faili, 2008: 26). Thus, the intention of the Baathists became clear as they launched the start of the expelling campaign, and around 70,000 Faili Kurds were registered for deportation in 1969, 1970, and 1971. This is despite signing the March 11, 1970, agreement between the Baath authority and the Kurdistan Democratic Party, "in the autumn of 1971, up to 40,000 Failis were expelled" (Fawcett and Tanner, 2002: 15), the Kurdish leaderships could not stop the further pressures on the Faili Kurds from Baghdad. Consequently, according to "the Internally Displaced People of Iraq" report (Fawcett and Tanner, 2002: 15), in just one year, 40,000 Kurds were deported to the Iranian borders and many of them disappeared. Confirming what was stated in the report, there are many other sources who emphasize that as a result of the "promulgation of legislation and decisions of the Baath's Revolutionary Command Council in years 1969-1970-1971 has caused more than (70,000) displaced and also the Faili villages and towns has been evacuated and its most Faili residents who have been expelled in 1975 as a collective punishment to the south and western Iraq" (Al-Faili, 2008: 2).

There was a decision to expel the rest of the Faili Kurds; therefore, the annual report contains a long explanation as follows: "Let it be clear, anyone who is not from Iraqi origin, we will act with them as we have acted with those Iranian traitors when they turned their back on this homeland, which gave them their identity and good deeds" (BASP, 1982: 65). Following this admission of past acts and future threats, the biggest campaign started in 1980 after Saddam Hussein become the first powerful man to practically seize power as Iraqi president, and he had a lot of power in his possession. In this year "1980," the aggressiveness against the Faili Kurds took on a new and dangerous scale, specifically at the beginning of the Iraq/Iran war, with its political, economic, and social circumstances. Here, the resort to aggressive public discourse began to appear more visible because of the Mustansiriya incident. This incident, according to many documents, was taken as a pretext to launch the next steps (Majeed, 2009). Accordingly, the first step was the issuing of resolution No. 666 of May 7, 1980 in which Saddam Hussein as Chairman of the Revolutionary Command Council decided to determine the fate of the Faili Kurds. In addition, the resolution includes that "in accordance with the provisions of paragraph (a) of Article 42 of the Interim Constitution:

The Revolutionary Command Council, resolution No. 666, have decided in their session held on 07.05.1980 the following:

1. The Iraqi nationality shall be dropped from any Iraqi of foreign origin if it appears that they were not loyal to the homeland, people, higher national and social objectives of the Revolution.
2. The Minister of Interior must order anyone whose Iraqi Nationality has been dropped under paragraph 1, unless he is convinced with sufficient reasons, that their stay in Iraq is a matter required by judicial or legal necessity or for preservation of the rights of other individuals which are officially authenticated.

3. The Minister of Interior shall undertake to execute this resolution. Saddam Hussein" (IR-SJC, 1980).

This kind of legal procedure is reflected in Saddam's announcement when he admitted that the Faili Kurds

"went to the dustbin of history, they went to a non-return. Uprooted from the land of Iraq, not to profane the Iraqi weather, nor profane the Iraqi flag when mixing their blood with the blood of Iraqis by intermarriage. Thus, they have been eradicated by the revolution from their roots to terminate their existence and to remain pure national Iraqis, who do not accept humiliation upon the forehead" (Hussein, 1981).

As a result of this policy, the number of victims from 1968 onward increased, and "130,000 deported Failis Kurds and approximately 5,000 male individuals aged 16 to 40 have been kept back in Iraq in various prisons" (Kreyenbroek and Sperl, 2005: 102). In addition, "the vast deportation in 1980 more than 500,000 Failis without legal justification. 15,000 to 20,000 people were put in the secret detentions without any clue of their fate" (Al-Faili, 2011).

THE DEPORTATION

In the previous part, the historical developments and the causes of genocide of the Faili Kurds in Iraq have been investigated in relation to the stages and steps the Baathists took toward the Faili Kurds in Bagdad and other Faili areas.

However, the process against the Faili Kurds was not separate from the rest of the Kurds. This is because alongside the Faili Kurds, the ongoing effort of the Arabization of the oil-rich areas and the deportation of its Kurdish residents was in progress. This attempt was in preparation for the coming steps to reduce and restrain the Kurdish region and strengthen state control over the means of violence and taxation. In this regard, the Baathists, with its advent to power, attempted to engage the Kurdish political movement in negotiations. Thus, the negotiations were in full swing, while the genocide of Faili Kurds was ongoing, and at the same time the process of Arabization was in progress. The unsuccessful March 11 agreement in 1970–1974 refers to this dilemma. It is because of the Baath's Machiavellian policy "End justifies the means," or the slogan of the Baath "Everything for victory" to stabilize its domination over state organizations and institutions. Here, they needed political negotiations according to the Baath's allegations to investigate the issues of non-Arabs who are "according to the 'cultural program for third stage of youthfulness of secondary school,' "living in the Arab homeland" (Cultural Program, 1983: 114).

Additionally, the allegation of "Arab identity of the land, where these minorities live" (BASP, 1983: 115), provides a justified indication for assimilating or expelling the Kurds from their homeland. Thus, "Iraq's territorial integrity" under the hegemony of the "party leader," within the unity of the Arab homeland and Iraq, as an important and undivided part of the Arab homeland, did not allow for compromise or concessions. All these principles are concealed in the Baath's motto "one Arab nation with an eternal message" (Aflaq, 1987: 105), which is contained throughout Aflaq's writings—a form of "exalted we-ideal" (Fletcher, 1997: 149). This Nazi ideal "was also more exclusive than other national ideals in emphasizing the primacy of one race and one nation" (Fletcher, 1997: 149). Here, what Michel Aflaq has announced about the Arab nation is close to the ideas of the Nazis as he concludes: "It is (the nation) the same as before thousands and thousands of years ago, it is (the nation) advantage is the united of its origin and race when the unity was the only powerful relation" (Aflaq, 1987: 106). Here, when the Baathists succeeded in weakening the Faili Kurds and announced the March 11 agreement in order to stabilize its authority, five to seven years after the Baath's coup, they neglected all obligations toward the Kurds and the March 11 agreement.

The Baathists, in their push for Arabization and Baathification of the highest number of people, and after their success in stabilizing their authority, turned to the Kurdish movement using all possible tactics and techniques. In this regard, "the Nazis made extremely effective use of several techniques, including terror, which was a short-term instrument of rule, concentration camps to remove dissenters and to intimidate the rest and a belief and behavior tradition which reinforced the effectiveness of these techniques" (Fletcher, 1997: 155). Baathists have pursued the same techniques, including terror, deportation, and gathering people in concentration camps. Thus, besides the Baath's attempt to annihilate the Faili Kurds, the dodging, twisting, and turning, according to many interviewees, was the nature character of Baath Party in relation with any issues of non-Arabs. Thus, "Baath Party was attempting to implement the process of Arabization of all Iraqi citizens and building a single nation in Iraq" (Qadir J., PI, June 8, 2015).

As a consequence, if this was the strategy of the Baathists, it is imaginable that all attempts that were in contrast to this strategy were considered as twisting and turning. The Baathists wanted to create a society according to their standards and conditions. Additionally, "Baath's ideas, its organization and belief in molding the society was a type of Nazism" (Karim A., PI, June 7, 2015). For these reasons, "The 11th March agreement was a tactic. It was under the pressure of the Kurdish political movement. They were forced to yield to this agreement temporarily, otherwise there was no conviction from the Baathists to deal with the Kurdish question properly and it was a temporary containment" (Saad C., PI, June 4, 2015).

In addition, there was unanimity among the interviewees that the Baathists spent time stabilizing their authority in order to pursue their strategy in the form of pan-Arab-centrism at an appropriate time. What is gradually noted here is the countercurrent in the civilizing process. It could be the disorder in the civilizing standards, when the state resorts to extreme violence toward its citizens or some of its citizens, based on ethnic or other grounds. This occurs "while the state continues to monopolize the exercise of violence, and promotes and protects civilized modes of behaviour and expression in society, at the same time it perpetrates massive and organized acts of extreme violence towards specific categories of its citizens" (Lash et al., 2001: 265).

The bias of the state against some of its country's citizens, which was practiced by the Iraqi state under the leadership of the Baathists, was practiced in Nazi Germany. It should be noted that the Nazis gained power in Germany through a legal election, whereas the Baathists seized power through a military coup. Accordingly, the Ba'athist rule until its end suffered from a lack of legitimacy, yet both of them militarized society and targeted specific categories of their citizens. Therefore, when the Baath authority was in negotiations with the Kurdish political movement to solve the Kurdish issue within the civilizing standards, at the same time, they were expelling Faili Kurds from their homes in Baghdad and other places. When they were announcing the national institution, particularly the national army, they were absorbed in building the different armed militias, even among the educational institutions through the Baath's youth organizations and Union of Students and Youth of Iraq (Faust, 2012: 93). Thus, they were militarizing society, launching Arabization in the contact areas, especially the oil-rich areas of Kirkuk province, and deporting Kurdish civilians from Kurdish areas to Arab areas in south Iraq.

This behavior was offensive and flagrant when "Baathists resorted to Arabizing the province of Kirkuk by bringing Arab tribes in order to change the nature of the demography. They also encouraged Arab citizens from various parts of Iraq to live in Kirkuk and pledged to give each Arab family that agreed to live in Kirkuk a piece of land for free with a grant of ten thousand dinars to build a house. They did the same thing in Khanaqin, Sinjar, Sheikhan and where they construct resident camps under Arabic names to accommodate the Arab tribes" (Al-Hamdani, 2007: 91). In contrast, "Baathists prevented the Kurdish citizens from building new homes and even the restoration of the old buildings. They came to falsify the census records of 1957, which was agreed to be adopted as the basis for the census" (Al-Hamdani, 2007: 91).

This countercurrent led the Baath regime to terminate the March 11 agreement (McDowall, 2004: 336) and to attack the Kurdistan region in 1974, which is known by the Kurds as Gulan's revolution. Thus, the March 11 agreement was necessary for the Baathists to stabilize their authority, as has been mentioned by an eyewitness who was participating in the Kurdish movement at that time as one of the closest family members to the Kurdish leader; he said: "Saddam Hussein has used the four years of the peace process as a gift from the Kurdish leadership that followed the statement of March 11th, to strengthen his power and the influence of the Baathists, including his security and military apparatus. This stage has been represented through the liquidation of its internal enemies on a large scale, to build a strong army that included the process of Baathfication inside the army and to place the security and police forces under his command" (Barzani, 2011: 361). Ultimately, the Ba'athists, through a long-term process of a totalitarian policy based on the monopoly of state institutions, including the monopoly of violent apparatus, attempted to centralize pan-Arabism as a state ideology.

EVACUATION AND FORCED CAMPS

It would be impossible to understand the Baath's conduct in Kurdistan without examining the interrelationship between colonialism and the occupied population. Failure to consider Iraq as an extension of British colonialism, which occupies a part of the Kurdish homeland, then transferring its power to the Arabs in Iraq, letting the Kurdish people face a sinister fate, led to the incomprehensible results. Therefore, recognizing colonial behavior is an important criterion for knowing what has happened and is happening in the Kurdish homeland, in the "four parts that been divided by the mother colonialism." Furthermore, the policy of Arabization adopted by the successive Iraqi authorities, particularly Baathism, reminds us of colonial behavior toward the indigenous people of America and Australia. Thus, "central here is the question of colonialism and imperialism, the ways in which nation states have established a brutal and violent relationship between their own 'civilization' and the supposedly 'barbaric' cultures of subjected peoples" (van Krieken, 1999).

The Arabization policy that the successive Iraqi authorities have followed in the direction of the Kurdish regions, whether systematic or not, remains an imperialist face of the Iraqi state, because it did not attempt to stop the Arabizing of the lands of the Kurdish peasants. It is notable that "since the 1930s, but particularly from the 1970s onwards, successive Iraqi administrations have forcibly displaced hundreds of thousands of ethnic Kurds, Turkomans (a Turkish-speaking Iraqi minority), and Assyrians from northern Iraq, and repopulated the area with Arabs moved from central and southern Iraq" (Mufti, 2004). It is distinguishable, with the advent of the Baathists to power in 1963, that this policy took a clear form, with the governmental formality in recruiting tens of thousands of Arabs to the Kurdish territories and the provision of compensation to those Arabists who built homes in the city of Kirkuk and other Kurdish territories. From this standpoint, as part of genocide procedures, three kinds of deportation were in progress. The first one was against the Faili Kurds; second, the deportation of the Kurdish residents from the Kurdish territories in Kirkuk, Khanaqin, and Shingal to be replaced by Arab emigrants. Third, the evacuation of the vast Kurdish territories adjacent to the international borders with Iran, Turkey, and Syria, in accordance with the Algiers Agreement that was concluded between Iraq and Syria against the Kurdish movement. This stipulated that "the two parties shall restore security and mutual confidence along their joint borders" (IMCM, 1981: 56). In this regard, the UN report concludes: "In the mid and late 1970s, the regime again moved against the Kurds, forcibly evacuating at least a quarter of a million people from Iraq's borders with Iran and Turkey, destroying their villages to create a cordon sanitaire along these sensitive frontiers" (HRW/Middle East, 1995: 22).

The authorities in Baghdad took advantage of the well-known colonial behavior, in an attempt to beautify the forcible deportations of Kurdish citizens, within a programmed methodology, under the title of developing the northern territories, in order to build modern camps for the villagers. This allegation started under the name of "The campaign of the development of the northern region" and it labeled the concentration camps "modern villages" (Muhammad, 2013: 18). This colonial approach was not hidden by the United Nations, but rather emphasized in its report on the Middle East and Iraq that "in their propaganda, the Iraqis commonly refer to them as 'modern villages'; in this report, they are generally described as 'complexes'" (HRW/Middle East, 1995: 22). In this context, the Iraqi allegation was that these areas are far away from the cities, and they deserve prosperity like the rest of Iraq, such as better schools and hospitals. At that point in time, within a dark media blackout, "there was no overall policy of forced assimilation to the Arab majority, but there was rather the deliberate annihilation of traditional Kurdish rural life and its economic basis by the wholesale destruction of Kurdish villages and the deportation of their inhabitants (i.e., those that were not killed) to strategic villages, 'new towns,' or concentration camps" (van Bruinessen, 1994: 1).

This is an important gesture in van Bruinessen's study that the deportation did not include Arabs. In this context, for someone who is unfamiliar with southern Iraq, they may believe that there are no deserts and all the lands are arable. On the contrary, Michael Field, the person who traveled through these areas, confirms that "travelling through central and southern Iraq one is struck by how uncultivated most of the land appears" (Field, 1995: 18). Despite such a situation, there is no indication that any Iraqi Arab villages were exposed to the deportation until the invasion of US troops in Iraq in 2003. Instead, regardless of the existence of agricultural lands, dense forests, areas rich in all kinds of fruits and vegetables, in addition to animal husbandry, and beautiful summer resorts for tourism, those lands were destroyed, and "most of the displaced Kurds were relocated into mujamma'at, crude new settlements located on the main highways in army-controlled areas of Iraqi Kurdistan" (HRW/Middle East, 1995: 22).

These procedures, which were followed by the Baath's authority in Baghdad, are strictly applicable to the concept of the civilized offensive that was implemented in Australia against the children of indigenous people. This method was also applied to the hundreds of thousands of Kurdish villagers for certain reasons if we accept the argument that the Kurds were removed from their homes in order to develop the northern region under the name of "Campaign of the development of the northern region" and building for them "the modern villages." Based on this rule, if the children of original people were abducted by the white authorities in Australia, in order to educate them in the way they wanted, thinking that their parents were backward and they have to create a time gap between these and their children, then the Baathists were intending to Arabize the Kurdish citizens by throwing them into concentration camps, in addition to aggressive security and military objectives against them. In this context, Ali Hassan Al Majid, "the chemical," admitted: "I am keeping them close to me, to let them hear my voice to implant in their minds what I want of thinking, culture and consciousness" (Majid, 2009: 5).

This means the Baathists did not conceal their "national ideal" of pan-Arab-centrism in the form of "one Arab Nation, with an eternal message." These Baathist national ideals are so close to those of the Nazi National ideal and "were also more exclusive than other national ideals in emphasizing the primacy of one race and one nation" (Fletcher, 1997: 149).

"Civilizing offensive" is a theoretical framework that has been derived from Elias's work, and it has been developed by Dutch sociologists and historians to refer to a wide range of phenomena, from nineteenth-century bourgeois efforts to elevate the lower classes out of their poverty and ignorance and convince them of the importance of domesticity and a life of virtue, to the oppression of popular culture in early modern times and, in general, "the attack on behaviour presumed to be immoral or uncivilized" (Persak, 2016: 14).

Additionally, if any community has been forced to move to a different place than where they are settled, under any kind of circumstances, it is considered to be a civilizing offensive. This rule was implemented on the Australian stolen generation, who "were forcibly removed from their families in order to 'civilize' them to become more like the European colonists" (Rohloff, 2011: 74). Thus, the "stolen generation" of the Australian authority, from many aspects, became the source of inspiration for many authoritarian regimes characterized by Nazi Germany, and the Baathists, with their chauvinistic ideology, followed that policy in order to deport thousands of Kurdish villagers to the new concentration camps. In this regard, "It is important to supplement, systematically, the concept of civilizing processes with that of civilizing offensives, to take account of the active, conscious and deliberate civilizing projects of both various powerful groups within societies and whole societies in relation to other regions of the world" (van Krieken, 1999: 303).

Here, the relationship becomes counterproductive and centrifugal between the civilizing process and the de-civilizing process to gain an understanding of the civilizing offensive. In the same field, but from another aspect, the resort to aggressiveness and the discharge of the Kurdish inhabited region are typically the result of a decline in power and due to identity issues, as "the deeply conditioned responses of aggressiveness and destructiveness in crisis situations prevalent in Nazi Germany were the result of a long intergenerational tradition bound up with successive defeats, a decline in power, uncertain national identity and an orientation towards the past" (Fletcher, 1997: 149). Based on this statement, the Arab defeat in the Six Day War in 1967 was considered as an insult to the Arab dignity (Al-Hamdani, 2007: 81). In the same direction, the resort to the genocide process is a kind of revenge for what struck the Arab nationalists at the core. This falls into the criterion that Elias stresses, with regard to long-term change in the psycho/sociogenesis during the crisis facing societies (Fletcher, 1997: 149). The political and security instability did not initiate with the advent of the Ba'athists only, but rather with the establishment of the Iraqi state, and the mobilization of military and economic forces for the sake of the pan-Arab nationalist ideology. This mentality developed upon the establishment of the State of Israel and the initiation of the Arab-Israeli conflict. During that period, all democratic issues were postponed, which was accompanied by the strengthening of the totalitarian rule in Iraq and other Arab countries.

THE KURDS: THE FUEL OF OTHERS' WAR

Although there is a deep-rooted historical enmity between Arabs and Persians, and attributing the general reason for the outbreak of the Iran-Iraq war to the ethnic and religious division, which has "separated Arabs and Persians, Shi'i and Sunni Muslims since at least the seventh century" (Karsh, 1990: 256), the roots and direct causes of the war may reside in another field. It may lie in the essence of the nation state, in that its inception was linked to the crisis. Over time, crises also developed. Among those states, Iraq, which is considered to be one of the failed states, their failure continued to be expressed and extended beyond 2003. If we look closely at the chronology of events, and the causes of the conflict between Iraq and Iran, we may find there are traditional, historical, ethnic, and sectarian reasons, but the Kurdish question, after the formation of the Iraqi state, has always been one of the main reasons for the lack of a good relationship between Iran and Iraq (Pelletiere, 1992: 30). But how and why?

The most sensitive phase between Iran and Iraq began after the Ba'athists seized power in Iraq, but in the new era, the Baathists continued their offensive: "Baath's Party, by all means of war and around 60% of the Iraqi army has attacked the Kurdish areas in November 10, 1968 in all directions" (Jalal, 1999: 257), as an expected result of the extent of the hatred that the Ba'athists had toward the Kurdish liberated movement based on their one-dimensional ideology, which cannot carry in its flanks anything other than chauvinism. When the Ba'athists seized power in 1968, they were facing serious challenges, and they soon knew that the war in Kurdistan was not in their favor. Therefore, they started negotiations with the Kurdish movement: "for a temporary peace" (Jalal, 1999: 259), to save time in terms of stabilizing their rule in Baghdad. Here, even the Baathists acknowledged the serious difficulties in this context, and this is set out in a specific Baath booklet regarding the March 11, 1970, agreement, which affirms: "The Party has found itself in front of a lot of problems, namely: The colonialism and Zionism devote most of their activities to expanding the fighting, even allowing them by passing their known settlement and authoritarian plans" (CLCF, 1975: 79).

After the collapse of the March 11 agreement, the Iraqi army began moving its troops toward the Kurdish areas and fighting resumed in 1974 between the Kurdish Peshmerga forces and the Iraqi troops. The most dangerous stages of the interrelationship between Baghdad and the Kurdish movement started with the Algerian Agreement in 1975 between Iran and Iraq, under the surveillance of the United States and Arab countries including Algeria. This agreement was to pave the way for the crushing of the Kurdish liberation movement. In essence, it was considered a concession to Iran, "the traditional enemy of Arabs in the eyes of the Baathists in the first place," in order to encourage Iran to close its borders in front of the Kurdish fighters, to surrender the Kurdish movement and to end its resistance. The result was the signing of the agreement in Algeria, under economic, political, and social pressure. The strangest thing about that agreement is that if the Ba'athists had conceded to the demands of the Kurdish movement, who considered Iraqi citizens according to the law, they would have saved themselves the concession to their traditional enemy, Iran; likewise, even if they spent the money that the Iraqi government spent on the Iraq war against the Kurdish movement, in the reconstruction of Kurdish areas, and they followed the peace and harmony process in the region, the results would have been impressive.

In the late 1970s, events accelerated, including the declaration of Imam Khomeini in 1979, after the revolution and the rise of the Islamic Republic in Iran. Likewise, Saddam announced the abolition of the agreement and the termination of its obligations. This declaration was also after the destruction of the rural areas along the borders with Iran, Turkey, and Syria between 1977 and 1979. In this campaign, all Kurdish rural areas were completely evacuated of Kurdish citizens. Consequently, all justifications for the termination of the agreement, including the Kurdish question, have been published in a booklet by the BP under the title "Why the Algerian Agreement between Iraq and Iran Has Been Cancelled" (IMCM, 1981). The consequences that followed the setback of 1974, which were a direct result of the Algiers Agreement, on Kurdish society, were bitter and murderous. As a result, "Baghdad embarked on brutal repression and forcible resettlement campaigns in the rural areas" (Rogg and Rimscha, 2007: 827). The entire Kurdish rural areas were destroyed, and the population gathered in forced compounds, under very harsh conditions for the citizens, who lost the professions that they used to occupy and were deprived of the natural environment that they enjoyed. This process led to thousands of non-pet animals dying or becoming homeless, due to the destruction of all water sources and the drying up of agricultural lands, which is described as ecocide.

After the war intensified, the war in which the Kurdish people had no direct or indirect relationship to claimed tens of thousands of young Kurds who were driven to the battlefields forcibly, to become fuel for the war against their will, without being a party to it or believing in it. In addition, there was constant bombardment on both sides of the border between Iraqi Kurdistan and Iranian Kurdistan, and the victims on both sides were innocent Kurdish citizens. An example is the Kurdish city of Sardasht, which was "attacked with several (chemical) bombs in July 1987 and June 1988" (Razavi et al., 2014: 166). The official toll of the Iraqi bombardment on the city of Sardasht is 119 dead and 1,518 injured.

The Kurdistan Region of Iraq, on the other hand, become a constant target of the Iraqi regime during the eight years of the war, starting with the Faili Kurds in 1980, passing through the annihilation of the Barzani males, and ending with the Anfal Campaign in 1988, including continuous arrests, executions, demolition of homes, and the transformation of Kurdish villages and cities into large prisons. The war ended, as usual, with devastation and destruction of the people and the country, without punishing those responsible for starting the war, and the citizens were the ones who paid the price.

The effects of that war to this day remain, and minefields in the mountains of Kurdistan still claim the lives of innocent people daily. The goal of the Algiers Agreement was to get rid of the Kurdish liberation movement, and the war was for the sake of liberation from the restrictions of the agreement, and in the end, the two parties returned to the starting point, with countless human and material losses.

BARZANI GENDERCIDE

The Barzanis are a large Kurdish clan who live in a mountainous area in the northeast of Iraqi Kurdistan. For many reasons, they have been able to lead the Kurdish movement, within the Kurdistan Democratic Party, since the establishment of the Iraqi state. Therefore, it was a natural consequence for them to fall under the attention of the successive Iraqi authorities. As previously explained, "As part of the Algiers Agreement of 1975, Iraq, Iran and Turkey agreed to create a security belt around and to move the all the population living within 10-20 km from the border" (Ahmad, 2014: 173). The agreement led to "resolving the Shatt al-Arab dispute, and paving the way for the suppressing of the Kurdish rebellion" (Karsh, 2002: 8). Within the framework of the implementation of that agreement, and after a short period of time, "the Ba'athist regime implemented this plan immediately and started by deporting the Barzanis by moving the clans of Harki binejeh, Nizari Baroshi and few Mizuries to the south of Iraq by helicopters, military personnel carriers and also by train from Mosul" (Ahmad, 2014: 173).

Consequently, the definition of the patterns of displacement entered the implementation phase following the specific international legislation through the Algiers convention under the surveillance of the United States. It is classed as international legislation because more than one country had an influential role in the success of this agreement, including Iran and Iraq as two members of the United Nations. It is included in the third act of the Algeria Agreement: "Accordingly, the two parties shall restore security and mutual confidence along their joint borders. They shall also commit themselves to carry out a strict and effective observation of their joint borders so as to put an end to all infiltrations of a subversive nature wherever they may come from" (Dilip Hiro, 1991: 301).

Thus, the Iraqi procedure and the Iraqi authority's behavior contradicted one of the points of the Convention on the Prevention and Punishment of the Crime of Genocide (CPPCG), as it includes the act of "deliberately inflicting on the group conditions of life calculated to bring about its physical destruction in whole or in part" (Kreß, 2006: 481). Additionally, beside the deportation of some Barzani people to southern Iraq, according to Mohammad

Ihsan, "the forced displacement campaign continued on 26 June 1978. The entire population of Argush Village, more than 300 families, was deported to the concentration camp in Harir. On 7 July 1978, the entire population of Mizuri tribal villages was deported along with other the population of some Sherwani villages" (Ahmad, 2014: 173). Thus, the process of deportation did not subside and did not stop until the Kurdish rural areas alongside Iran/Iraq and Turkey/ Iraq were entirely evacuated. Regarding the Barzani Kurds who were deported to the south of Iraq, "the Baath Party discovered that there is a kind of sympathy between Barzani people and Shi'a residents of the province of Diwaniyah. Thus, after five years of their difficult residency in the province of Diwaniyah, Barzani people for the 2nd time in 1980 have been transferred by the military trucks toward Qushtapa, which is a half hour away from Erbil city" (Abdulla, 2011).

Here, what is remarkable is the two prepared complexes under the names of "Qudis"[2] and "Qadisiya,"[3] which are two names carrying the nature of Arabization and religious characteristics. The important point here is the purpose of the Baath's transferring of these Barzani people from south Iraq to Erbil, besides those Barzani people who had been transferred to the concentration camps of Harir, Bahirka, and Diyana, as has been explained previously. This gathering of all Barzani people into a few complexes, including those who had been brought back from southern Iraq to Erbil, is a clear move in the framework of the stage of concentration camps.

Here, it has been noticed that the deportation of the other Kurdish components continued, but the deportation of the Barzani people was sustained until July 1983, when, according to a letter to the secretary of state dated March 29, 1989, the director of general security reported on the situation in the Harir area as follows:

In July 1983, an Iranian, Zionist aggression on the Haji Umran front, substantiated by the participation of the clique descendants of treason, the group who are mostly from the Barzani family, an order from the former Director of Public security "Dr Fadhel Al-Barrak" was sent to the Directorate of General Security to assemble a big unit consisting of members of security from the directorates of the autonomous region on a top secret mission to commence at down on the next day. The mission commenced on the 1st of August 1983 with members of the Republican Guards surrounding Al-Quds, Al-Qadissiya and the Qushtappa compounds, which were specifically built for the Barzani families. All males over the age of 15 from the Barzani families were arrested and transported using large army vehiclesaccompanied by military force. (Ahmad, 2014: 174)

Thus, those assembled Barzani people from Quds and Qadissyia were suddenly kidnapped from their concentration camps for a reason that is revealed in the same document, as follows: "The Barzani clan is known for their disloyalty to the Party, Revolution, and the country for decades, they have persistently resisted the unity of the nation and they were the real traitors. They consider themselves the legitimate representatives of the Kurdish people; they are full of hatred and animosity" (Ahmad, 2014: 174). What we realize in this context is the dehumanization of the Barzanis, as they were stigmatized by the director of public security, throughout the ongoing conflict between the authorities in Baghdad, because "political elites with grievances against ethnic minorities may curtail their freedoms, expel them from the country, or kill them" (Campbell, 2011: 287). This violence, which was imposed by the Baathists, is not considered a justification for the conflict that was raging between the Kurdish political movement and the authorities in Baghdad, as it has been pointed out that "since violence is often a response to a conflict, it can be explained with theories of social control" (Campbell, 2011: 288). The violence that the Kurdish people have resorted to is a natural result of arbitrary measures and the digestion of the natural rights of a group of people. If the Ba'athists were concerned about a threat to the Arab identity that they imposed on Iraq, then the Kurds could not pose a threat to that identity, let alone a tribe residing in the high mountains! Therefore, it can be said that the process of mass extermination followed by the Ba'athists was deliberate in order to impose racist policies and a specific culture on all the citizens of Iraqi Kurdistan.

For these reasons, "the process of Barzani gendercide as the fourth and final phase of annihilation started to be implemented, and according to the description by definition, it involved, Extermination mobile killing operations in extermination camps" (Finchelstein, 2005: 19). In a carefully planned operation, all Barzanis were gathered in a few forced concentration camps in Qadisiyah and Quds in the Qushtapa area, including the camps of Harir, Diana, Bahirka, and Quarto, and they besieged and deported everyone to the places of extermination. In two military campaigns, the first one on July 31, 1983, and the second one on August 10, 1983, every single Barzani male above seven years old was forcibly arrested and transferred to their fate. In the third phase, Barzanis were buried alive, according to the commandment of the general director of public security, at that time (Fadel al-Barrak) at the beginning of August 1983. He states that the Judgment of the Nation had been implemented against some 667 Barzanis in 16 cases, and they were executed. The others were killed in mass graves in the desert of Busaiya. The process of killing Barzanis was under the supervision of Major Assi Ibrahim Assi al-Dduri, who was transferred to Busaiya and remained there for two weeks (Abdulla, 2010: 59). This operation was carried out "in August 1983, [and] all men aged between 8 and 70 of this group, eight thousand in total, were rounded up in the camps and driven off in army lorries" (van Bruinessenl,

1994: 6). However, what exactly happened to the Barzani Kurds is still partly unknown. A report by a preparatory committee has stated that on July 30, 1983, 8,000 male Barzani Kurds "have they been reported, imprisoned, tortured or massacred? Still no one knows" (A preparatory Committee, 2005: 9). In addition, and horrifically, "according to information confidentially leaked by Iraqi military sources, at least some of them were used in experiments with chemical arms; there is little hope that any of them are still alive" (van Bruinessen, 1994: 7).

In the end, like the behavior of the despotic rulers, who have become a symbol of blood and racism in their country, and clearly, Saddam Hussein admitted on Iraqi television that "some, who were called Barzani, who cooperate with them (Iranian), so they have been severely punished and have gone to hell" (YouTube, 2020). This kind of recognition was a foolish weakness that followed the Iraqi state because they did not eliminate those who were leading the Kurdish movement but, rather, innocent people who were subjected to the crime of deportation in their places and put in difficult conditions under constant surveillance by the Iraqi security forces. However, those human masses of men were arrested in front of their children and relatives and led to their fate, which was mass graves.

THE MARTYR HALABJA[4]

Chronologically, the chemical attack on Halabja is part of the Anfal Campaigns, but because of its enormity, it has been given a specific position even by the Iraqi High Tribunal (IHT). Regarding this crime, the Iraqi Baath's authority, through its absolute ruler, Chemical Ali, was absorbed in the definition of the areas that were supposed to be exposed to genocide, "At this stage, the Iraqi warplanes for the first time in the middle of April 1987 and for a period of 18 months, launched 14 chemical attacks on civilians in Kurdish villages" (Salih Khaled, 1995: 151). The campaign was comprehensive, and the attacks included many areas. Before gassing Halabja, chemical weapons were used to attack dozens of villages throughout various areas in the depth of the Iraqi Kurdistan far from the warzone. This means these areas were intentionally targeted for ethnic reasons and within the Anfal operations.

There is incorrect information about the bombing of some areas in May 1987, in that they were subjected to a chemical attack "in an attempt to deter the civilian population from collaborating with the advancing Iranian forces" (Karsh, 2002: 55). This information may not be accurate for two reasons: the first one is these villages were outside the warzone and many of them were far away from the borders. Second, the residences of these villages, as he mentions, were a "civilian population" and mostly women and children.

How could these civilian populations outside the warzone collaborate with the Iranian forces?

Therefore, the goal of the entire campaigns was to kill as many citizens as possible, before the security forces arrived, because the intention in all cases was to kill these citizens, whether it was inside their villages or by taking them to the detention camps and then killing them in mass graves. Regarding Halabja, there are rumors and controversy about whether the bombing of Halabja with chemical weapons was part of the Anfal Campaigns or not.

While the result was the same, the Halabja operation, in terms of timing, took place "in the afternoon of the 16th, the Iraqi air force launched a massive chemical strike against the area of Halabja and Khurmal" (Hilterman, 2008: 5), and this means that it falls within the first Anfal Campaign, which "took place between 23 February and 19 March 1988" (Hardi, 2012: 19).

Contrary to the previous opinion, there are other arguments that consider Halabja an independent operation, because, on the one hand, it is not located in the target area of the first Anfal Campaign, and on the other hand, many towns and villages had been exposed to chemical weapons prior to the Anfal Campaigns. In this context, in April 1987, the first Kurdish village to be attacked with chemical weapons (apart from napalm) was Sheikh Wisan in the Balisan Valley (Makiya, 1994: 164/165). In addition to this argument, even the UN report states: "The Iraqi regime did not consider Halabja to be part of Anfal" because "Halabja was a city, and Anfal was intended to deal with the rural Kurdish population" (HRW/Middle East, 1995: 97).

This issue became the focus of discussion by many interested researchers, in that "the attack on Halabja was not considered part of the Anfals because, in the bureaucratic mind-set of the Iraqi government, Halabja was a city" (Kelly, 2008: 33). Thus, as a consequence of these arguments, Halabja is different to the process of the Anfal Campaigns because it was a city, and it can be considered an independent process and an extension of the demolishing of the Kurdish cities, alongside the demolishing of Kurdish rural areas. This is because the demolition of the cities continued even after the Anfal Campaigns. In addition, this argument does not change the magnitude of the tragedy, the number of victims, or its position in international or national law, which according to the IHT is considered genocide.

In any case, the enormity of the bombing of Halabja with chemical weapons, according to Michael Kelly, "was costly, however, as Iraq bombarded the town of 80,000 with gas, killing as many as 5,000 civilians" (Kelly, 2008: 57). In this regard, the first statement to announce the bombing of the city with chemical weapons came from the Islamic Republic of Iran News Agency, where it stated that Iraq "chemical bombed Halabja town . . . twice Wednesday evening" March 16—killing and wounding "hundreds of . . . defenseless women and children" (Hiltermann, 2007: 116).

SUMMARY

In order to establish ethnic-Arab-centrism and to Arabize Iraq, a series of procedures were implemented in the framework of the process of genocide. In this regard, the Baathists initiated several stages for the preparation and adoption of violence to implement their ideology. This stage could be considered as part of the de-civilizing process. Thus, when the Baathists took power in 1963, they launched the first act of violence by establishing a militia in order to strengthen their authority. In this regard, for the first time, they utilized the legitimacy of state institutions to build a NG; Article (2) of the Act provides that "the National Guard is an organized popular force, that has been trained in the use of arms and its pillars are the believing people in their right to a free and dignified life" (al-Iraq, 1963: No. 35). In this context, we can understand that the Baathists' tendencies were to impose their ideology by force, which they did not conceal in their rhetoric and discussions. Hence, they showed their intention clearly, that the NG was an instrument for Arabization in the form of protection of the Arab existence in Iraq. As a consequence, the Nationalist Guard, as has been revealed in this chapter, approved of the atrocities against the Kurdish nation. However, the dramatic growth of this militia reflected the Baath's belief in a national ideal, involving the elimination of the obstacles in the way of Arabization.

Since the formation of the state, violence has been one of the most prominent political and social phenomena, particularly throughout the period of the 1960s, when the violence continuously increased and "the Baathists returned to power by organizing two coups, one on July 17 and the other on July 30, 1968" (Batatu, 1978: 1074). Additionally, the Baathists turned state institutions into platforms for developing their ideology and oppressing non-Arabs in order to idealize its slogans and to promote pan-Arabism. However, "When the rulers are perceived to be working for themselves and their kin, and not the state, their legitimacy, and the state's legitimacy, plummets" (Rotberg, 2010: 9).

These kinds of circumstances also caused a specific vision of the "outsider." Moreover, according to the stages of genocide in the framework of the de-civilizing process, the Bathists, dependent on the principle of "divide and conquer," had a particular vision and genocidal plan for every Kurdish component in order to guarantee their success at every stage. Additionally, the Baathists started with the definition of the Faili Kurds throughout, as "the political report of the eighth region Conference for Baath Arab Socialist Party, 1974," purposefully explained all of the justifications for expelling the Faili Kurds from Iraq, identifying them as dangerous foreigners. This violent vision toward the Faili Kurds occurred due to four main factors, which are ethnic, economic, political, and religious factors. Here, in terms of extermination, the Faili Kurds were considered to be "fifth columns," and due to this grievance, some of them were killed and others expelled and their property captured.

The other point is the forcible displacement of hundreds of thousands of Kurds in a deliberate deportation process, both the Faili and non-Faili Kurds. This stage of Arabization was initiated through a huge campaign of deportation of the Kurds and replacing them with Arab citizens. This process was applied in the framework of the civilizing offensive, which reiterates the ideology of pan-Arab-centrism. Regarding the impact of the Iran-Iraq war, and the Kurds, the "control of territory and population became even more crucial on both sides than it had been before the war" (Van Bruinessen, 1986: 14). However, this war paved the way for the continuation of the Arabization policy against the Kurds and the implementation of the process of genocide. Here, the genocide of the Barzani Kurds is another dilemma for the interrelations between the Iraqi authority and the Kurds. The Barzani Kurds were forcibly deported to concentration camps and then arrested and transferred to an unknown place in Southern Iraqi in order to execute them in silence.

The issue of the genocide of Halabja is another tragic act that occurred when the city was bombed in cold blood: 80,000 people, mostly women and children. None of the international laws, which clearly prohibit the targeting of civilians in the war, were respected. Halabja remains a stain on those responsible for the crime, and everyone who kept silent about its conduct at a time when they were able to stop it, but did not. The result was that 5,000 civilians were killed, tens of thousands were wounded, and the survivors are still suffering from the consequences of inhaling the deadly gases.

NOTES

1. The term "Ahl al-Bayt" literally means "people of the House of Hashmi, the descent of Prophet Muhammad." This term indicates Shi'a Muslims as followers of Muhammad's family in front of the Sunni Muslims (El Sandouby, 2008: 28).

2. Quds or al-Quds is the Arabic name for the city of Jerusalem; al-Quds in Arabic means "to be holy." Arabs consider it to be an Arab city; therefore, Arab nationalists in Iraq have utilized it as a symbol for their pan Arab purposes.

3. Al-Qadisiya is the name of a previous battle of Arab Muslims force against the Sassanid Empire army. Saddam Hussein chose this name for his war against Iran, which started from 1980 until 1988.

4. This is the traditional name of the city of Halabja, after the chemical bombardment in 1988.

REFERENCES

Abbud, Zuher Kadim. Al-Masuliya Al-Qanuniya Fi Qadziyat Al-Kurd Al-Failiyyin. *Al-Hiwar Al-Mutamaddin*, December 6, 2007. Accessed December 12, 2020. https://bit.ly/380pgiL.

Abd, Jassim, Al-Saadi. Iraq is between two cultures, a civil society culture, and a culture of violence. *Journal Researcher Journal* 1, no. 3 (2007): 19–30. https://bit.ly/2KUm259.

Abdulla, Rebwar Ramazan. *Barzani's genocide in the twentieth century, compared with the domestic and international conventions, 'Cenosayîdî Barzaniyekan, be berawird legel Rekkewtnname Newxoyî u Newdewletîyekan'*. Erbil: Minara Publisher, 2011.

Abdulla, Rebwar Rebwar. *Extermination storm of the Barzanis, Barovî Lenawbirdinî Barzaniyekan*. Erbil: Aras Publication, 2010.

ABSP. al-Taqrir al-Siyasi al-Sadir An al-Mu'tamar al-Qutri al-Thamin, January 1974.

ABSP. *ul-Taqrir al-Markazi lil-Mutamar al Qutri al Tasi*. Baghdad: Arab House, 1982.

ABSP. *Cultural program for third stage of youthfulness of secondary school*. Baghdad: ABSP, 1983.

Ahmad, Mohammed. *From blueprint to genocide*. University of Exeter, 2014.

Ahmed, Kadim Mohammed. Ankawa. *Nabtha Tarikhiya an Al-Milishiyat Fi Al-Iraq*, April 24, 2016. Accessed December 12, 2020. https://bit.ly/2W65w7A.

Akhavi, Shahrough, ed. *Middle East studies: History, politics, and law*. New York, London: Routledge, 2004.

Al-Ali, Nadje, and Nicola Pratt. *What kind of liberation? Women and the occupation of Iraq*. University of California Press, 2010.

Al-Faili, Ahmad Nasir. *Al-Kurd Al-Failiyyun Bain Al-madzi Walhadzir*. Baghdad: Shafaq Institution, 2005.

Al-Faili, Al-Alawi, and Jaafar Zaki. *Tarikh al-Kurd al-Failiyun wa Afaq al-Mustaqbal*. London: Gilgamish, 2008.

Al-Faili, Riyadz Jasim. Jarimat Al-iabada Al-jama'yia Lil-Kurd Al-Faylyin Wa Atharuha Al-dawliya. *Al-Hiwar Magazin*, January 18, 2011. Accessed December 12, 2020. https://bit.ly/3qOmbuF.

Al-Fazil, Munthir. Al-Kurd Al-Failiyun Wa Huququhum Fi Mustaqbal Al-Iraq. *Al-Hiwar Al-Mutamaddi*, December 1, 2002. Accessed December 12, 2020. https://bit.ly/3a0Aqql.

al-Hamdani, Hamid. *Sanawat al-jahim, Arbauna Ama min Hukm al-Baath fi Al-Iraq 1963–2003*. Vaxjo: Veshun Media Sweden, 2007.

Al-Iraq, Durar. Qanun Al-Jinsiya Al-Iraqiya Raqm (43) Lisanat 1963. *Al-qawaneen Wal-Tashri'at Al-Iraqiya*, 1963. https://bit.ly/2Wv7VZj.

Al-Iraq, Durar. Qanun Al-Haras Al-Qawmi No (35) year 1963, 1963. http://bit.ly/3a2QU1e.

Al-Musilli, Munthir. *al-Qaziya al-Kurdiya fi al-Iraq, al-Baath wal-Akrad*. Dar al-Mukhtar, Damascus, 2000.

A Preparatory Committee. *Progress report of the missing 8000 Kurds in Iraq.* London: WKA, 2005.

Blamires, Cyprian P. World fascism: A-K. United Kingdom: ABC-CLIO, encyclopedia, 2006.

Campbell, Bradley. Genocide as a matter of degree 1. *The British Journal of Sociology* 62, no. 4 (2011): 586–612.

CLCF. *al-Qaziya al_kurdiya wa al-Hukm al-Thati.* Baghdad: Committee in the Labour Culture Foundation, 1975.

Dunham Jr, William H. Doctrines of allegiance in late medieval English law. *NYUL Rev* 26 (1951): 41.

El Sandouby, Aliaa Ezzeldin Ismail. *The Ahl al-bayt in Cairo and Damascus: The dynamics of making shrines for the family of the Prophet.* Los Angeles: University of California, 2008.

Faust, Aaron M. *The Baathification of Iraq: Saddam Hussein and the Bath party's system of control.* Boston University, 2012.

Tanner, Victor., Fawcett, John. The Internally Displaced People of Iraq. United States: Brookings Institution-SAIS Project on Internal Displacement, 2002.

Field, Michael. *Inside the Arab world.* Harvard University Press, 1995.

Finchelstein, Federico. "The Holocaust Canon: Rereading Raul Hilberg." New German Critique, no. 96 (2005): 3-48. Accessed March 24, 2021. http://www.jstor.org/stable/30040977.

Fletcher, J. *Violence and civilization: An introduction to the work of Norbert Elias.* Cambridge: Polity, 1997.

Gibson, Bryan R. *Sold out? US foreign policy, Iraq, the Kurds, and the Cold War.* Springer, 2016.

Gunter, Michael M. *The A to Z of the Kurds.* Scarecrow Press, 2009.

Hanna, Batatu. The old social classes and the revolutionary movements of Iraq: A study of Iraq's old landed and commercial classes and its communists, bathists and free officers (1978).

Hardi, Choman. *Gendered experiences of genocide: Anfal survivors in Kurdistan-Iraq.* Ashgate Publishing, Ltd., 2012.

Hilberg, Raul. *The destruction of the European Jews, Holmes & Meier.* New York, 1985.

Hiltermann, Joost R. The 1988 Anfal Campaign in Iraqi Kurdistan. In *International Conference on Genocide against the Kurdish people.* Erbil: Arras, 2008.

Hiro, Dilip. *The longest war: The Iran-Iraq military conflict.* Psychology Press, 1991.

HRW/Middle East Watch. Iraq's crime of genocide: The Anfal Campaign against the Kurds. *Human Rights Watch*, 1995.

Hussein, Saddam. *The speech of (Saddam Hussein) in the (al-thawra) newspaper.* Baghdad: al-Thawra Newspaper, 1981.

IMCM. Boçî Rêkewtinnameî Cezair Le Nêwan Êraq u Êran Helwešayewe. *Iraqi Ministry of culture and media edn.* Baghdad: Al-Hurriya House Publishing, 1981.

IR-SJC. The Interim constitution of 1968. *The Supreme Judicial Council*, March 25, 2010. Accessed December 12, 2020. https://bit.ly/379it6Y.

Jalal, Ibrahim. *Xiwarui Kurdistan u Shorishi Eylul, Bunyatnan u Haltakandin, 1961–1975*. Sweden: Herman Publisher, 1999.

Karol, R. Iraq 1963: The short rule of the Bacth. *Asian and African Studies* 18, no. 1 (2009): 16–39.

Karsh, E. The Iran–Iraq war 1980–1988. United Kingdom: Osprey Pub., (2002).

Karsh, Efraim. Geopolitical determinism: The origins of the Iran-Iraq war. *Middle East Journal* 44, no. 2 (1990): 256–268.

Kelly, Michael J. *Ghosts of halabja: Saddam Hussein and the Kurdish genocide: Saddam Hussein and the Kurdish genocide*. ABC-CLIO, 2008.

Kirmanj, Sherko. *Anfal-Sirinewei Kurd le Parezgai Kerkuk* 18 (2013): 10.

Kreß, Claus. The crime of genocide under international law. *International Criminal Law Review* 6, no. 4 (2006): 461–502.

Kreyenbroek, Philip G., and Stefan Sperl, eds. *The Kurds: A contemporary overview* (vol. 4). Routledge, 2005.

Lash, Scott, and Mike Featherstone. Recognition and difference. *Theory, Culture & Society* 18, no. 2–3 (2001): 1–19.

Majid, Mohemmed. The heroic of Anfal operations. *Al-Qaswa Lada Saddam Husein*, April 13, 2009: P5. https://bit.ly/2YD0Jxe.

Makiya, Kanan. *Cruelty and silence: War, tyranny, uprising, and the Arab World*. WW Norton & Company, 1994.

McDowall, David. *A modern history of the Kurds*. London: IB Tauris, 1992. Parenthesis added (2004): 402.

Michel, Aflaq. *Fi Sabeel al-Baath*. al-Tali'a Publisher, (V.1), 1987.

Mohy Alheims, M. State under formation; exile dialogue, proof of existence (Iraqi Kurdistan as a model) 14 (2013).

Mufti, Hania. *Iraq, claims in conflict: Reversing ethnic cleansing in northern Iraq* (vol. 16, no. 4). *Human Rights Watch*, 2004.

Muhammad, Omer. *Pelamare Serbaziyakanî Anfal le Heshit Qonaxda*. Sulemani: General Directorate of Libraries, 2013.

Nakash, Yitzhak. *The Shi'is of Iraq*. New Jersey: Princeton University Press, 2003.

Nalepka, E., and S. Manoukian. Saddam is Iraq and Iraq is Saddam: Saddam Hussain's cult of personality and the perception of his life and legacy. *January* 10 (2014): 2016.

NWE. Naturalization. *New World Encyclopedia*, 2008, November 5, Naturalization edn (2008). https://bit.ly/2KjrOjS.

Pelletiere, Stephen C. *The Iran-Iraq war: Chaos in a vacuum*. New York: Praeger, 1992.

Persak, Nina, ed. *Regulation and social control of incivilities*. United Kingdom: Routledge, 2016.

Post, Jerrold M., and Amatzia Baram. *Saddam is Iraq: Iraq is Saddam*. No. 17. USAF Counterproliferation Center, Air War College, Air University, 2002.

Razavi, Seyed Mansour, Mahdiyeh Sadat Razavi, Mohsen Pirhosseinloo, and Payman Salamati. Iraq-Iran chemical war: Calendar, mortality and morbidity. *Chinese Journal of Traumatology* 17, no. 3 (2014): 165–169.

Rogg, Inga, and Hans Rimscha. The Kurds as parties to and victims of conflicts in Iraq. *International Review of the Red Cross* 89, no. 868 (2007): 823–842.

Rohloff, Amanda. *Shifting the focus? Moral panics as civilizing and decivilizing processes*. London & New York: Routledge, 2011.

Rotberg, Robert I., ed. *When states fail: Causes and consequences*. Princeton University Press, 2010.

Salih, Khaled. Anfal: The Kurdish genocide in Iraq. *Digest of Middle East Studies* 4, no. 2 (1995): 24–39.

Sassoon, Joseph. *Saddam Hussein's BP: Inside an authoritarian regime*. Cambridge University Press, 2011.

Scholtyseck, Joachim. Fascism—national socialism—Arab "fascism": Terminologies, definitions and distinctions. *Die Welt des Islams* 52, no. 3–4. Leiden, (2012): 242–289.

Taneja, Preti. *Iraq's minorities: Participation in public life*. Minority Rights Group International, UK, 2011.

Tejel, Jordi, Peter Sluglett, and Riccardo Bocco, eds. *Writing the modern history of Iraq: Historiographical and political challenges*. World Scientific, Singapore: 2012.

Van Bruinessen, Martin. The Kurds between Iran and Iraq. *MERIP Middle East Report* 141 (1986): 14–27.

Van Bruinessen, Martin. Genocide of the Kurds. *The Widening Circle of Genocide. Genocide: A Critical Bibliographic Review* 3 (1994): 165–191.

Van Krieken, Robert. The barbarism of civilization: Cultural genocide and the 'stolen generations' 1. *The British Journal of Sociology* 50, no. 2 (1999): 297–315.

Waqa'i Al-Iraq. Qanun Al-Haras Al-Qawmi, Rama (35) Listant 1963. *Dorar-al-Iraq*. Accessed December 11, 2020. https://bit.ly/3a2QU1e.

YouTube. *Thahabu ila aljaheem*, February 2, 2020. Accessed December 16, 2020. https://bit.ly/3mol9SQ.

Chapter 4

Genocide and the De-Civilizing Process in Iraq

The Anfal Campaigns[1]

In the previous two chapters, two important notions have been explored with regard to nation building. The first notion is the process of the Iraqi nation state under the circumstances of the hegemony of the Sunni Arab minority in order to create a national identity within the characteristics of pan-Sunni and pan-Arab nationalism. Throughout chapter 3, the notion of Arabization and its implementation through the different instruments and the process of one Arab state nation building have been explored, particularly in relation to Arab identity. In this chapter, there will be an attempt to complete the discussion of the Arabizing of Iraqi identity through the process of the last solution, which is the Anfal Campaigns.

If we take into consideration the process of Arabization, we also see the de-Kurdification of Iraq on the other side, through the policy of assimilation, evacuation of the Kurdish areas, and the large-scale destruction of the Kurdish people. Additionally, at the level of the theory of the civilizing process, according to the framework of state formation, how the process of nation building collapses during the de-civilizing process will be explored. This means that the "de-civilizing process is what happens when the civilizing process goes into reverse" (Mennell, 1990: 205). The Iraqi regime in the 1970s and 1980s was moving in the same direction, and the Anfal Campaigns were one of the signs of the de-civilizing process. On the other hand, if we examine the process of the Anfal Campaigns, we can recognize the applicability of all angles examined in chapter 2. In this regard, it has been argued, "The destruction process has inherent patterns. There is only one way which a scattered group can effectively be destroyed" (Hilberg, 1985: 1064).

This chapter is divided into five sections including the conclusion. Primarily, the definition of Anfal and its essence is considered, followed by an introduction to the Iran-Iraq war and the possible relationship with the

113

Anfal Campaigns. The stages of Anfal include the preparation of the final solution, concentration, and the process of annihilation, which is an important part of the chapter. Finally, a short explanation from some of the survivors and their circumstances will be presented.

THE ESSENCE OF ANFAL

What does the concept of Anfal mean, and why were these campaigns implemented under this religious name? Certainly, it is possible to find one of the origins of the campaigns behind this concept. The concept of Anfal is the name of the eighth chapter (surah) of the Quran and the first verse (ayah) of the chapter. Additionally, the text or the verse of Anfal in the Quran includes: "They ask you (O Muhammad) about the spoils of war (al-Anfal). Say: 'The spoils (al-Anfal) are for Allah and the Messenger.' So, fear Allah and adjust all matters of difference between you, and obey Allah and His Messenger (Muhammad), if you are believers" (Ali, 2003: 7). This refers to when Prophet Muhammed and his companions were confronted in a battle for the first time by the non-Muslim Arabs who had been persecuting them in the battle of Badr in 624. Later on, this verse became part of Sharia law. Dependently, ISIS mobilized this understanding of the Quran against the Ezidi Kurds in 2014 and kidnapped more than 5,000 Kurdish Ezidi women as slaves, according to international sources (Spencer, 2014).

However, it is worth mentioning that the concept of Anfal existed before Islam for the same purpose, which is spoils of war, but what does spoils of war mean? The majority of Islamic interpreters are unanimous about the meaning of the concept being money and property or everything moveable, but according to some traditional sources, the "spoils of war" exceed "money and property" to prisoners and taking them as slaves. In this regard, the historian Ibn Katheer one of the prominent traditional interpreters has explained "what is deviated from the infidels to Muslims without a fight from the slave, female or chattel or spoil" (Ibn Katheer, 2000: 5–12). Here, he is admitting without a fight because everything in the moment of fighting is permitted. Accordingly, the Prophet Mohammad stated, "the spoils of war have been made permissible for me, whereas they were not permitted for any before me" (Abdul-Rahman, 2009: 97). The problem with this and many other texts of the Quran is they can remain absolutist, and every Islamic group interprets them according to their own perspective and interests.

In terms of the recent use of the name Anfal within its religious background, which was a war waged by the Iraqi government, led by the Baathists, it involves different interpretations. In addition to the use of the concept of Anfal for the purpose of the intended insult of the targeted people and stripping them of their humanity, or in other words, the purpose of "dehumanization" and to consider those people as objects or property. However, the "Dictionary of Genocide" states that "the Anfal campaign was the name of a series of military campaigns undertaken by Saddam Hussein's (1932-2006) Iraqi Baathist regime against the Kurdish population residing in northern Iraq" (Totten and Bastrop, 2008: 13). It should also be noted that the use of the term "Anfal" in its original sense was in reference to a battle between opposing sides (the Battle of Badr) and not an assault on a civilian population.

Regarding the campaigns being given a religious name, the Baathists carried in their essence a unique model; therefore, the Anfal Campaigns also appear to be unique campaigns. Hence, as based on the literature of the Baathinsts and its founder Michel Aflaq and also according to the secretary general of the National Islamic Front in Iraq and the Iraqi Baath's representative Khudair al-Murshidi, "ABSP based on an organic connectivity between Arabizm and Islam. The Baath Party, since its inception, was based on these three principles (humanitarian nationalism, National Socialism, the connection between Arabizm and Islam), therefore, when Islam came, it created the nationalism, a new creation" (Muawad, 2016).

If we look at the issue from the angle of this statement, based on figurational sociology, the Ba'athists have always wanted to employ the past and have always been inspired by the past. They connect the past with the present and mobilize its religious and cultural dimensions as tools for the purpose of its ideology. The term Anfal can be considered part of this policy. Here, having explored in the previous three chapters how the Baathists expressed themselves as having a unique model of thinking, the issues are now being examined in order to confirm their behavior theoretically and practically. From this point, we can explore the dimensions of the Anfal Campaigns; however, "it was an odd choice of terms, for the Kurds, themselves are Muslim and Iraq, at the time, was a secular state" (Totten and Bartrop, 2008: 13).

MOOD OF THE WAR: DOES IT MATTER?

Having explored the origins of the Iraq-Iran war and its impact on Kurdish society in chapter 3, it is now necessary to examine the relationship between this war and the Anfal campaigns for two reasons: to understand the position of the genocide process under the circumstances of war and to explore whether the Anfal Campaigns were a consequence of the war or vice versa.

In terms of circumstances, both sides—Iraqi Kurdistan and Iranian Kurdistan—were under pressure due to the war, and on both sides of the border, the victims were Kurdish citizens (van Bruinessen, 1986: 14), but on two different levels, as explained later in the chapter:

Regarding the first level, since the Kurds are considered as Iraqi citizens, they were under pressure to join the army units, the popular army (official militia), and the popular militia (semiofficial militia). Tens of thousands of Kurdish men, who were under military conscription, were forced to move toward the front line, or they were used as reserve forces to protect state institutions. Most of them were employees, workers, and ordinary people, or they were used as reserve forces to protect state institutions. If a person refused to join these forces, he was considered a fugitive, and desertion, according to the law, was a punishable crime. In some cases, they returned to their units, but in the latter years of the war, cutting an ear was one of the punishments for the fugitive; also, the fugitive had to accept losing his job and risking his life and the life of his family.

The second level can be called the internal level, which is the pressure that was exerted on activists and opponents. Thus, arrests, prosecutions, and a state of emergency were a daily phenomenon, continuing without interruption, and this is in addition to the systematic extermination process. The components were regularly targeted. Likewise, throughout the war, the Arabization process did not subside on the first and second levels. In addition to the possibility of "seeing the increasingly brutal treatment of the whole of Iraqi society caused by the Iraq-Iran War can be seen in the evolution of Iraqi government policy toward its Kurdish population during the 1980s" (Makiya, 1994: 163).

Additionally, the most important question is what kind of relationship exists between the war and the Anfal campaigns? Here, two different principles must be taken into consideration:

First: The historical and strategic tensions in the frame of the nationalistic and sectarian conflict between Arabs and Persians, or in other words, between the Iraqi authority and the Arab political elite on the one hand, and the Iranian authority and its political elite on the other hand. During the twentieth century, several conventions and agreements were signed, but all of them failed. Thus, the Arab-Persian conflict exceeded the Kurdish case.

Second: The Baathists were following the ideology of creating a permanent enemy, whether external or internal, or both together. Regarding the parties opposed to the Baath authority, which were operating outside the Baath's will, or any political parties not satisfied with the leadership of the Baathists in the political process, these were considered enemies of the Baath's revolution (ABSP, 1972: 37). In addition, the existence of an enemy in the Baath's literature is described throughout. The "cultural curriculum: the third phase of youth 'Futuwwa' students of first, second and third years of secondary school," is one example, as it has been confirmed that "the commander and the father-leader Saddam Hussein once asked a group of elementary school students; who is our first enemy? Some of them answered the Persian regime; others said the Zionist entity and others included traitors of the nation. The commander Mr. President, answered, the Zionist entity (Israel) is the first enemy of the Arabs, and then the Iranian regime and the traitors of the nation" (ABSP, 1983: 27).

According to this method, the Baathists with their many nationalist tendencies were attempting to create persistent enemies, because enemies are necessary for "having an enemy is our principal means of acquiring an identity" (McKim, 1997: 79). Therefore, it is difficult to find any Baathist discourse that is free from the concept of the enemy or describing the out-group using multiple adjectives. For example, they described the Iranians as "Persians Magi[2] racists" (al-Iraq, 1988). It is a kind of portrayal of inferiority that suggests a conversion away from Islam to justify killing them. In this context, they portray the Kurds as the inner enemy, traitors, and agents of this Iranian enemy, the Magi, or the client's pocket. The aim of this discourse was to prepare, ideologically, Iraqi public opinion in order to target the Kurds. Thus, they made the Kurds the group that should be destroyed like dogs. It has been pointed out by Ali Hassan al-Majeed that "dogs are not linked to any rights in Islam" (Jihani, 2007: 18).

The relationship between the Anfal Campaigns and the Iran-Iraq war as causality has mostly been shown to be nonexistent. In this regard, the developments of the war proved that the Anfal Campaigns were not part of the arrangements of the war's termination, but rather "after eight years of fighting, the Iran-Iraq War had finally come to a halt, but the fight continued for the Kurds" (Miller, 2014: 60). This continuity of the campaigns, for the High Iraqi Tribunal Court, was one of the most important reasons for considering the campaigns to be genocide (High Iraqi Tribunal Court). In addition, if the campaigns were part of the war, continuity should have been considered a violation of the ceasefire, not only that but the eighth phase was one of the deadliest campaigns, as "Saddam continued his genocide against the Kurds with the eighth and final Anfal phase" (Miller, 2014: 61).

We can consider that the war of genocide that was being waged in secret, and claimed the lives of tens of thousands according to a bureaucratic plan, makes it a unique model that has parallels with the Holocaust from several aspects. Thus, we come to the conclusion that "al-Anfal were not the product of a defined political and a military of Iran-Iraq war or to put the pressure on the Kurdish movement to surrender but it was Baathist strategy inspired by the bloody legacy of culture and national project and to declare the death of the Kurds as Aflaq has confirmed for their biggest project, which was the

Arab unity" (Suleiman, 2002: 7). For the sake of Arab unity and all of the Baath's goals, the Ba'ath slogan "everything is for victory," "the Iran-Iraq war provided the crucial element with which Baghdad could cover-up its opportunity to bring to a climax its long-standing efforts to bring the Kurds to heel" (Salih, 1995: 149).

THE PREPARATION

The preparation for the Anfal Campaigns took a specific course under specific circumstances. The specific circumstances, as has been explained in chapter 3 and the previous section, are that despite the lack of causality between the Iraq-Iran war and the Anfal Campaigns, the circumstances of the war were exploited in order to support the implemention of the genocidal plan. The state was facing a difficult test, and the Baathists were wounded to the core because of the war and the human and material losses they incurred, and as "the war has passed its 7th year, therefore, the Baath leaders gathered in order to put the final solution plan for the Kurdish case" (Muhammad, 2013: 15). Thus, the atmosphere of the war provided an appropriate base for the Iraqis to implement their ideological policy of Arabization and extermination. The "documents unequivocally show, the genocide of the Kurds, such as the geno-cide process in Rwanda and Yugoslavia in 1990, 'along on the same lines in wartime,' previously have been studied and planned by the Iraqi regime and then have been implemented by the chosen Baath men" (Hiltermann, 1999: 19). Thus, all the indications, evidence, documents and eyewitnesses confirm that an intended and deliberate plan was drawn up before the implementation of the Anfal Campaigns. Among those indications are that the authorities were given an opportunity to implement the final solution, "as they were thinking" that the atmosphere of the "Iran-Iraq war could provide the crucial element with which Baghdad could cover-up its opportunity to bring to a climax its long-standing efforts to bring the Kurds to heel" (Salih, 1995: 7).

Here, if we go back to the theoretical basis, as has been shown in chapter 1, in preparing the atmosphere to target a specific component, there are many factors in the discipline of genocide that form the causality of human destruc-tion. The main characteristic of social division is ethnocentrism, which is the central phenomenon within the dominant group. The indication toward eth-nocentrism here is important for two reasons: the first is Ali Hassan Majeed's behavior toward the targeted areas and the victims. The second is utter hatred toward unarmed civilians who are at the same time citizens of the state; although it does not compare to a modern state with its citizens, it tends to be the behavior of a primitive tribe against strange people. Additionally, the behavior of the Iraqi forces under the leadership of the Baathists, particularly under the leadership of Al-Majeed, followed the ideas of ethnocentrism, which "is the technical name for this view of things in which one's own group is the center of everything, and all others are scaled and rated with reference to it" (Sumner, 1906: 41). With regard to the relationship to the preparation of the genocide, the Anfal Campaigns can be divided into two phases, with the first phase, starting on April 21, 1987, and ending on June 20, 1987 (Kirmanj, 2013: 11). This division, according to the sequence of the campaigns, is significant, and an attempt to structuralize the events will be made.

Specific Legislation

The legislation regarding the Anfal Campaigns started with the first meeting of the "Revolution Command Council" through the appointment of Ali Hassan al-Majeed, as follows: "The Revolution Command Council decided in its session held on 03.29.1987 as follows:

First: Comrade Ali Hassan Al-Majid, a member of the region (al-qutrr)[3] leadership of Baath Arab Socialist Party, represented the national command of the Party and the Revolutionary Command Council in the implementation of their policies throughout the region of the North, including the Kurdistan region of autonomy in order to protect law and order and to ensure stability by implementing the autonomy of law in the region." (Majid, 2009)

Thus, the legislation for the Anfals under the guise of ethnic-Arab-centrism began, after "Saddam Hussein appointed his cousin, Ali Hassan al-Majid, to become the overlord of the North" (Hiltermann, 2007: 3); with a fanatical tribal background and a weak level of education, he has been installed as "the brutally effective and efficient head of Iraq's secret police" (Miller, 2014: 53). This ethnic background was prominent in Al-Majeed's mind when he announced, "I am going to the north, though I wear pants[4] or force them to wear Iqaal"[5] (Kirmanj, 2013: 14). The prominent element in Al-Majid's confession is the identification of the "symbols" that distinguish Kurds from Arabs. Traditional clothing is a prominent part of the difference in culture and identity, along with the entire language and ethnic background. All this is in order to facilitate the goal of the Iraqi soldier and to ensure an effective campaign.

Hence, this legislative step is considered a crucial move taken by Saddam Hussein, within the stage of preparation for further resolutions before taking any other steps. In order to implement the provisions of the legislative step, "on March 18, 1987, Saddam replaced the governor of the Northern Bureau in Kirkuk, who had weakly overseen security in northern Iraq, with his own cousin Ali Hassan al-Majid" (Miller, 2014: 53). Considering that the Kirkuk governor during that period was a weak person deserves to be examined, because what was happening in Kirkuk due to the Arabization policy and the deportation of thousands of indigenous people did not convince Saddam Hussein regarding a crucial development in Arabization.

This is what has been presented in chapter 1 in relation to the theoretical relationship in the model of patterns of genocide, as the "destruction process has inherent patterns. There is only one way which a scattered group can effectively be destroyed" (Hilberg, 1985: 1064). In addition to this framework, there is a strong characteristic of the perpetrator, which is "the perpetrator was a collective or organized actor or commander of organized actors" (Fein, 2015: 134). Thus, it is clear that "the Iraqi Revolution Command Council" was a collective leadership and an absolute power holder, and that its orders could not have been rejected or criticized. Dependent on this model and other models of theoretical explanation, the Anfal Campaigns have been designated as genocide, even as the perpetrators were aware of these theories. Accordingly, the nomination of Al-Majid for the position of secretary of the northern office of the Baathists was accompanied by the definition of the target group according to the contents of the instructions, as a basic plan to implement the genocide, with the knowledge and intention of the first person of the state and the party.

Identification

The prominent meeting of the Baath's "Revolutionary Command Council," which was the highest authority in Iraq, considered within its resolution a clear plan for the final solution to the Kurdish question in Iraqi Kurdistan. In this regard, the 1993 Human Right Watch report entitled "The Anfals against the Kurds" states, "In the first three months after assuming his post as secretary general of the Baath Party's Northern Bureau, Ali Hassan al-Majid began the process of defining the group that would be targeted by Anfal, and vastly expanded the range of repressive activities against all rural Kurds" (HRW/Middle East, 1995: 24). Moreover, the HRW's report is based on the study of 14 tons of documents, as the report emphasizes that "the PUK cache consists of fourteen tons of documents contained in 847 boxes" (HRW/Middle East, 1995: 24). In addition, these documents were "remaining under the joint custody of the PUK and the Middle East Watch" (HRW/Middle East, 1995: 17). According to the documents, this first stage of Al-Majeed started with two important steps, which are discussed in the following sections.

The Census

To identify those people who are included in the target group, conducting a census was indispensable. The Iraqi authority took the first step through the formation of a committee to enumerate the general population for the year 1987 under the category: Revolutionary Command Council resolution, No. Legislation: 272. "The title of the legislation: the decision to form a committee of the General Census of the population for the year 1987" (Al-Iraq, 1987). The census that was conducted within the decennial census of Iraq in October 1987 "the regime gave it an important secondary purpose" (Hiltermann, 2008: 3). There may be many purposes for this census, but the most important purpose as, the UN report states, is "in terms of defining the target group for destruction, no single administrative step was more important to the Iraqi regime than the national census of October 17, 1987" (HRW/Middle East, 1995: 25). Hence, this extra attention to the census took on serious dimensions because "those who failed to register in the 1987 census were no longer considered Iraqi citizens and thus the road to their destruction was paved" (Hardi, 2012: 16). Therefore, this census did not include the prohibited areas, which were previously designated as prohibited areas.

Consequently, Ali Hassan Al-Majid ordered his intelligence officials to prepare detailed case-by-case dossiers of "saboteurs" "families who were still living in the government-controlled areas" (HRW/Middle East, 1995: 25). Here, despite families not living in prohibited areas, and having participated in the census, they were transferred because one of the family members could be participating in the Kurdish movement or, as the UN report confirmed, "when these dossiers were complete, countless women, children, and elderly people were forcibly transferred to the rural areas to share the fate of their Peshmerga relatives" (HRW/Middle East, 1995: 25).

Prohibited Areas

The scope of the prohibited areas was broad and manifold. If we take a province such as Suleimaniyeh, in the 1977 census according to the UN report, it consisted of 1,877 villages, and "by the time of the 1987 census, this number was down to just 186 only during 10 years. Almost 1,700 villages had thus disappeared from the official map. Of these, several hundred had been destroyed during the border clearances of the 1970s and at various stages of the war against Iran" (HRW/Middle East, 1995: 81). This statement confirms two issues: the first one is that the dimensional process of the de-Kurdifikation of the Kurdish areas remained in progress. Second, the horrific situation of these areas' residents, which on the micro level, affected their social interrelationships and interdependency chains. However, "most of their inhabitants had been resettled in the nine complexes that were also listed in the 1987census. The remaining villages were simply not counted because they now lay in 'prohibited areas'" (HRW/Middle East, 1995: 81). In this regard, these nine complexes were living under controlled conditions.

The prohibition of these areas, within the administrative plan, was to justify the legitimacy of the destruction and extermination of tens of thousands of families in these rural agricultural areas. With the initiation of the evacuation of these areas, a record in one of Ali Hassan al-Majeed's meetings with members of the Northern Bureau of Baathists and the mayors of Kurdistan, the autonomous region/ Iraq, April 15, 1988, states that he shouted:

Next summer, we must not remain a village here and there with the exception of complexes. It must be like a chicken when it enters her baby chickens under her wings, they will calm down in silence. We must bring these people to the camps and watch them. We do not let them stay in the villages. Why let them live there like donkeys. Do they know anything? For wheat, I do not want their wheat. It is about twenty years we buy wheat from abroad. Let's add another five years. I will make this vast and large area, the prohibited areas. I do not let anybody remain there. (Suliman, 2014)

This record leaves no doubt about dehumanizing the targets in order to facilitate their elimination by following specific bureaucratic procedures, whereby "victims were selected because they were members of a group, were victims selected Irrespective of any charge against them individually" (Fein, 2015: 134). Thus, the only crime they committed was their belonging to specific areas. To carry out this selection, here is the official resolution of the Iraqi authority:

The issue of Resolution No. 4008
    Date 20.6.1987
    From the leadership of the Northern Secretarial to the leadership of Legion One, the leadership of the Legion II, the leadership of the Fifth Corps.
    Subject / dealing with the villages of forbidden areas in terms of security:
    Because the official duration identified for assembling these villages, will expire on 21 June 1987 we will decide to start fast action from June 22, 1987, as follows:

1. All villages will be considered as prohibited areas in terms of security, areas that reside, Iranian agents, saboteurs, and traitors, who have betrayed Iraq.
2. It is prohibited to stay in these areas for any human being or animals. These areas are considered prohibited areas; shooting in the areas is permitted without restriction or condition and without instructions, unless other instructions are issued in this regard by our headquarters.
3. Any movement from here to there and from there to here, or agriculture, industry and animal husbandry, is absolutely forbidden. The related institutions have to pursue this matter, and everyone according to their specialty.

4. The corps must be ready for the particular bombardments, sometimes with guns, aircraft and helicopters. It includes twenty-four hours, night and day, in order to kill the largest amount of those who exist in the forbidden areas and were previously warned.

This resolution includes three extra points in detail. It exists in the appendix.

Ali Hassan al-Majid
A member of the Regional (Qutrr) leadership
Presidential Office of the Northern

(Muhammad, 2013: 219)

This resolution covers all elements of the crime of genocide, because "the destruction of group members was undertaken with intent to kill and murder, it was sanctioned by the perpetrator. The importance here is the direct evidence of orders or authorization, for the destruction of the victims" (Fein, 2015: 135).

The Anfal Campaigns can be divided into two stages:

The first stage, starting from April 21, 1987, and ending on June 20, 1987, when 703 villages controlled by the Iraqi authority were destroyed, and the residents who lived in these areas were deported to the forced complexes, and the evacuated areas were to be entirely Arabized, particularly the mixed areas (Kirmanj, 2013: 11).

The second stage, which started on the day of the census, coincided with October 1987 and is identified as the last day for the surrender of those who were living in the forbidden areas. The regime called that day "the day of return to the national grade" (Kirmanj, 2013: 11).

In this regard, the UN report states that "two government instruments the October 1987 national census and the declaration of 'prohibited areas,' covering more and more of the Kurdish countryside like a crazy-patterned quilt were institutional foundations of this policy" (HRW/Middle East, 1995: 6). It is worth mentioning that the UN report includes an argument comparable to the categorization of the two stages, as it has been stated: "These instruments were implemented against the background of nearly two decades of government-directed 'Arabization,' in which mixed-race districts, or else lands that Baghdad regarded as desirable or strategically important, saw their Kurdish population diluted by Arab migrant farmers provided with ample incentives to relocate, and guarded by government troops" (HRW/Middle East, 1995: 6). This recognition does not leave any doubt that the Anfal Campaigns were an extension of a process of Arabization during the rule of the Baathists.

The critical question here is how did the targeted people return to the prohibited areas that had been evacuated in 1976? The UN report has covered this issue and explains that "(1). After the start of the war with Iran, which began with the Iraqi invasion of September 22, 1980, Baghdad's campaign against the Kurds faltered. (2). Army garrisons in Iraqi Kurdistan were progressively abandoned or reduced, their troops transferred to the Iranian front; (3). Into the vacuum moved the resurgent Peshmerga.[6] (4). Villages in the north began to offer refuge to large numbers of Kurdish draft dodgers and army deserters. (5). Increasing stretches of the countryside effectively became liberated territory" (HRW/Middle East, 1995: 43). However, many areas were for the first time considered to be prohibited zones. There were other rural areas in the heart of the Kurdish region, and not close to the border with Iran, but these were also considered prohibited zones. The Baathists, based on their Arab centrism, knew what they wanted and planned all their steps with precision and care. What they were intending goes beyond what was announced because "by the mid-eighties, the villages in the border areas were not the only villages being razed, but those villages in the oil-producing regions in the heart of northern Iraq were also being razed and their inhabitants resettled" (Makiya, 1994: 154). With the 1988 Anfal Campaign, all residents of the areas that the Ba'athists used to call the prohibited areas were gathered and treated with a craft similar to what the Nazis did in Auschwitz, but with the differences in technology and the cultural differences that the Ba'athist Arabs possessed. They were simply living in areas designated "prohibited for security reasons" (which now extended to virtually all rural areas in northern Iraq and included, incidentally, areas inhabited by Assyrian Christians who are not Kurds) and "entering these areas would be like having a death sentence" (Makiya, 1994: 154).

Thus, these dimensions of the Baath's intentions are significant, because the goal was to address not only the areas adjacent to the border but also all Kurdish rural areas, and the regions of Kirkuk, Diyala, and Mosul provinces, particularly the areas "those in the oil-producing regions in the heart of northern Iraq." This situation possessed a serious threat to the existence of the Kurdish people in the region in the long term, because the rural people are more involved in their land and its region in comparison to those who live in the city. Those who live in the city have a house, and it is not difficult for them to sell their houses and buy another one in another area, but the villagers in contrast are bound to their village by the land, memories, and the historical dimension, and it is difficult to get rid of this.

CONCENTRATION CAMPS

According to Raul Hilberg, the deportation and concentration camps are the fourth stage of the procedure in order to annihilate an out-group. The purpose of the process of the Anfal Campaigns, according to what has been examined of the procedure, confirms the de-civilizing process. It is the dissociation of the interdependency chains and the dismantling of Kurdish community structure, and its dismemberment. Regardless of Al-Majeed's warning of June 22, 1987, the villagers were attached to their land, their cultivation and the jobs that they used to occupy in their ancestral areas, and they had "learned to live with the climate of war and take care of their crops. Even the inhabitants of the villages that had been destroyed earlier, and had accepted deportation to the mujama't were rounded up, they were expelled to the 'prohibited zone'" (Hardi, 2012: 29); however, the aggression reached a level of collective annihilation that was previously unthinkable.

Here, it is worth mentioning that "indeed, the Anfal cannot be understood without an awareness of the half century of Kurdish armed struggle against the central government of Iraq, through various political regimes" (HRW/Middle East, 1995: 3). Binding these military operations to the past is unavoidable because of the nature of the events, which complement each other. The Kurdish resettlement camps, despite the difference between the previous resettlement camps and concentration camps, in terms of their temporary nature, could be considered a prison for the classification of the victims. They enabled the preparation of the final stage of destruction, remaining focused on one goal, which is the Arabization of the region, and grabbing the large territory that was evacuated from its residents. Additionally, "as all the horrific details have emerged, this name has seared itself into popular consciousness—much as the Nazi German Holocaust did with its survivors" (HRW/Middle East, 1995: 5).

Before delving into the essence of the process, there are two points that should be noted, which is that a distinction must be made between the forced compounds that the Baathists established in the 1970s, which have been discussed in the previous chapter, and the temporary concentration camps that were established when the military attacks were carried out on the targeted areas in the Anfal operations in order to reorganize the detainees, dispersing them and transferring them to mass graves. In this context, what took place in 1987–1988 was a kind of final uprooting. Or, in another sense, "the Anfal were carrying the characters of anti-Kurds (de-Kurdification). The targeted areas were totally Kurdish areas. I must add that those who were not exposed to any harm in the Anfal areas and not killed at the hands of the regime did not relate to the lack of confidence, but because they were not Kurds. In the Anfal period, no Arabs been subjected to arrest or murder. At a time, even the villages that were trusted by the regime have been subjected to genocide besides the villages that were destroyed and the families wiped out" (Hiltermann, 2008: 20). The nature of the de-Kurdification of the Kurdish region is based on the principles and various documents from the Anfal Campaigns, and even the multiple eyewitnesses who are still alive—witnesses that include some of the participants in this research. The first step in these operations began with the destruction of villages and the countryside, and gathering their inhabitants into specific concentration compounds (1). A racist statement by Chemical Ali in this regard is clear when he ordered the forces to "do not keep one house in the Kurdish villages in Erbil's plain, except the Arab villages" (Suleiman, 2002: 9). What is strange about this racist statement is that there is not a single Arab village in the plain of the Erbil Governorate. Chemical Ali's affirmation, in this regard, regarding excluding the Arab villages from the demolition process, emphasizes the goal of Arabizing the land and exterminating its original owners.

The De-Kurdification of the Region

Here, despite the de-Kurdification process occurring as defined by the genocide convention, which appears in General Assembly Resolution 961: Genocide is "a denial of the right of existence of entire human groups" (Smith, 2013: 228), the stage of deportation and concentration camps was still in progress, along with the preparation for the military being well underway. Hence, the second stage was reached, which can be described as an attempt to evacuate the entire areas that had been prohibited. This stage included or preceded the military action of destroying the villages, countryside, and everything useful to humans and animals in accordance with the scorched-earth policy, according

Table 4.1   The Names of the Complexes

	The Name of the Complex	Places
1	Al-Ssumud (resistance)	Between Kufri and Kalar
2	Al-Nnasir (Victory)	Sharazur
3	Al-Ukhuwa (Brotherhood)	Sharazur
4	The New Halabja	Sharazur
5	Shorish (Revolution)	Chamchamal
6	Takiya	Chamchamal
7/8	Bazian 1 & Bazian 2	Bazian
9/10/11	Bainjan, Kubala, and Alai	Bazian
12	Piramagrun	Dukan
13/14	Haji-Awa and Saruchawa	Pishdar
15/16	Tasluja and (Qadisiya)[1]	Bakrajo

(1) A list of the forced complexes before the Anfals in the province of Sulemaniya (Suleiman, 2002: 10).
[1] **Al-Qadisiya**: This is a historical name of an Arab-Islamic battle against the Sassanid Empire. Hence, on April 2, 1980, at the Mustansiriyyah University in Baghdad, Saddam was drawing parallels to the seventh-century defeat of Persia in the Battle of al Qadisiyyah when he announced:
"In your name, brothers, and on behalf of the Iraqis and Arabs everywhere we tell those [Persian] cowards and dwarfs who try to avenge Al-Qadisiyya that the spirit of Al-Qadisiyah, as well as the blood and honor of the people of Al- Qadisiyah who carried the message on their spearheads, are greater than their attempts" (Zweiri and Zahid, 2007: 10).

to chemical's order in the "clause five of the first directive instructed the armed forces to kill any human being or animal present in these rural areas" (Rabil, 2002: 22). In order to implement that, these areas were besieged from all sides and then attacked under the policy of "shoot-to-kill" as "the first of the Chemical's directives bans all human existence in the prohibited areas, to be applied to a shoot-to-kill policy" (HRW/Middle East, 1995: 24). In the context of the plan studied, and despite the ferocity of the battles that were taking place with Iran: "Saddam's regime had barely finished the five battles with Iran, consequently, he turned to the Kurdistan region. The heart of Saddam Hussein was filled with malice against the Kurds as he issued his orders to the Republican Guard forces, led by the offender ancient Ali Hassan al-Majid, the (Chemical Ali),[7] which his name has been linked to the using of chemical weapons against the Kurdish people" (Al-Hamdani, 2007: 115).

After the initiation of the Anfal Campaigns, Chemical Ali expressed his intention, after becoming the absolute ruler of what was called the northern region, as follows:

I told [the village leaders]: "I cannot let your village stay. I will attack it with chemical weapons. Then you and your family will die.". . . I will kill them all with chemical weapons! Who is going to say anything? The international community? F--- them! This is my intention. As soon as we complete the deportations we will start attacking them everywhere according to a systematic military plan, even their strongholds. . . . I will not attack them with chemicals just one day, but I will continue to attack them with chemicals for fifteen days. Then you will see that all the vehicles of God himself will not suffice to carry them all. (Totten and Parsons, 2004: 392)

This ultimatum issued by Ali Hassan al-Majid contains words and attitudes that reflect three important points: the first one is the pan-Arab ideology, which involved applying violence as one of its decisive principles; the nature of this ideology has for decades been a source of education in Iraq. Second, the use of these types of bad words in a conservative society is an expression of the extent of the barbarity of the person and that he has never received an education. Third, although the international community always emphasizes "never again" (Budick, 2012: 9), such atrocities have occurred many times, with their knowledge and within their sight, but the story has been repeated without end. This issue leads us to the third parties who were deaf, blind, and dumb, in the face of the infernal horrors that the Iraqi state created against the Kurdish civilians in the Kurdistan region. Chemical Ali or his partners in the governance gave no value to the international or regional community, and they persisted in their destructive plans.

This type of attitude is in accordance with the ideology of "national ideals," which was also propagated in Nazi Germany, which is considered "a firmly established centuries old tradition of absolutist rule had generated an implicit requirement for national ideals, beliefs, principles and standards that could be obeyed absolutely" (Fletcher, 1997: 148/149). There was no compromise, no mercy, and no postponement because the authority had to be obeyed absolutely. Accordingly, the UN report, "Under this bitter regime, the inhabitants of the prohibited areas struggled to survive. During al-Majid's first eight months in office, the groundwork for a 'final solution' of Iraq's Kurdish problem had been laid. Its logic was apparent; its chain of command was set in place" (HRW/Middle East, 1995: 82). Furthermore, the mission was well underway at the highest levels to do what was necessary. Thus, the events of 1987 were just a preliminary step and they highlight the admission of a former intelligence officer, or in Arabic al-Istikhbarat, explaining, "Because the war was still going on. The Iraqi government was not so strong and many troops were tied up on the front. They postponed the anger and hate in their hearts . . . but only until the beginning of 1988, when the major winter offensive that Baghdad had feared failed to materialize, and Iran's fortunes on the battlefield began rapidly to decline" (HRW/Middle East, 1995: 82). Thus, during this period, they were calculating the condition of the weather and military logistics because of the wild and mountainous geography of Kurdistan.

Here, it is worth mentioning that Ali Hassan al-Majid was continuing his satirical style of dehumanization of the targeted people in terms of the psychological preparation of his men, as he announced, "When we started to implement our job, we were expecting to meet some good people, because we are sharing the citizenship, but we did not meet any good people, we never met any good people of them" (Hiltermann, 1989: 20). Chemical Ali's descriptions of the Kurdish people do not differ from the descriptions of the Nazis of the Jews. This transgression against the Kurdish people by the Ba'athists had become routine, and among them was Chemical Ali. For them, "Kurds were routinely described as donkeys or dogs or human cargo" (Spencer, 2012: 81). This kind of language, including the psychological preparing of the army and security units, according to Elias, "always takes a considerable time to unfold in relatively civilized societies. Terror and horror rarely appear in the societies without any long process of social disintegration" (Fletcher, 1997 through Elias, 1988c: 197).

Now, with the deadline approaching, announcements were sent to the military units and security forces to be ready for zero hours. This was the next step, as confirmed by the UN report, as "On October 18, the day after the census, Taher Tawfiq al-Ani,[8] secretary of the RCC's Northern Affairs Committee, issued a stern memorandum to all security committees in Kurdistan, reminding them that aerial inspection would ensure that Directive no.4008 of June 20 was being carried out 'to the letter'" (HRW/Middle East, 1995: 82; Muhammad, 2013: 19). Despite the day of the census, which coincided with October 1987, it was identified as the last day for those who would surrender from the forbidden areas; the regime called that day "the day of return to the national grade" (Kirmanj, 2013: 11). This kind of rhetorical language has been included by HRW in its report to highlight the similarity between Baathists and Nazi Germany, as it states that, "like Nazi Germany, the Iraqi regime concealed its actions in euphemisms." Where Nazi officials spoke of "executive measures," "special actions," and "resettlement in the east," Ba'athist bureaucrats spoke of "collective measures, "return to the national ranks," and "resettlement in the south" (HRW/Middle East, 1995: 82). Al-Ani instructed the security forces and the army to be ready immediately to kill the largest possible number of people in the forbidden security areas. Accordingly, people were exposed to attack from the ground and the skies, and chemical weapons were used, including comprehensive annihilation weapons such as cyanide and mustard. The orders were very harsh and strict, as Al-Ani threatened the security forces that if "any committee that failed to comply would 'bear full responsibility before the Comrade Bureau Chief'—that is to say, Ali Hassan al-Majid" (HRW/Middle East, 1995: 82).

More than nine months after the appointment of Al-Majid as the absolute ruler of Kurdistan, on February 22, 1988, the military operations started overwhelmingly to begin the first stages of destruction called the Anfal Campaigns, under the leadership of Ali Hassan al-Majid, and under the direct care of Saddam Hussein and Adnan Khairallah. The operation continued until the beginning of September, according to the documents of the Iraqi authority. "On September 6, 1988, the Iraqi regime made its de facto declaration of victory" (HRW/Middle East, 1995: 26). However, "the series of eight military campaigns conducted from February to August 1988 together constitute one of the most concerted and tragic series of events in the history of human affairs" (Newton, 2007: 1524/1525).

THE ANFALS, OR IN KURDISH "ANFALEKAN"

The Anfal Campaigns started with eight destructive campaigns from February 22 to September 6 in order to kill or assemble the survivors in forced and temporary camps. However, the distance between the census and the operation was four months, as has been confirmed by the UN report, the "Anfal campaigns began four months after the census, with a massive military assault on the PUK headquarters at Sergalou-Bergalou on the night of February 23, 1988" (HRW/Middle East, 1995: 25). This means the targeted areas and its residents were placed accurately and with pertinacity. The measures taken for this campaign were at the highest level and with the conscious participation of the state authority in Baghdad. However, in regard to the participation and knowledge of Saddam Hussein, it must be taken into account that Al-Majid was appointed by order of the president and his signature, which includes his staff of the Revolutionary Command Council. The UN report states that "from March 29, 1987, until April 23, 1989, al-Majid was granted a power that was equivalent, in Northern Iraq, to that of the President himself, with authority over all agencies of the state" (HRW/Middle East, 1995: 20). This absolute power for Al-Majid, who describes Kurds as donkeys or dogs or human cargo (Spencer, 1912: 81), is a clear message that the final solution was underway.

Hence, to carry out the military operations accurately, the Iraqi troops "tore through rural Kurdistan with the motion of a gigantic windshield wiper, sweeping first clockwise, then counter-clockwise, through one after another of the prohibited areas" (HRW/Middle East, 1995: 25). This description confirms the magnitude and size of the force that was running the processes that transformed the entire Kurdish region into a closed military area.

The First Anfal

As is clearly highlighted on the map of the Anfal Campaigns, the first operation took place in Jafayati valley. It was initiated "at 2.00 A. M. on the night of February 22-23, 1988 in the village of Yaakh Simar near Sulaimanniyya" (Makiya, 1994: 166). Yaakh Simar is located in the Jafayati valley. On that day, the "Baathist regime has started its first attempt towards implementing a plan in sending the first and fifth military corps to the area of the first Anfal in Jafayati valley in southern Kurdistan" (Muhammad, 2013: 25). It has "centered on the siege of the PUK headquarters, took more than three weeks. Subsequent phases of the campaign were generally shorter, with a brief pause between each as army units moved on to the next target" (HRW/Middle East, 1995: 26). The authorities in this campaign relied on the participant forces in this military campaign, and it is possible to see the seriousness and accuracy of the state's plan to complete this military attack successfully.

> The attack was led by Lt. Gen. Sultan Hashim, who was commanding the first and fifth Legion. The Participants in this attack was 20 Brigade of the military include the brigade of (2,3,4,5,6,7) and a brigade of 65 and 66 Special Forces. The forces included the Command and General Armed Forces, which include the Commando Brigade Corps (2,4,6) and a brigade (19,31,72,116, 438.445) and commando battalions Corps 4-5. In addition to about 30 Regiment reservists and the strength of emergency include the mercenary forces. (Muhammad, 2013: 25/26)

The Iraqi regime relied on all its forces. In addition to these huge military forces, chemical weapons were used against civilians, including children and elderly, innocent people who could not escape and did not have a plan to escape.

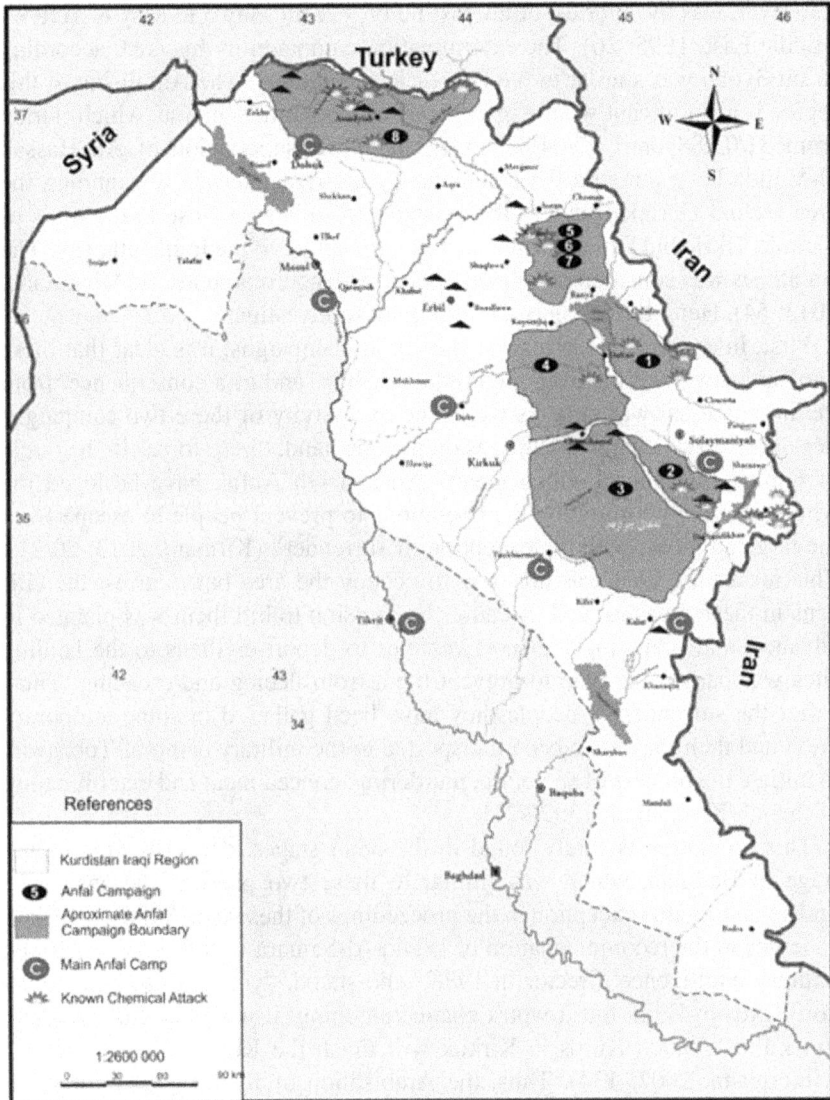

Figure 4.1   Map of Anfal Campaigns, Indicating the Target Zones in Numbers for All Eight Stages. *Source:* Hoshiyar M. Rashid and Sardar Abdulrahman (2021).

The Second, Third, and Fourth Campaigns

The characteristics of the second, third, and fourth Anfal Campaigns were very specific in terms of the severity for the victims and the purposes of Arabization. The "third Anfal, which covered the hilly plain known as Germian, took from April 7 to April 20; the Fourth, in the valley of the Lesser

Zab river, was the shortest of all, lasting only from May 3 to May 8" (HRW/ Middle East, 1995: 26). The extermination campaign in this area, according to survivors, was similar to the Day of Resurrection: "The Anfalising of this region is a significant wound in the body of the Kurdish nation, which started from 31/03/88 until 20/04/88 under the direct supervision of Ali Hassan al-Majid. They initiated the campaign by a circular terrify surrounding the area around Germian, due to the existence of this area close to oil wells of Kirkuk, Tikrit and Diyala, which has a major centre to the Iraqi authority. The Ba'athists was considered Germian as a very dangerous centre" (Muhammad, 2013: 54). Here, three points are important to investigate.

First, in examining the map of the Anfal Campaigns, it is clear that these two campaigns are far from the borders of Iran, and as a consequence, from the international war zone as well. The exclusivity of these two campaigns lies in these two characteristics, as on the one hand, "Iraqi forces in the circle of Kirkuk (Germian), which means 3rd and 4th Anfal, have besieged the whole area before initiating the operations to prevent people to escape from the targeted areas, with the exception of surrender" (Kirmanj, 2013: 20/21). This means the goal was not only to occupy the area but to arrest the citizens in these areas as well, because the decision to kill them was planned in advance, and preparing transport vehicles to deport civilians to the landing sites was part of the plan to prevent them from fleeing and escaping. Thus, "after the surrender of people they have been gathered in some temporary areas and then they have been transported to the military camp of Tobzawah to initiate the process of secretion, murdering, concealment and extermination of them" (Kirmanj, 2013: 20/21).

This regulation is rarely found in the other stages, except for the eighth stage of Badinan, which was similar to these two phases. The answer to understanding this exception in the proceedings of these two Anfals in Kirkuk zone lies in the recommendation of Wafiq Al-Samara'i,[9] the deputy of Iraq's military intelligence director in 1988, who stated, "you can kill half a million Kurds in Erbil, but it won't change anything: it would still be Kurdish. But killing 50,000 Kurds in Kirkuk will finish the Kurdish cause forever" (Hiltermann, 2007: 134). Thus, the Arabization of Kirkuk city in order to minimize the extent of the Kurdish areas and to besiege them into three cities without the rural dimension was a prelude to suffocating the Kurdish region and confining it to these three cities. In this context, Ali Hassan Al-Majid and the other Baathists were clear and did not hide their intention to besiege the Kurdish cities by any means possible, to empty the Kurdish demands of their effectiveness, and to humiliate the rest of the Kurdish citizens, as has been expressed by Chemical Ali in various ways and on numerous occasions.

Accordingly, the following statement gives a clear purpose to the Baath's authority to keep the Kurds under their control; however, rather than educating them, they were mass murdered. In this regard, according to one of the state's official statements from Ali Hassan al-Majid numbered (289 on 11/4/1988), the villages of the third Anfal area were those most affected by the Anfal operations, as the disappearance of the population included the highest proportion of women and children in comparison to other regions attacked in the Anfal Campaigns. The state's official statement confirms:

> Assembling points have been made for civilians who have been arrested or have surrendered in the villages of the region before being sent to the security headquarters as described, as stated in the book, for example, the leadership of the oil protection force No. 289 on 11/4/1988 "to the security directorate of al-Tamim[10] (Kirkuk); we are sending you the families listed in the attached, who surrendered to our military units on April 11, 1988, please take the necessary steps in respect of the regulations of the North Office and let us know of their receipt." (Majid, 2009: 8)

The Fifth, Sixth, Seventh, and Eighth Anfal Campaigns

Every military campaign has its characteristics and is carefully designed, both geographically and logistically. Therefore, to address the essence of every campaign in detail separately would require at least one chapter for every operation. Therefore, in order to prevent prolongation, I will provide a summary of the campaigns.

The attacks were successive, meaning that not all campaigns took place at once, which may have been due to the Iraqi forces' preoccupation in the war with Iran. Therefore, the same forces that were used in the Anfal operations in the early stages were mobilized in the operations that followed. Regarding the fifth, sixth, and seventh operation, its destination was the Erbil Governorate, which targeted "the valleys of Shaqlawa and Rawanduz in the Erbil district, on the border of Iran. This consisted of three consecutive offensives, which started on 15 May and ended on 26 August" (Hardi, 2012: 21). These campaigns were carried out respectively, in areas adjacent to each other. However, the victims in these areas were much less in number in comparison to the previous campaigns, due to the rugged region, on the one hand, and on the other hand, according to Omer Mohammad, "the majority of the residents had left the areas before the beginning of the military offensive" (Muhammad, 2013: 164). Perhaps many were able to head toward the borders and enter Iran, or they were able to reach the old forced camps in order to hide among the citizens in the compounds near the area of the operations.

In terms of the eighth or the final Anfal Campaign, which "took place between 25 August and 6 September" (Hardi, 2012: 21), this was characterized by particular cruelty and even more civilian casualties; strangely, in addition to that, this area is located on the border of Turkey, which is very far from the war zone. Therefore, "even after concluding the Iran-Iraq War, Saddam continued his genocide against the Kurds with the eighth and final Anfal phase, which targeted the heavily populated Badinan region of the KDP in late August and early September" (Miller, 2014: 61). This means that the campaign was characterized by several peculiarities, including conducting it after the end of the Iran-Iraq war, which helped the authorities to gather a greater force in their campaign, and this made the campaign more brutal and cruel, and it was conducted in the last populated rural area.

THE PROCESS OF ANNIHILATION

With respect to the Baathist's perpetration of the entire annihilation of the targeted people in the death zone, I will attempt to approach Elias's framework of violence. There is a religious peculiarity, which can be considered as part of psychogenesis in the civilizing process, which ought to prevent a Muslim from targeting innocent people or inciting them to do so. How did the Baathists dare to attack the masses of people, on the one hand, and on the other hand, some Arab Muslims, and even Islamists congratulated Saddam for his victory over what they called the rebellion in the north? It may be that they were coerced to do so and also living in fear of disobeying the regime. Even so, we can understand the reason for the name of Anfal, as the Baathists considered Kurdish citizens to be infidels as soon as they disobeyed the state, and thus they deserved to be killed and exterminated. It is worth mentioning that these citizens did not leave the state's obedience, and they were living in safety in their areas. Rather, the state could do nothing to protect them, provide services for them, and grant them the freedoms that are considered the basic rights of citizens. The state in Iraq has borne the seeds of the decline of civilization due to the reduction in the dependent chains between individuals and groups, which led to a decline in cooperation between the components on the one hand, and between them and the state on the other hand; therefore, the name Anfal and the impression of a religious color provide a window on the social characteristics and their transformation in the long term, as according to Elias's theory.

Thus, if, according to Elias, the process of state formation with its characteristics is considered to be a civilizing process, and with Elias's examination of the process of genocide in the framework of the breakdown of the state, it is difficult to find an independent process of state formation due in part to its failed characteristics. In other words, state formation in Iraq constantly carried in its matrix the seeds of the collapse. Hence, to the extent of the state's cruelty toward a segment of its citizens, there is the cruelty of those who collaborate with the state, and there is the silence of the majority that does not move to stop the bloodshed against thousands of innocent people. From here, and in the same direction, Elias is raising a confusing question about what happened in Nazi Germany as he states:

> How was it possible that people could plan and execute in a rational, indeed scientific way, an undertaking which appears to be a throwback to the barbarism and savagery of earlier times—which, leaving aside all differences of population size and provided one is allowed posthumously to grant slaves the status of human beings, could have taken place in Ancient Assyria or Rome? But in the twentieth-century one no longer expected such things. (Fletcher, 1997: 158)

In addition to the unique aspects of the Nazi mass killing, there are certainly unique aspects to the mass killing that the Iraqi Baath leaders committed in the absence of the international community. If there are philosophical and historical dimensions for Nazi Germany and its ideology, there are at the same time levels of philosophical and historical dimensions for Iraqi Baathists and their ideology. Based on the above discussion, "genocide was a calculated action which served to reduce the enemy's military strength" (Fletcher, 1997: 158).

Therefore, there is a great similarity between the Nazi and Baathist models on the subjective and objective levels. They can be compared at the macro and micro sociological levels, including the similarity between the two models concerning their marginal position in the countries that host them as citizens or as subordinates. There is another great similarity that can be compared, which is the division of the Kurdish homeland among more than one country, dividing them, and making them an "international colony" (Beşikçi, 2004). It is possible to put it in the context of the de-civilizing process in the way that "Elias places the Nazi mass murder of the Jews in the context of inter-state processes and the dynamics of established-outsider relations" (Fletcher, 1997: 160). Hence, there are two important characteristics: the interstate and the established-outsider relations, and both exist in the Anfal Campaigns. First is the cooperation of the international community with the Iraqi authority politically, financially, and militarily.

There is another peculiarity in the Anfal Campaigns, which are related to a great extent to the Holocaust. This is the use of toxic gases to kill Jews and Kurds, with the difference in mechanism. The Baath's authority in Iraq carried out massive bombing operations from the sky with toxic gases, but the Jews were killed through the poison gas chambers. The medium was gases, and only the mechanism was different. Several European Union companies have supplied Iraq with internationally banned weapons, and among those countries is Germany. These weapons were used against defenseless citizens in dozens of urban areas, and on top of it was the city of Halabja. This means that "the use of chemical weapons on the defenseless rural population of Iraqi Kurdistan was both the first use of chemical weapons by a state on its own civilian population (without a legitimate military target) and the first direct chemical gassing of a town or village" (Miller, 2014: 54).

What attracts our attention here are the bystanders, internally and externally, who have been congratulating the regime in an unprecedented way, given that "genocide does not take place in a completely closed system but in a global context" (Spencer, 2012: 50). The Iraqi media was announcing the operations of the army and mercenaries, consequently, in the name of the "heroic Anfal campaigns" (Miller and Meiselas, 1993). It means, they were boasting about the killing machine that they were perpetrating disgracefully. Operations were not against foreign or internal armed forces, but against unarmed civilians and farmers, and in the depth of Kurdish areas. In contrast, "there are both internal and external bystanders and the inaction of those outside may be more important than that of those inside" (Spencer, 2012: 50). In this regard, there is much discussion about the classification of bystanders in a wider sense, to include helpers (those involved directly), "gainers" (those who benefited directly or indirectly from the despoliation of victims), and onlookers (those who watched passively) (Edgren, 2012: 54).

In addition to this classification, the international community was aware of the acts of genocide that Iraq was practicing in the Kurdish regions. The United States was aware as "the United States certainly knew about this prohibited use of chemical weapons, and issued weakly-worded statements of disapproval, but took no actionable steps to stop them" (Miller, 2014: 48). The strangest thing is that, and opposite to the Iraqi authority themselves, the United States during the period of using the chemical weapons confirmed that Iran is the country that had used chemical weapons, and this was their position until the US Congress announced that it was the Iraqis' responsibility. Consequently, this case confirms the interstate nature of the Anfal Campaigns, including the internal emphasis on the established-outsider relations, which have previously been noted, in that the relationship between successive Iraqi authorities and the Kurds led to the genocidal action. At that time, many European countries not only were aware but were the ones who supplied Iraq with these weapons. In addition to the United States and the Europeans, Arab and Islamic countries, led by the Organization of the Islamic Conference and the Arab League, many of the leaders of the Islamic movements were either silent or congratulated the success of the Anfal Campaigns. There is one exception, and that is the former Algerian president Ahmed Ben Bella, who issued a warning to the Iraqi government and public opinion on

9/3/1988 stating: "I call on the Iraqi government to stop the war of genocide against the Kurdish people, and I call on governments and political forces in the Arab and Islamic world to break their silence and apply pressure to stop the massacres" (AL-Mada, 2010).

The other important point, based on this theoretical explanation, the fourth and the final phase with regard to the Anfal Campaigns, is the annihilation, which consists in the "extermination mobile killing operations in extermination camps" (Finchelstein, 2005: 19). In this regard, Ali Hassan al-Majid was not hiding his intention to eliminate the targeted people, as he emphasized "taking care of them means of burying them with bulldozers. That's what taking care of them means. Those people gave themselves up" (Makiya, 1994: 167). Here, an important question arises regarding the question of Elias: "How was it possible that people could plan and execute in a rational, indeed scientific way?" (Fletcher, 1997: 158): Yet does it matter for killing whether it is in a rational or in a scientific way? The answer is that the perpetrators cannot resort to genocide without a rational and scientific method for their purpose. It is true that the Holocaust was carried out in a highly rational and scientific way, insofar as it is "a textbook case of scientific management, a paradigm of modern bureaucratic rationality, exemplified by the department in the SS headquarters in charge of the destruction of European Jews, officially designated as the Section of Administration and Economy" (Shaw, 2007: 135). However, it is also true that more than one million people in Rwanda have been killed by militias who typically murdered their victims with machetes and machine guns, and far away from bureaucratic procedures, as these tools have proven quite as murderous as the gas chambers were, "without the need for bureaucracy on the German scale (although the organizer did employ modern political organization and mass media)" (Shaw, 2007: 136).

Thus, it is possible to determine all models of genocide as being unique in their method of killing and annihilation. However, despite the nature of rationality and scientific approach taken in the Anfal Campaigns, the primitive mentality in the Baathist rhetoric, particularly the rhetoric of Al-Majid, was still strongly apparent. As a consequence, it may be possible to state that the process of the Anfal Campaigns has combined both models of Rwanda and the Holocaust. This is because, theoretically, the tribal nature of the Rwandan mentality emerged in the Baathist literature, particularly in Al-Majid's rhetoric, and their behavior was in accordance with the tribal totalitarian model toward the outsider; also, practically, the modern implementation of technical administration was similar to that of the Holocaust in bringing the process to a "successful" end. Accordingly, dependent on the admission of one of the commanders of the mercenary forces, who has confirmed that Chemical Ali was fiercer than Saddam Hussein, "He was not respecting anybody and he was obeying the orders of Saddam only" (Jihani, 2007: 18). This is evidence of the lack of a structural mind in one of the state institutions, which is the army. Chemical Ali, in virtue of his family relations with Saddam, and the blood relationship of the tribe, would not listen to anybody except the words of his cousin Saddam Hussein. Hence, this kind of power relation is still the prisoner of the tribal mind.

The methods used for the transformation of victims were implemented in different ways, depending on multiple formats and in accordance with the process. Primarily, the victims were transferred to temporary camps, throughout several stages and locations. The victims were arrested and detained in areas near to the military campaigns (Fatih and Salih, 2003: 174), pending their transfer to military bases. This was done in difficult circumstances without food or drink or any kind of cover to protect them from the extreme cold. In the end, they were transferred to the camps allocated for victims in order to categorize them and separate families from each other (Fatih and Salih, 2003: 175). However, in some cases, some of those who were arrested from the villages and the surrounding areas were killed in the same place by the Iraqi forces (Resool, 2003: 122).

Temporary allocated camps

- Al-salamiyah
- Tobzawah[11]
- Nugrah Salman
- Nzarka Castle
- Abu Ghreb
- Dobbs
- Khaled Military camp
- Poseah

(Mzuri, 2011: 15)

On the micro level, it is very difficult to describe the events in several pages, because the mechanism was carefully planned, as "the state initiated to arrest the target people to turn them into detention centres and private camps. Then the state separated males from females to transfer them in groups in order to open fire and murder them by the special teams. This means that death in the AC was a cumbersome death and was not carried out directly in one place. Additionally, those who were involved in the process of the AC were not involved in direct murdering, but everyone carried out a function and the state arranged a special place and special squads to murder and genocide them" (Qani, 2008: 31). This means that bureaucracy, as was the case in the Holocaust, constituted the most important part of the process, as

victims were led to death in various stages, and in very complex psychological and life circumstances. People were transferred in closed vans from one place to another like animals. Then they were murdered and buried in mass graves. In such a moment, "bureaucracy provided the 'moral sleeping pills' that made possible the Holocaust's technical-administrative success" (Shaw, 2014: 136). Here, "the summit of the Baath's fascism, after the termination of all Anfal campaigns, tens of thousands of the Kurds men, and women, the elderly and children were transferred to a military complexes. Then they were deported for the second time in the southern Iraqi desert, Nugra Salman,[12] Rumadi, Samawah, and the desert of Arar, near Saudi Arabia. There is some information is indicating that many of the victims of Anfal were sold to the Arab countries" (Suleiman, 2002: 11).

Survivors

It is important to present the experiences of some of the survivors to understand the real circumstances in these military camps and prisons. One of those of survivors is Mam Anwar who had fifty-one members of his family disappear. He said, "When they took us to Topzawa they have separated us from each other. My oldest son was with me, when they came to take him from me I told him this is my son and he was always with me but they took him forcibly from my arms and he was taken crying, and I did not see him anymore. I do not know what has happened to him" (Ahmad, 2008: 260). Muhammad Kakamin is another survivor who said, "I have 21 members missing from my family, and 45 people missing from my extended family" (Ahmad, 2008: 261).

Mariam Malik (seventy-nine years old): four of her children went missing in the Anfal Campaigns. She spent the whole seven months in this prison and witnessed the huge insults, and the torture of prisoners in the camps of "Dobbs, Topzawa, and Nugrat Salman" in Arar. These prisons were full of women, children, and young people from the Anfal of Garmiyan.

She said: "What should I tell, who can tell what have happened? It was a disaster and even our memories are shattered," "When we arrived at Nuqrat Salman it looked like a hell, and I wish I could not even see my enemies in this place." Her husband, who was sitting next to her, said, "The prison was containing 8000 prisoners and the place was not fit for any kind of life. They were assaulting and torturing people in terrible ways. My mother died because she was not strong enough to bear the harsh conditions of the prison. I placed her body in a shallow ditch of half a meter depth, because they were not giving us enough time to bury her" (Arar, 2008: 235). The following chapters provide more accounts from the participants.

CHARACTERISTICS OF THE ANFAL CAMPAIGNS

The Anfals of 1987–1989 were characterized by the following consequences:

First: The Anfals were characterized by inclusiveness and continuity. It is a misreading of the Anfal Campaigns to believe that they involved the state with all its titanic resources, standing monitoring the villagers and arresting helpless people one by one. If the Anfal Campaigns on the surface were surrounding and arresting villagers, inwardly, they involved a dismemberment of the Kurdish cities psychologically, socially, economically, and logistically. Making the outside of these cities the military zones meant paralyzing the movement between cities entirely in order to restrict the mobility between cities, and to impose a psychological fatigue to push people to migrate toward the south to the Arab cities. In this regard, "if an analysis cannot tell us what the formation of the Iraqi authority is, the authority that the annihilation was one of its products, at the same time nobody can tell us why the destruction of the Kurdish towns after the Anfal operations occurred and how we can understand it. The authority, which has destroyed the villages and the fundamentals of its life, was the same authority that destroyed the cities of Qaladze, Sayed Sadiq, Rania and other cities in Kurdistan. Therefore, the target inherently was wider and further than the destruction of the villages" (Makiya, 1994: 166).

Second: The Afals were characterized by pursuing the scorched-earth policy for the purpose of planting despair and ruining the ground. Thus, the rural areas were completely and utterly demolished, the nature of its beauty completely eliminated, including the destruction of all that was owned by those villagers. It is estimated "that over 4,000 villages were completely destroyed in this campaign" (Miller, 2014: 62), and "roughly 80% of all the rural villages in Iraqi Kurdistan were destroyed" (Makiya, 1994: 167). This demolition, according to the UN report, included "the wholesale destruction of civilian objects by Army engineers, including all schools, mosques, wells and other non-residential structures in the targeted villages, and a number of electricity substations" (HRW/Middle East, 1995: 20).

Third: The widespread use of chemical weapons against civilians on a large scale during two complete years. During these two years, several kinds of chemical weapons were used as a UN report confirms: "Mustard gas and the nerve agent GB, or Sarin, against the town of Halabja as well as dozens of Kurdish villages" (HRW/Middle East, 1995: 188/189), and that "the first Kurdish village ever to be attacked with chemical weapons (apart from napalm), was Sheikh Wassan in the Balisan Valley . . . at April 1987" (Makiya, 1994: 164/165).

Fourth: Mass executions and the mass disappearance of tens of thousands of civilians, including large numbers of women and children, and sometimes the entire population of villages, because they were considered enemies and a legitimate target for killing and destruction; based on the chauvinist ideology that the Ba'athists relied on.

Fifth: The campaigns are characterized by announcing them in official military statements through the state media and as a heroic national military operation. The Ba'athists were proud of the victories they were reaping, and "there was nothing secret about the fact that something new was in the works because all through 1988 Iraqis heard over and over again, in all the major government-controlled media, about the (heroic Anfal operation)" (Makiya, 1994: 166).

Sixth: The majority of the Kurds are Muslims, and one of the character-istics of the Kurdish village is that there is no village without a mosque, so more than 4,000 mosques were destroyed in Kurdistan, but the Kurdish peo-ple did not find a single Muslim objecting to these crimes, and they did not move even for the destruction of the mosques that are part of their sanctities, let alone for the mobilization of religious discourse in the Anfal Campaigns.

Seventh: According to the decisions of the Iraqi Supreme Court, which considered the Anfal campaigns as genocide, it was supposed to compensate the victims, but the successive Iraqi governments after the year 2003 did not compensate any of the victims. Moreover, there is always a general Arab dis-course that tends to deny genocide, which is characterized by a generalized and vague context. This statement is merely diluting the issue and trying to forget the matter and not mentioning or denying the events.

SUMMARY

In this chapter, the final solution in the form of the Anfal Campaigns against the Kurdish people in Iraqi Kurdistan has been studied. This process lies within the framework of the process of the Arabization of the Kurds in Iraq, or in other words, de-Kurdification. The concept of Anfal is the name of the eighth chapter (Surah) of the Quran, which means spoils of war, and it has been misused as justification in terms of the Islamization of nonbelievers. This is based on figurational sociology, and the ideology of the Baathists, in order to mobilize its religious and cultural dimensions as instruments for the legitimization of their authority.

In addition, the difficult circumstances of the Kurdish region in the period of the Iran-Iraq war doubled because of the Baath's pressure on Kurdish society, on the one hand, and because of transferring the war to the Kurdish borders on both sides of Iraqi and Iranian Kurdistan. It has been noted that the "control of territory and population became even more crucial on both sides than it had been before the war" (van Bruinessen, 1986: 14). However, if the war had created an extra difficultly for the Kurdish people, at the same time, it has been argued that there is no relationship between the war and the Anfal Campaigns. This means that "after eight years of fighting, the Iran-Iraq War had finally come to a halt, but the fight continued for the Kurds" (Miller, 2014: 60).

The Anfals as a process were implemented according to the four theoretical stages of Raul Hilberg. Hilberg has effectively set out a model for the pattern of genocide, as he argues that the "destruction process has inherent patterns. There is only one way in which a scattered group can effectively be destroyed" (Hilberg, 1985: 1064). The first stage is the preparation, which is an intentional plan that had to be drawn up before the implementation of the Anfal Campaigns. The second stage is the legislation, and it started with the first meeting of the "Revolution Command Council" through the appointing of Ali Hassan al-Majeed as absolute ruler of the Kurdish region. The third stage is identification, which means "the definition of the group that would be targeted by Anfal, and vastly expanded the range of repressive activities against all rural Kurds" (HRW/Middle East, 1995: 24). This stage started with a general census, and as a consequence, the prohibition areas were designated in preparation for the destruction of the residents of these areas. However, according to Raul Hilberg, the deportation (or seizure) and concentration camps was the fourth stage of the procedure in order to annihilate an out-group.

This procedure fits with the General Assembly Resolution 961, which is a denial of the right of existence of entire human groups. Thus, this denial has been implemented practically through the eight Anfal military campaigns, which led to the annihilation of hundreds of thousands of victims and the destruction of entire Kurdish rural areas.

NOTES

1. Before commencing my PhD, my master's dissertation was on the same topic under the name of "Religion and Nationalism: A critical examination of the way in which religion was mobilised in the Anfal campaign."

2. Magi is a reference to a Magi tribe who were Zoroastrian clergy (the magi), and the Muslims used it when they struck Iraq as a synonym for the worship of fire, and it was a negative against them (Jackson, 1899: 7).

3. The Baath Party believed in the Great Arab state; therefore, they were calling Iraq *Qutrr*, which means branch, region, or part of the Great Arab state.

4. Kurdish pants consist "of baggy pants tied at the shoe, a shirt with heavy belt and cummerbund, long embroidered jacket and a tribal-distinctive turban" (Wagner, 1992: 5).

5. Arab Iqaal or Agal: this is "worn by Bedouin Arabs to keep the keffiyeh in place" (Kennedy, 2004); it is a piece of thick cord known as an igal or agal.

6. *Peshmarga*: Kurdish (pêshmerge from pêsh before, in front of + merg death). A member of a Kurdish nationalist guerrilla organization (Speake and LaFlaur, 2002). The Peshmerga have been an important part of the larger development and refinement of the Kurdish national identity (Gillette, 2010: 12).

7. Ali Hassan al-Majid (1941–2010) is known as "Chemical Ali" the cousin of former Iraqi president Saddam Hussein. Al-Majeed was one of the Baath Party's leaders and he was elevated to the post of Iraqi defense minister in the mid-1990s. Ali Hassan Al-Majid Al-Tikriti (Majid) is known around the world as Chemical Ali for his role in the use of chemical weapons against Kurdish villages (Newton, 2007: 1525).

8. Taher Tawfiq al-Ani was an Iraqi Baathist politician who served as the governor of Mosul and the secretary of the Revolutionary Command Council (RCC)'s Northern Affairs Committee (HRW/Middle East, 1995: 82) during the al-Anfal campaign. He was one of the co-defendants who remain on trial for the AC (Kelly, 2007: 237).

9. Wafiq Al-Samara'I, who is living in UK, was deputy director in the military of intelligence responsible for the Iran branch (Woods, 2009: 71).

10. Within the policy of Arabization, the Baath authority changed the names of many places into Arabic, with political connotations. Based on this policy the name of Kirkuk has been changed to al-Tamim.

11. *Tobzawah* is one of the worst military bases which were built according to the proposal submitted by the Soviet Union and their planning in order to keep the city of Kirkuk safe. This castle is composed of a large fort containing 2,500 soldiers. In some places there are 2 or 3 castles (Resool, 2003: 122).

12. Qalat Al-Salman Prison is sited in the middle of the desert, about 150 kilometers from Samawa and 80 kilometers from the Saudi border in Ar'Ar region (see map of Iraq) and has no access road. This prison was built in the early 1980s, about 5 kilometers from the prison of Nugrat Al-Salman (which has now been converted into a warehouse for building material). Until testimonies were received from some of the hostages released in the late 1980s, Qalat Al-Salman was thought to be Nugrat Al-Salman (Al-Hattab, 2012).

REFERENCES

Abdul-Rahman, Muhammad Saed. *Tafsir Ibn Kathir Juz'22 (Part 22): Al-Azhab 31 to YA-Sin 27* (vol. 22). London: MSA Publication Limited, 2009.

ABSP. *al-Hizb al-qaid fi al-Nadariyati wa-altatbiq*. Beirut, Lebanon: Arab Institution for Studies and Publishing, 1972.

ABSP. *Cultural program for third stage of youthfulness of secondary school*. Baghdad: ABSP, 1983.

Ahmad, Karwan. Jalamord, the village that called the second Halabja. Sulaimaiya: Ar Ar, 3rd Year (3), (2008): 260.

al-Hamdani, Hamid. *Sanawat al-jahim, Arbauna Ama min Hukm al-Baath fi Al-Iraq 1963–2003*. Vaxjo: Veshun Media Sweden, 2007.

Al-Hattab, Jawad. Nukrat Al-Salman, Yur'ib Al-Iraqyin. *Al-arabiya*, November 19, 2012. Accessed December 26, 2020. http://bit.ly/3pmXjbL.

Ali, Abdullah Yusuf. The meanings of the Holy Qur'an. *Surah* 90, London: (2003): 8–20.

al-Iraq. Persians Magi racists. *The National Newspaper of Press/Politics*, no. 3729, Baghdad: (1988, April 24).

Al-Iraq, Durar. Qarar Tashkil Lijnat lil-Ta'dad al-Am li-ssukan. *Al-qawaneen Wal-Tashri'at Al-Iraqiya*, No. 272, Baghdad: (1987). https://bit.ly/3oKluRe.

AL-Mada D. N. Wahdaha Al-Adalat U La Tamut. Baghdad: *AL-MADA Daily Newspaper*, 2010. Accessed November 23, 2020. https://bit.ly/3kZDrc8.

Arar. Arar Magazine Vol 3. Sulaimani: *Magazin*, 2008. Accessed December 25, 2020. http://bit.ly/37Q23Ro.

Beşikçi, İsmail. *International colony Kurdistan*. Taderon Press, 2004.

Edgren, Henrik. Looking at the onlookers and bystanders: Interdisciplinary approaches to the causes and consequences of passivity. Sweden: *Forum för Levande Historia*, 2012.

Fatih, Latif and Majid Salih. *Extermination of the Kurds, Ibadat al-Kurd*. Silemani: Publisher and Offset Tishik, 2003.

Fein, Helen. *Human rights and wrongs: Slavery, terror, genocide*. Routledge, 2015.

Finchelstein, Federico. The Holocaust Canon: Rereading Raul Hilberg. Published By: Duke University Press: *New German Critique* 96 (2005): 3–48.

Fletcher, J. *Violence and civilization: An introduction to the work of Norbert Elias*. Cambridge: Polity, 1997.

Hardi, Choman. *Gendered experiences of genocide: Anfal survivors in Kurdistan-Iraq*. Oxford: Ashgate Publishing, Ltd., 2012.

Hilberg, Raul. *The destruction of the European Jews, Holmes & Meier*. Yale University Press, 1985.

Hiltermann, Joost R. (Iraq u Kurdekani), Genocide, Hawtawani Bedengi, Sulemani: Rahand (1999) (7): 17.

Hiltermann, Joost R. *A poisonous affair: America, Iraq, and the gassing of Halabja*. Cambridge University Press, 2007.

Hiltermann, Joost R. The 1988 Anfal Campaign in Iraqi Kurdistan. In *International Conference on Genocide against the Kurdish People*. Erbil: Arras, 2008.

HRW/Middle East Watch. Iraq's crime of genocide: The Anfal campaign against the Kurds. *Human Rights Watch*, 1995.

Ibn Katheer. *Tafseer Ibn-Katheer* (vol. 7). Giza, Egypt: Qurtuba Institution, 2000.

Jihani, Samzini. *Summary about Anfal, Kurte Basek leser Anfa*, Erbil: The East, 2007.

Kirmanc, Şêrko. *Identity and nation in Iraq*. Boulder, CO: Lynne Rienner Publishers, 2013.

Kirmanj, Sherko. Anfal-Sirinewei Kurd le Parezgai Kerkuk 18 (2013): 10.

Majid, Mohemmed. *Al-Qaswa Lada Saddam Husein*, April 13, 2009: P5. https://bit.ly/2YD0Jxe.

Majid, Muhammed. Alqaswa Lada Saddam Husein-Amaliyat Al-Anfal. February 25, 2009: P2. Accessed December 25, 2020. http://bit.ly/34M9pTY.

Makiya, Kanan. *Cruelty and silence: War, tyranny, uprising, and the Arab World*. United Kingdom: Norton, 1994.

McKim, Robert, and Jeff McMahan, eds. *The morality of nationalism.* Oxford University Press on Demand, 1997.

Mennell, Stephen. Decivilising processes: Theoretical significance and some lines of research. *International Sociology* 5, no. 2 (1990): 205–223.

Miller, Judith, and Susan Meiselas. Iraq accused: A case of genocide. *New York Times Magazine* 3 (1993): 12–17.

Miller, Judith, and Susan Meiselas. Iraq accused: A case of genocide. *New York Times Magazine* 3 (2014): 12–17.

Muawad, Hassan. Dr Khudair Al-Murshidi. *Al-Arabiya*, February 26, 2016. Accessed December 25, 2020. http://bit.ly/3rmQUiR.

Muhammad, Omer. *Pelamare Serbaziyakanî Anfal le Heshit Qonaxda.* Sulemani: General Directorate of Libraries, 2013.

Mzuri, Rekar. *Al-Anfal, al-qatil al-jama'I wa al-ta'thirat al-nafsiya.* Erbil: Minarah Publication, 2011.

Newton, Michael A. The Afal genocide: Personal reflections and legal residue. *Vand. J. Transnat'l L.* 40 (2007): 1523.

Qani, Mariwan. Anfal wek Genocide, Anfal wek Brinêkî Neteweyî. Sulaimaniya: *Er Er* 3 (2008): 22.

Rabil, Robert G. Operation 'termination of traitors': The Iraqi regime through its documents. *Middle East Review of International Affairs* 6, no. 4 (2002): 14–21.

Resool, M. S. *Anfal: Kurd u dewleti Iraq.* London, 2003.

Salih, Khaled. Anfal: The Kurdish genocide in Iraq. *Digest of Middle East Studies* 4, no. 2 (1995): 24–39.

Shaw, Martin. *What is genocide?* Cambridge: Polity, 2007.

Shaw, Martin. Genocide and large-scale human rights violations. *The Handbook of Global Security Policy* (2014): 145–159.

Smith, Rhona K. M. *Textbook on international human rights.* Oxford University Press, 2013.

Spencer, Philip. *Genocide since 1945.* Routledge, 2012.

Spencer, Richard. Isil carried out massacres and mass sexual enslavement of Yazidis, UN confirms. *The Daily Telegraph* 14 (2014).

Suleiman, Khalid. Nahwa Tasees Qira'a Kurdiya lima jara'. *Kurdish Papers* 5: 2015. doi: amude.com/ewraq, 2002.

Sumner, William Graham. *Folkways: A study of the sociological importance of usages.* Boston, MA: Manners, Customs, Mores, and Morals, Ginn & Co., 1906.

Taha Suliman. *Al-Ibada al-Jamaiya Lil-Alsha'b al-Kurdi; al-Buhuth wal-Ihsa'at wa-lma'lumat wa-lwathaiq.* Erbil: Jin Publisher, 2014.

Totten, Samuel, Paul Robert Bartrop, and Steven L. Jacobs. *Dictionary of genocide: MZ* (vol. 2). Greenwood Publishing Group, 2008.

Totten, Samuel, and William S. Parsons, eds. *Century of genocide: Critical essays and eyewitness accounts.* Routledge, 2004.

Van Bruinessen, Martin. The Kurds between Iran and Iraq. *MERIP Middle East Report* 141 (1986): 14–27.

Chapter 5

Personal Views and Experiences in the Process of Iraqi State Formation and Ideology

In the preceding two chapters, through the literature and documents of the Baath Party, the notion of state formation as a civilizing process has been examined, along with analyzing the Baath's ideology and the stages involved in the process of genocide against the Kurds. This chapter builds on the previous two chapters by analyzing the developments in knowledge and the experiences of individual people and their perceptions of genocide and the Baath's behavior toward individuals and groups in Iraqi Kurdistan.

In this chapter, there is an attempt to approach the most important causes of the genocide in Iraq by focusing on state formation and the Baath's ideology. For this reason, thirty-four participants have been selected and interviewed, from different levels and based on two conditions: their age and residency in Iraq under the Baath's rule. Five participants who were involved in the Baath's authority in Iraq, or who worked for the government, have been interviewed. Seven participants involved in the opposite spectrum of the Baath's rule have also been interviewed. It is worth mentioning that attempts were made to interview women as well, especially those who have studied in this field or lived through the scourge of genocide.

As has been confirmed in the previous three chapters, the genocide was carried out during a long-term process. In this regard, Mam Qadir (age seventy-nine), who is one of the victims, was jailed for five years on charges of belonging to Peshmarga guerrillas; also, his birth place was destroyed twice, and some of his family members were mass murdered in 1988. He described these stages through his own experience of these events, with deep sadness and sorrow. Mam Qadir is illiterate but has an excellent memory and significant experience, and he lived among Sunni Arabs for more than ten years under the Baath's order of his exile. The importance of Mam Qadir's description is that he counts the stages and difficulties of these periods under the rule of Iraqi authority as follows: "Primarily, the Baathist's started by Arabizing the land and the people everywhere and everything, specifically in the contact[1] areas. However, Arabizing was and still depends on an ascending order and does not have more stages. It is an ascending order of a continuous Arabizing in a single-stage, before Baath's power and still" (Mam Qadir, PI, June 25, 2015).

In addition, including Mam Qadir, all the participants agreed on, and the documents confirm, the eyewitnesses' experience that when the Ba'athists seized power, they started with the Faili Kurds, deporting and killing them and looting their property. The nature of the Baathists was procrastination and resorting to all available methods to postpone the confrontations in order to strengthen themselves, and at the right time, they started a ferocious war on the Kurdish region and began to empty the villages and rural areas to establish a security belt at a width of 20 to 40 kilometers along the Kurdistan border with Iran, Turkey, and Syria. As Mam Qadir confirmed,

> They would have shown more aggression and destruction towards the Kurds if they had stayed in power for a longer period. (Mam Qadir, PI, June 25, 2015)

THE ESTABLISHMENT AND THE INSTABILITY

Despite the passage of a long time from the establishment of the Iraqi Kingdom to the later stages of state formation, the second generation still recounts many political, social, and economic events from different eras of Iraqi state formation. However, the era of the BP and its effects are still evident to the present day, as the victims still remember the entirety of both macro and micro events. Many of the participants have been involved in intellectual, political, and social activities and suffered directly and indirectly from the Baathists having hegemony over elements of their freedom. The establishment of the Iraqi state from the beginning, and its unilateral behavior toward the Kurds, was consistently one of the key issues raised by the interviewees. The previous MP Chinar Saad (PhD) explained that she has suffered because of her father's Peshmerga affiliation, and after the national uprising against the Iraqi Baath regime in 1991, she became the "Minister of Martyrs and Anfal affairs" in the Kurdistan region. Later, she established the "Kurdish Institute to Prevent Genocide." She argues: "If we want to understand the coup led by the Baath in terms of the Iraqi state, and if we justify it in the case of the Baathists, what about the previous stage? The Arabs were behaving normally with the Kurds, even during the era of the Iraqi Kingdom at the beginning of the Iraqi state's formation; the conduct of Arabs and their view of the Kurds were similar" (PI, June 4, 2015).

Citizen's behavior is linked to the state's behavior and its perception of the basic issues that the state is going through in terms of influence, which, based on the process of state formation, brought with it changes in the way people were connected with one another. This leads eventually to greater integration and greater interdependence between people, which brings with it changes in relations between them, or greater decline and greater division between people with the same criteria, according to the civilization process. We may find a great contradiction in the views of many Arab citizens concerning the attitude of colonial behavior, when it oversaw the division of the Arab region after the fall of the Ottoman authority and established countries in the region such as Iraq, Syria, Jordan Lebanon, and so on. At the same time, they consider the international borders of these countries sacred when it comes to the Kurdish people.

Later, because of the colonial powers and England, as well as the political interests of the international community vested in the region, an effect on the conduct of Arabs emerged as it was comparatively less aggressive. Otherwise, the Kurds under the pressure of these successive regimes, under a similar Arab mentality, were suffering. Therefore, I do not think that the coup is the only reason for the genocide, but they were already thinking and behaving in that direction. This type of mentality has always existed. (Saad C., PI, June 4, 2015)

This quote highlights two important postulates: the unipolar state that was ruled by the Sunni-Arab minority from its establishment, inclusive of the Baath's rule after 1968. Hence, the Kurds were driven away from power sharing. In addition to the persecution, it led to the genocide in different forms. Thus, this figure of the state and its different characters includes unipolar eradication through violence and other forms of conduct. Here, the main issue that has been focused on by the interviewee is the Arab mentality. Thus, the whole quote is expressing pan-Arab-centrism, not only through the marginalization of other groups but also in order to mobilize everyone and utilize every tool in realizing their vision. Here, another interviewee, who is a Sunni-Arab Iraqi thinker from al-Anbar, and an academic in Political Sciences, Prof. Dr. Tayseer Abdul Jabbar Al Alusi (age sixty-two), primarily focuses on the state that failed because of the absence of harmony between the Iraqi groups, as he argued:

The emphasis on building a modern Iraqi state was not implemented in the correct manner. The reason is because of the patriarchal authority of the Kingdom, and its falling under the influence of some elements that had contradictory purposes, making them tired from what those elements wanted to push the state towards concerning the different conflicts. The implications of this are that it fell

upon the shoulders of the Iraqi components, especially the non-Arabs . . . then
dragging the state institutions towards a tyrant authority, instead of following
legal and constitutionally proper principles. (PI, May 24, 2015)

Thus, according to Al-Alusi, non-Arabs became the victims of the power
conflict between the Arab ideological tendencies and the most prominent
goal of all Arab political factions centering on Arab-centrism. His concept
of "tyrant authority" is a useful summary of a nondemocratic and totalitarian system that marginalized non-Arabs and put them under tremendous
pressure. In this regard, the Kurdish historian professor Dr. Jabar Kadir (age
sixty-nine), who is from the city of Kirkuk, having been intensely exposed to
the Arabization process, stated:

The process of nation building, or the process of a nation under the name of the
Iraqi nation, has completely failed. Primarily, as King Faisal and his followers
were struggling, this continued when the Arab nationalist movement in Iraq in
the form of its fascist and Nazi model of the 1930s emerged. As a result, the
non-Arabs' reaction led to even more affiliation with their language and ethnic
culture. This kind of state policy compelled the Kurds to hate the country that
had become a big prison and full of suffering. (PI, June 8, 2015)

Here, we can understand that one of the main causes of the failure of the
state institutions was the rise of pan-Arab nationalism and the monopolization
and exploitation of state institutions in the interests of an Arab-centric ideology. This situation led to despair with the state among the non-Arabs, and a
lack of the cooperation with the Arab nationalists. Thus, this unilateral rule of
the state led to the dilemma of political legitimacy. Moreover, the failure of
the state led to the persecution of the Kurds who strongly opposed the regime,
having marginalized them and gradually tightened the pressure. In addition,
Kadir stated that

during the period of the republic, particularly during the period of the reign of
the Baath, the common sense that existed was terminated. We must admit that
there is no nation called the Iraqi nation, and there is not even a common Iraqi
culture. For example, in Kurdistan, no one has felt that he is part of a state called
Iraq and no one has felt that he has membership of a nation called the Iraqi
nation. (PI, June 8, 2015)

The feeling that the participant presents indicates an internal bitterness
regarding this authority that treated all non-Arabs in an inhumane manner
and made them hurt to the core. Building the nation at the expense of a component who was forced to live under the same roof as a partner who did not

respect their rights, and did not treat them as human beings, is in itself a crime against humanity, and colonialism bears part of the moral responsibility for those torments that affected the Kurdish component—not only inside Iraq, but within the four countries, each of which occupies a part of Kurdistan. Hence, according to Kadir, a sense of affiliation from the Kurds is absent. In the same trend, Al-Alusi added:

> The Baath is an Arabized and chauvinistic party, par excellence. This party has exploited the tyrant authority mechanisms to impose its influence, as the predominant task. However, the subject of building an Iraqi nation failed as the predominant aim, except in the case of assimilating the non-Arabs and non-subordinates to the tune of their philosophy, and also in the interests of Arab chauvinism, disadvantaging the people and commensal nations historically in this region. There is no neutrality for the Baathists, and no cultural background that believes in pluralism. Baath is a party, with a totalitarian unilateral discourse, having entered into fascist territory, and its performance reflects that. (PI, May 24, 2015)

Thus, the most prominent point from al-Alusi is that he believes that the Baath Party was a nondemocratic party, and pan-Arab-centrism was a very strong part of its ideology. Therefore, the assimilation of other non-Arabs is one of the constant principles of Arab-centrism. In addition, the Baath's view of a nation state is the hegemony of Arab culture under the leadership of a president commander. Kadir also reiterated this idea as he argued: "The Arab nation state in Iraq was imposed upon the non-Arabs, particularly upon the Kurds, without an agreement. Government officials in Iraq, in terms of the nation state concept, only considered the Arab nation. They were attempting to prepare Iraq to include Kurdistan as a central place for Arab nationalism" (Kadar J., PI, June 8, 2015).

The importance of Kadir's statement lies in two points: the lack of an agreement between the Iraqi components, as Sunni Arabs had monopolized the Iraqi authority for more than eight decades, and Iraq was considered to be a central place for all Arab nationalists. This attitude did not arise out of a vacuum, but it was encouraged and highlighted by the Baath's authority, as announced by the Baath's "Revolutionary Command Council" on law decisions called "Legislation Title: The Arab Citizen Naturalized by Iraqi Citizenship, Has a Number of Privileges," which stated:

> According to the provisions of paragraph (a) of Article-42 from the Constitution, the Revolutionary Command Council held on 09.14.1985 decided the following: First—the Arab citizen naturalized by Iraqi nationality, enjoys the following privileges: 1,2. The grant of a piece of land (200^{m2}) in any province of Iraq

even Baghdad after 5 years living in Iraq. 3. Giving them a disposal from the land bank in both cases referred to in 1 and 2 above.

Second-the privileges have been provided in this resolution apply to Arab citizens naturalized by Iraqi nationality before the date of issuance (The decision no. 1906, 1985). This is a clear decision, in line with Kadir's statement, to prepare Iraq to be a central place for Arabs from all of the Arab countries. This decision could be interpreted as one of the most important mechanisms for Arabization of the non-Arab areas in Iraq, as the decision was to "grant a piece of land in any province of Iraq. (UNHCR, 1985)

Another participant confirmed the dilemma of the Iraqi nation state and its consideration as a failed state. Dr. Muhammad Sharif (age eighty-five), who was part of the Iraqi authority and worked for the Iraqi Ministry of Endowment and Religious Affairs as a deputy minister claimed:

Of course, Iraq is a failed state because of these reasons:
First: from its establishment, the state was a vacuum concerning the meaning of a state. It has been built on three wrong bases. In addition, Iraq could not become a suitable environment for democracy because of the hegemony of the Arab element.
Second: because the Arabs were the majority, they wanted to build an Arab state, and for this reason they have marginalized the Kurds. In contrast, this situation from the beginning has been refused by the Kurds. They have considered themselves as being oppressed and they have struggled for salvation from this situation. (PI, June 6, 2015)

There are several examples that we can investigate in these statements from the participants. First, there is unanimity among the participants with regard to considering Iraq to be a failed state, with terms such as "the absence of harmony" and "Arab nationalism," as well as concepts such as chauvinism and Nazism. Second, all of the participants focused on the Arab hegemony that led to monopolizing the state institutions and marginalizing other components, particularly the Kurds.

ANNEXATION AND UNITY

The previous section has discussed part of the vision of the participants regarding Iraqi state formation. In this section, the issue of Mosul province, which is indivisible from the Iraqi state, will be examined. The issue of Mosul province discussed in chapter 2 has been clearly set out. In this respect, the explanation of Dr. Sharif includes important points, as he claimed:

In my view, it can be hailed as the crime of the century. Jamal Abdul Nasir has described the Balfour promise when Palestine was given to Israel as: "they gave something to someone which was not their right." We "as Kurds, as Kurdish nation or as residents of Mosul province," were not part of the war. This means the decision on war was not in the hands of the Kurds, so why did they make us part of the equation in this political war? They handed us over to Iraq, and the Iraqi authority did not have the right to accept us as part of them. (PI, June 6, 2015)

It is worth mentioning that the decision to annex southern Kurdistan to Iraq was the will of two British colonial representatives, and specifically, the role of Percy Cox, the new High Commissioner for Mesopotamia at that time; specifically, in the conference that was held in Cairo on March 12, 1921, and continued until the end of the month. Strangely enough, four of the seven British officials who attended the conference "were in favour of the alternative of a separate Southern Kurdistan not subordinate to Arab rule" (Eskander, 2001: 155), including Winston Churchill, but in the end, it was Cox's position that won, and his decision to annex southern Kurdistan to Arab Iraq. This decision, according to Sharif,

was a historical crime in depriving a nation from its basic right to live as any other nation, and in time this became was known. The decision of self-determination was not something new. The 14-points of the US president for self-determination, one of these points was that every nation has a right to self-determination. However, he commented that the Kurds were given to Iraq and other nations to someone else; they are not property to be distributed. This is a crime and a continuous crime. In criminology, this is a continuous crime. It has been 100 years, and the Kurds want to eliminate this crime. (PI, June 6, 2015)

This statement from someone who was close to the Baath's authority and party members of the Baath has important indications. He, as a legal expert, has pointed out that the annexation of Mosul province to Iraq is a continuous crime. In addition, he included the fourteen points of Woodrow Wilson regarding the new world order as evidence for Kurdish rights and determination. He mentioned the information on Woodrow Wilson's twelfth request to assure the security of the life of non-Turks, as Woodrow Wilson declared: "The Turkish portion of the present Ottoman Empire should be assured as a secure sovereignty, but the other nationalities which are now under Turkish rule should be assured an undoubted security of life and an absolutely unmolested opportunity of autonomous development" (Wilson, 1918: 3). Mosul province provided an opportunity because of its multidimensions. In this regard, it was announced that King Faisal requested to integrate

Mosul province with "Arab Iraq" in terms of a kind of stability. Therefore, regarding this request, "King Faisal had such a request to save the balance between Shi'a and Sunni Arabs, but this is an Arab problem. What were the benefits? The Kurds were not ready to support Sunni-Arabs against Shi'a Arabs" (Sharif, PI, June 6, 2015). Sharif, despite his religious background as a former Sunni cleric, refuses this assumption and claims that the Kurds were not ready to support an Arab minority when they were against any rights of the Kurds. In addition, this annexation could have created deep anxiety for Arabs regarding the redivision of Iraq. Therefore, the Baathists constantly focused on the unity of Iraq, as Sharif asserted:

> Yes. Saddam Hussein "psychologically" in his mind had a theory of impossibility that the Kurds would never accept the current situation and they will separate one day. Therefore, he wanted to create a specific situation to make this an impossible goal. He faced two impossibilities, one of them was physical and the other was moral. The physical one was to evacuate Kurdistan. For example, five million Kurds should be screaming we want Kurdistan, but where do they want Kurdistan? (PI, June 6, 2015)

From this extract, we can understand that the focus on the unity of Iraq by Iraqi leaders did not come from nowhere, as there were continuous attempts to prevent the division of Iraq. This rhetoric involves rejecting everything that is related to separation, even a kind of cultural separation, influenced ordinary people, who consider separation as betrayal, or at the very least, an unpleasant quality for everyone accused of separation. Chinar views the issue from another angle as she claimed that

> I wish they handled us as a colony because when the colonial powers occupied a region, they always had a sense that they were guests but they were coming for issues of economics and to expand their authority. They never thought that they are occupying a country, but they came to reconstruct the country. In contrast, when Kurdistan was annexed to Arab Iraq, they did not handle Kurdistan like that. They believed that Kurdistan is their personal property and a region called Kurdistan is non-existent. Therefore, the Arab view was more chauvinistic than the colonists. (PI, June 4, 2015)

In this context, Churchill's concern did not come from a vacuum "who expressed his fears about ignoring Kurdish sentiment and the oppression of the Kurdish minority by a Sharifian ruler with the support of his Arab army" (Eskander, 2001: 155). Terms such as "Sharifian ruler" and "Arab army" should be considered. That is, they were aware of the intentions of Al-Sharif and his Arab army. This statement means that when the Iraqi state was established and institutions were built, the Kurdish citizens were not given any role, and they were marginalized throughout all these changes. They were not only marginalized, but rather, the British army participated with the Arab army against the demands of Sheikh Mahmoud, whereby the "deliberate use of gas bombs and air raids against civilian targets in the period 1922-25 were clear indications of British desperation quickly to restore stability to Southern Kurdistan" (Eskander, 2001: 176). Thus, the dilemma not only concerns the annexation of Mosul province, but she also believes that the Arabs viewed this province as their property, and it is shown in the Baath constitution that Mosul province is included in the borders of the Arab homeland. According to this belief, they referred to the Kurds in the constitution of the Baathists in Article 7 which states that "the Arab National Homeland is that part of the earth inhabited by the Arab Nation and which lies between the Taurus mountains, the Zagros mountains, the Persian Gulf, the Arabian Sea, the mountains of Ethiopia, the Sahara Desert, the Atlas range and the Mediterranean Sea" (ABSP, 2015).

As per this article, even Arabs did not inhabit the Kurdish region, and the Kurds never belonged to Kurdistan as they migrated to this area. From this point, the viewpoint of Chinar explains the Arabs' fear. This fear meant that they tried to refuse to recognize Kurdistan as an occupied area but saw it as part of Iraq, and Iraq as directly part of the Arab homeland, as she claims:

> Of course, this fear accompanied Arabs constantly because of the sense of deprivation that existed among the Kurds, and the Arabs knew that. Fear from the Kurdish activities, political movements, fear from their history that they had never been controlled, led to such a fear. In terms of the Arab sense and their view of the Kurdish land and the Kurdish nation, it is problematic because this nation, according to the Arabs is emigrant, and the Kurdish land has been considered as Arab land. Still, many Arabs do not recognise Kurdistan but believe it is Iraqi land. (PI, June 4, 2015)

Thus, two points are important here—the fear of division and the foreignness of the Kurds in Iraq. "This annexation was in the benefit of Arabs and as a result you have to convert to an Arab or be a good Iraqi in accordance with Arab standards, or it is impossible for you to exist. You are a foreigner. You are a guest" (Saad C., PI, June 4, 2015). All of these terms, in the Iraqi Arab nationalist memory, confirm the impression of the dominant ethnocentrism in the reins of the Iraqi state. In order to ensure that hegemony, the Iraqi Arab political elite always present the Kurds in a frightening triangle, as separatists, agents of Israel, and saboteurs of the Iraqi state—that is, in their view, the reason for the failure of the Iraqi state. Based on this belief, they resorted to the final solution.

Falakaddin Kakayi was one of the main Kurdish political figures and a journalist and writer. He was an MP and later minister of culture of KRG. In 2013, after conducting this interview with him, he died at the age of seventy. I have the transcript of a long, uncompleted interview with him because later on, the questions on state formation were added to the previous questions. Regarding the annexation of Mosul province, Kakayi claimed: "This became a strategy, but where did it come from? Why did they inflict Mosul on Iraq anyway? They told us you are a nation but they inflict us on the Arab nation. What is the issue? The issue is oil as the economic and geopolitical strategy. In fact, England was behind the annexation of Mosul Vilayet to Iraq" (Kakayi, PI, May 27, 2015). This statement from Kakayi is another different view on the dilemma of Mosul province. It is a view from different angles. He is viewing the issue both economically and geopolitically. He continued: "When Iraq became a new state, they wanted us to be a new state. It was for a goal, or Iraq itself was a goal and this goal should have the ability to protect itself" (Kakayi, PI, May 27, 2015).

This view of Kakayi's starts from the belief in the existence of a super power that does as it pleases, but on the other hand, it is closer to pessimism rather than optimism. In addition, he is highlighting the economical aspect as the main cause of the annexation. In relation to the issue of balance between Shi'a and Sunni Arabs, he also has a different view, as he admitted: "I could not believe in this balance. It is not true that the Shi'a and Sunni Arabs are different. For them, the Arabization is important. The Da'wa party existed and it might be that they are more backward than the Baathists, but they are not different in their belief in Arabizm" (Kakayi, PI, May 27, 2015). His thoughts were more radical as he believed that the state was built upon the pillars of Arab identity. In addition, the Arabs in Iraq are the majority, and the Kurds were annexed to them against their will. This issue of establishing a state upon a minority within its pan-Arab-nationalistic pillar at the expense of other components, who were considered outsiders, was problematic and exploitable for the majority of the participants. Here, Jambaz (age seventy), a senior lawyer, author, and a former MP of KRG parliament stated: "The annexation has had a very bad influence. The economic and geopolitical interests led to the re-division. This time we became the victims, as the assumption was that the majority of Arabs in Iraq are Shi'a Arabs so it was decided to annex the Kurds to Iraq to form a balance for Sunni Arabs" (Jambaz, PI, June 1, 2015).

This means that to increase the weight of Sunni Arabs, the weight of Shi'a Arabs should be reduced in order to create a parallel between both of them, but at the expense of the Kurds. Thus, it meant that the Kurds were a project used to manipulate, and their fate was utilized for the benefit of the ruler and the colonial power, including its allies in Baghdad. In this regard, this issue of creating a balance has been answered by the participant as he claimed: "Yes, the King had been told to assist with this demand. The trend of the King was pan-Arabism as he had never been emotional about the Kurds. The Iraqi constitution in 1925 did not mention Kurds. They issued a law called the 'law of languages' but it was for the membership of the League of Nations. The things were selectively directed and the only official language was Arabic" (Jambaz, PI, May 27, 2015). This claim has been confirmed in many documents, including the 1925 constitution; however, Mosul Wilayat was still not annexed to Arab Iraq, but at the same time, it confirms that the Kurds were utilized as outsiders, and in chapter 2, the king's position has been illustrated as being pan-Arab-centric. Therefore, the participant is referring to an important point, stating, "There was a phobia called the 'Kurdish phobia' and that led to the commencement of the Arabization of Kurdistan" (Jambaz, PI, May 27, 2015). This statement provides a clear perspective that all trends from the beginning led to the establishment of a unilateral state with Arab nationalist dimensions.

A serious attempt was made to include as many Arab participants as possible in this research, but most of them who were contacted were not ready to give their view or any information. This kind of circumstance and its consequences is not empty from the dilemma of the complexity of the inter-relationship between the components. This complexity was commented on by Alsamarrayi (age seventy-three), a Sunni-Arab individual, a university professor, residing under the Baath's rule for thirty years; he was not ready to provide an opinion and declined to give any information about the history of Iraq or even the Baath's ideology. Consequently, regarding the question of the annexation of Mosul province to Iraq, he claimed: "I do not have any information about the history of Iraq" (Alsamarrayi, PI, May 25, 2015). At the same time, this participant considered himself part of the opposition to Saddam Hussein's authority as he stated: "I was against Baathists from the beginning to the end; this is known. It is a real opinion without compliment (hahaha)" (Alsamarrayi, PI, May 25, 2015).

Perhaps fear, or objection to telling the truth, or any other reason, puts us in front of a big problem, which is acceptance of the interview, but he stated he does not know anything. The truth is that he knows a lot, shown by his academic background, as he holds a doctorate degree and opposes the Baathists; yet at a sensitive moment in time, he retracted from stating the facts. Perhaps he is right given his experience of living under the authority of the Baath— the authority that sowed terror in every aspect of Sethshetia, Iraqis, Arabs, Kurds, and others. Perhaps talking about genocide and the responsibility of the Iraqi state brings great risks. Likewise, the new political elite, after 2003, demanded an apology for the crimes committed against tens of thousands of rural civilians. Furthermore, the issue of compensation that the Iraqi state did not pay despite the Iraqi Supreme Court's decision that the crimes were genocide, including the compensation for all genocide survivors. However, the successor state to the Ba'ath regime did not move a finger, nor did it recognize the crimes and its responsibility for the events. This refusal, or marginalization, may be one of the reasons that the man is not allowed to speak.

Another Sunni participant is Al-Alusi, who acknowledged the rights of the Kurds, but his view regarding Mosul province and some other issues is that they are problematic for the reasons explained below, as he claimed: "In the context of the formation of Iraq, the poll in the state of Mosul was in favor of becoming part of the Iraqi state. Signals were installed in the Iraqi constitution and affirmation of the request was sent to the King to respect the identity and the particularity of the Kurds" (Al-Alusi, PI, May 24, 2015).

The British colonial authority, especially Percy Cox, the new High Commissioner for Mesopotamia, was approached on the issue of Southern Kurdistan's future from the Arab view point, and regarding supporting the territorial claims of the Sharifian family and the Sunni followers in Mesopotamia (Eskander, 2001: 154). Accordingly, his decision was clear concerning annexing southern Kurdistan to Arab Iraq, as we can see from the events of the Cairo conference. Furthermore, Cox was the de facto ruler in Iraq, so the United Nations Committee that was sent to the state of Mosul to investigate is a kind of deception for two reasons: first, the British were intent on joining southern Kurdistan to Iraq. The fact-finding committee that came to Mosul Vilayat was limited to tribal chiefs (feudal lords), sheikhs, and religious notables; therefore, the majority of the population was excluded (Rafaat, 2017: 3), although under the supervision and protection of the British forces. Britain's attempts were evident even to the fact-finding committee, whereby "the League Commissioners held Great Britain responsible not only for public outbursts, but also for the heavy police presence that accompanied the Commissioners wherever they went and kept them from sleeping" (Shields, 2009: 8). Although they knew this, in the end, the committee recommended that "Mosul should be under the rule of British mandate for 25 years" (Kibaroğlu and Kibaroğlu, 2009: 23). This means that the committee did not preserve its independence, but they turned a blind eye to the violations that they recorded. In addition, there was no revival of the common legal concept, and the citizens' desire was not respected when the people of Sulaymaniyah voted against joining Iraq. Finally, they submitted to the British will and decided according to what they wanted.

The fundamental question here is: Can we regulate the impartiality of these people who were interrogated while under the domination of colonialism? In the same context, in addition to all this confusion and many question marks about the formation of this committee, the participant who has acted as a barrister for Anfal victims, Abdul Rahman Haji Shaban (fifty-seven) stated:

The referendum was inherently wrong and an encroachment on the Kurdish rights. They gave the Kurds just two options; the sweetest was bitter. Both options were void. The question was: do you want to be with Iraq or with Turkey? It does not contain a question about them wanting to be independent: I want to be with myself. Thus, the referendum was invalid. (Haji Shaban, PI, July 4, 2015)

In contrast to this decision, the British mandate, according to a treaty with the Iraqi authority for independence, was "signed on June 30, 1930; this treaty acknowledged an independent Iraq with complete sovereignty over its internal affairs" (Fattah and Caso, 2009: 172). Regarding this treaty, Haji Shaban stated: "In 1932, Iraq officially became a member of the League of Nations. According to the treaty, some of the pledges were imposed on Iraq, especially Article X, which says there should not be any Iraqi law contrary to this treaty. In contrast, Iraq throughout the 20th century has violated the terms and the laws of the treaty continuously" (Haji Shaban, PI, July 4, 2015). In addition to this admission, the British mandate, which depended on this treaty, did not lead to the finishing of their obligations in Iraq, particularly in relation to the Kurdish question. Despite this information, "No one respected the rights of the Kurds, and the State handled them unjustly, persecuted them, so it pushed them to revolt for their own rights. Thus, the chauvinists called it the separatist spirit, which means divisional, but it is certainly not true and the Kurds do not deserve such a diseased description. They have all rights to self-determination" (Al-Alusi, PI, May 24, 2015).

In the same direction, another participant, the Shi'a Arab political activist, Saad al-Mutallibi (age sixty), did not recognize this causality and said: "I do not think so. I do not think the geographical division had anything to do with this subject. If this view was right, all Arabs have participated in this opinion in southern Iraq, but they did not share their vision" (AlMutallibi, PI, June 24, 2015). Iraq is a country for all Arabs, even Sunni/Shi'a Arabs; it was and still is a united country and it is essentially indivisible. This is what I discovered from the majority of the interviewees, but the Kurds have been accused of being separatists, as expressed by the participant Al-Mutallibi: "The spirit of separatism exists in some of the Kurdish brothers only" (Al-Mutallibi, PI, June 24, 2015).

There are several points that can be explored from these extracts, but the most prominent point here is the division between the Kurd and Arab interviewees. This similarity emphasizes the historical dimension, common characteristics and interests between members of a group. The division also resides in the cultural dimension, whereby the Kurds believe that they used to own a homeland, but by virtue of colonialism it was divided, and part of this homeland was annexed to Arab Iraq. The Arabs, on the other hand, and as a whole, believe in the sanctity of the current borders of Iraq, and they consider Iraq to be part of the Arab world. This means that culture is an important element of the intellectual structure in which collective interests mature. In this regard, "Culture as equilibrium in a well-defined set of circumstances in which members of a group sharing common ancestry, symbolic practices and/or high levels of interaction" (Laitin, 2007: 64). This trend has been confirmed by an Arab university professor who I met in London; he refused to reveal his sectarian affiliation and identified himself as Dr. Al-zubaidi. He confirmed: "I am familiar with many Arab elite. There is no Iraqi Arab who believes in dividing Iraq. Iraq is not the property of an ethnic party or an ethnic group. Rather, Iraq is the property of the Arab nation in its current geography. Dividing Iraq means insulting the dignity of all Arabs" (Al-zubaidi, PI, June 28, 2015). Here, we face an established group or a cultural group who "are able to condition their behavior on common knowledge and beliefs about the behavior of all members of the group" (Laitin, 2007: 64). This belief of the participants is understandable in that they share a similar belief in a common issue under the influence of common interactions, even though it may be modulated or apocryphal. This commonality led to the sharing of knowledge, specifically about a set of ideological issues, which were reiterated through the internal state media on a daily basis.

BAATH'S IDEOLOGY

Chapters 2 and 3 examined aspects of Baath ideology according to the Baath's literature; here, the participants have also contributed and expressed their views on the issue. The focus now will be on the prominent concepts which were put forward by the interviewees.

Racism of the Baath Party

After the annexation of Mosul province and the process of state formation in Iraq, as a consequence of the Sunni-Arab domination and the hegemony of pan-Arab-nationalism, many Arab-centric trends emerged, including the Baath Arab Socialist party, as explained in chapter 2. Here, it is important to note that the ideological dimensions are based on the experiences of the participants in relation to the direct interrelationships between citizens and the authority. Al-Alusi, a Sunni Arab, without any hesitancy about confidentiality, stated that "the Baath is an Arabized and chauvinistic party" (Al-Alusi, PI, May 24, 2015). In this regard, Sharif being one of those participants who has had direct experience with the Baathists, as a deputy Iraqi minister, explained:

> The ideology of BP is Arab racism: Who lives on the Arab land, is Arab. The
> Arabs have a historic message. They consider the message of Islam to be their

message. When they have a message, it means they are the best people. It means Arabs are better than all others. When they become better than others, they should be dominating others. This is the theory of superiority and racism. (PI, June 6, 2015)

Sharif, who was actively involved in the Baath's authority, understood the aspects of the practical ideology of Baath members of the highest level. Therefore, he admitted that "they told us the history of Islam is the history of Arabizm" (PI, June 6, 2015). Sharif worked in "The Ministry of Endowments and Religious Affairs," and he has studied the required program of religious clerics. He knew what his statement meant and what the Baath's intention was regarding outsiders. Hence, he stated: "Those who believe in the Baath ideology are serving this party as a religious task" (PI, June 6, 2015). From this claim, it is possible to explore the religious language and symbols which the Baathists adopted, specifically in the Anfal Campaigns. Kakayi, who belongs to an old Kurdish religious minority, announced: "In 1969, Saddam Hussein's uncle and his Mentor, Khairulla Tulfah, who is one of the Baathist leaders, appeared on TV with his newly publicised book, and he claimed that: Three kinds, God should not have created them: The Jews, the Persian and the Flies" (PI, May 27, 2015). This statement of Tulfah coincided with the eight-year-long war against Iran and the Baath state media against Israel. This language during the Baath era confirmed their Arab superiority, as there are dozens of documents and newspapers calling the Persians "Persian Magi or Shu'ubi." Kakayi showed his astonishment as he declared: "This arrogance comes from a primitive ideology. It is a racist tribal ideology. It comes from blindness and a spellbinding arrogance. I do not know where it comes from, possibly it comes from history" (PI, May 27, 2015).

Thus, Kakayi, along with the other participants, accused Baathism of being a racist ideology because of several theoretical and practical evidences. In addition to that, Dr. Khalil Faili (age seventy), author and university history professor, who belongs to the Faili Kurdish minority and suffered from the Baath's policy against the Faili Kurds, depending on his memory, argued that "Khairallah Talfah has honestly claimed that Arabs are the best nation raised up for mankind. This is a Quranic verse, 'You are the best nation raised up for mankind.' It means Arabs are the best nation as Nazis" (PI, Jan 2, 2015).

This point has been reiterated by Aflaq indirectly as he claimed: "Our nation has guaranteed the past because it is combined with a message of humanity and this is something unique to the Arabs alone" (Aflaq, 1987: 155). Thus, the uniqueness, according to Aflaq, is limited to the Arab nation and the other nations have no relationship with humanity. Here, Aflaq continues that "Arabs with Islam became a great nation but the Arab nation has carried the message of Islam and its strength is from the strength of Arabs and its weakness is from the weakness of Arabs." Thus, Aflaq here is closer to narcissism and claims that Arabs are at the center of Islam and even humanity. They overtly believe in the superiority of the Arab nation, as they are "one Arab nation with an eternal message." The eternality makes Arabs the best nation from the whole of mankind, exactly as the Nazis claimed their superiority due to their origins going back to the Aryan race, and as the Nazi leaders were obsessed by "semi-religious beliefs in a race of Aryan god-men" (Goodrick-Clarke, 1992: X). Here, if we compare Saddam Hussein to Adolf Hitler, it is possible to find several common characteristics between the two, as, "malignant narcissism and psychopathy are common among génocidaires in modern history. Consider Adolf Hitler, whose stunted, injured ego found transcendence in the holocaust" (Jones, 2010: 262).

Kadir, as one of the residents of Kirkuk, the oil rich city that was exposed to Arabization on a large-scale, and Kadir's house, like many other Kurds, was demolished and its habitants expelled. Regarding the ideology of the Baath and its dimensions, Kadir stated:

> Baath nationalism was based on reactions. It was always bound to the past of the Arabs. They have been defeated by the Mongols. They have been defeated in front of Ottoman power, which was a dark era for the Arabs. When the Baath emerged, they wanted to bring the old history back. Baath was working on a history. When Saddam took power, he was talking about rewriting history. Rewriting the history from the beginning or forming it differently, or at least creating history as the Baathists wanted it, and not the real history which has happened and should have ended. (PI, June 8, 2015)

Thus, it could be the humiliation and historical defeats, according to Kadir, that had a major influence on the people's behavior. As in Germany, this kind of reason and the "largely unexpected defeat of 1918 brought great humiliation and trauma for broad sections of the German people" (Fletcher, 1997: 122). In this regard, the politician, MP Aso Karim (age sixty-six), a previous Kurdish Peshmerga guerrilla and writer, added a different dimension to the Baath's characteristics in that "Baath ideology began in the forties. It has its dimensions based on the German school" (PI, June 7, 2015). Thus, anybody that has information about the process of the Holocaust refer to the characteristics of the Baathists. According to Karim's view, they followed German ideology, as he continued, "Their beliefs and organizations were molding the society. It was similar to the Nazis. They were beginning from the children to change them to vanguards. They must become the vanguards, the Union of Iraqi Students or Iraqi Youth" (PI, June 7, 2015).

Those who lived during the era of the Baathists could easily recognize these kinds of characteristics. The characteristics were "often tied to ethnically-based political parties [that] reflect and reinforce inter-ethnic hostility via propaganda, ritual, and force" (Horowitz, 1985: 243). In a similar direction, the MP participant, a previous Kurdish Peshmerga guerrilla and political figure, Saadi Pira (age sixty-nine), reiterated the similarities to Nazism, as he argued, "The principles of Baath ideology in 'its growing and learning' profited from the Nazis. Especially in using violence, burning the land, deportation, Arabization and Baathification, they were copying Nazism. The Baath's philosophy was: if I cannot rule a country, I can burn it. This is the summit of sadism and the most advanced Nazism" (PI, June 30, 2015). Hence, we can acknowledge that the concept of Nazism and fascism have been reiterated by most of the participants. Jambaz also confirmed this kind of conduct and argued:

> Baathizm was a very bad imitation of Nazism and fascism. They were arguing that they are "God's chosen people" and always reiterating Arabs and Arabic. For example, they were helping Yemen and other Arab countries. The strongest Baath organization was in Iraq, and they had excited some young men who believed in Baathizm. They believed in using force and they seized power through the armed forces. (PI, May 27, 2015)

Here, according to the majority of the participants, Nazism and fascism are two inherent traits of Baathism, particularly their conduct in relation to the non-Arabs, which was significant. Hence, Chinar presented a deeper and clearer view on this issue, as she argued:

> In his view of other components, Aflaq saw the Arabs as a superior race, civilised and the greatest. Be sure his view is not different from Hitler's view or the Nazis' view in relation to the Aryan race. Aryans took preference because their blood is pure and clean, and others are inferior. Even Saddam Hussein had a similar feeling. Therefore, in my thesis, I made a comparison between Hitler's and Saddam's discourse. There are massive similarities between them from reading their behavior in relation to other ethnicities. (PI, June 4, 2015)

Based on this data, it is possible to understand the intellectual background of Baathizm, and their fascist trends, which prompted them to erase all non-Arab culture, particularly throughout the rewriting of history, which resulted in the processes of genocide. These details show that non-Arabs have been considered as outsiders and they have been systematically assimilated, whether they wanted it or not.

Rewriting History

"We Arabs, therefore, are one nation, and the geography of our land is the entire Arab nation. This is the decisive result that we give our attention, and therefore our reading of history must be according to how it serves this truth" (Husain, 1978). This is what Saddam said in one of his speeches on rewriting history. The rewriting of history was a serious project for the Baathists in Iraq—to rewrite it according to their ideology. The project appeared after returning to power in July 1968, when the second Baathist regime organized a "Project for the Rewriting of History, headed by Saddam Hussein, ostensibly to re-appropriate understandings of Iraq's past that had purportedly been dominated by the writings of colonialists and their local underlings" (Davis, 2004). The project was one of the most serious Baath projects aimed at rebuilding the Iraqi collective memory according to the Baath's vision in order to centralize Arabism and to assimilate the non-Arab dimensions in Iraq. "The essence of the Baathist attempts to rebuild the historical memory lies in the so-called draft rewrite history. The Baath has started to implement this project immediately after its reins of power in 1968; however, it was officially not clear until 1979" (Davis, 2005: 235). This project was not something secret, and the Ba'athists were not ashamed of it. Rather, "Many writers, university professors, researchers and scientific research centers have moved for this purpose to begin rewriting the history of Iraq and the Arabs and their role in Iraq, the region and the world" (Habib, 2006).

The participant Saadi Pira described the policy of historical correction as under this policy they intended to embark on Arabizing the non-Arab population, specifically Kurdish religious minorities in the strategic or contact areas, as he explained:

> Primarily, they attempted to assimilate non-Arabs under the name of the correction of history because "according to Baathists" they were Arabs but they had changed their nationality to Kurdish nationality. If they were unable to succeed in this process, they would use force. This is by deportation, or by uprooting them from their roots. They cut-off all date trees and filled the water sources with cement to destroy the sources of life for the purpose of coercion. Now, most areas in West Tigris, which is Sinjar and the tribes as Ezidi's, Miran, Musa Resh, Hasnan, Gargari and Kiki, all of them are Kurdish tribes. Now they are wearing Arab clothes because they were forced to wear these Arab clothes. If they did not wear them, they would have been killed because of their identity. (PI, June 30, 2015)

Thus, in order to centralize Arabs and assimilate non-Arabs, a systemic process was preferable; otherwise, resorting to violence in order to implement its policy was the last solution or a security solution. Here, it is can be understood that the BP was attempting, through dozens of writers and postgraduate projects, to de-colorize the history of Iraq in order to implant the idea of pan-Arab-centrism in the minds of future generations and remove all kinds of diversity from the memory of the people who reside in Iraq.

> Hitler was speaking about history and saying that they will rewrite the history of Germany; we are rewriting it in order to serve the future generations. Saddam, in a similar trend, said we are not rewriting history for dead people but for those who are alive. Look, he will deviate from the history to show the greatness and beauty of Arabs in the framework of rewriting history. Therefore, in Aflaq's view, the Arabs are a great race, intellectuals and followers of Islam. The prophet is Arab; thus, Arabs must remain superior and lead the other nations with no possibility of equality. (Saad C., PI, June 4, 2015)

Ideology for Unification and Power

One of the main ideological principles is unification, and to unify all Arabs as an established entity, therefore any outsiders should be assimilated. Chinar is not far from the previous statements about the Baath's ideological principles, including its desire to use hegemony and authority, as she focused directly on the central dilemma in the Baath's view, which is unity through power: "The unity of Arabs is in raising the Arab nation. The unity is in the frame of Arab nationalism. The greatness of Arabs is part of Baath ideology. Arab nationalism is strong; therefore, it must be predominant and ruling. All nationalities in the region should be under the hegemony of Arabs" (PI, June 4, 2015). Thus, the unity of Arabs may not be the end goal, but the hegemony and power at the expense of other nations is the ultimate goal of pan-Arab-centrism. In a similar direction, Khalil argued:

> It is the Arab ideology, which is "one Arab nation, with an eternal message." In the Arabs' view, the Arab state starts from the Pacific to the Gulf. This view led to the uprising of other non-Arab nations. We sought the south of Sudan, which is now an independent state. Therefore, there is a movement to get rid of this kind of ideology.
>
> This kind of ideology generally belongs to Arabs, because it is existent in other Arab countries. Because the universal policy is heading towards self-determination, and they could not stop other components gaining their self-determination. (PI, January 2, 2015)

Al-Mutallibi warned me in the beginning that the Arab Shi'as' view is different to that of the Arab Sunnis' view in relation to the Baathists, and his view here is more radical than that of the Kurdish participants, as he claimed: "The Baathists does not amount to having an ideology. They were some gangsters that seized power" (PI, June 24, 2015). This statement reveals a complex disagreement between Shi'a and Sunni Arabs. However, here, what is remarkable is that Shi'a Arabs have more hostile views on the Baathists than the Kurds have. In contrast, because this participant is an Islamist Shi'a Arab, he has a specific view about nationalism, and he claimed: "An ideological system or political thought is based on nationalism; the direct consequence is they are hostile to other nationalities" (Al-Mutallibi, PI, June 24, 2015). Thus, according to al-Mutallibi, nationalism is a typical cause of hostility and ethnocentrism. The Arab Shi'a were brave in accusing the Baathists of being gangsters.

However, Al-Samarrayi, while he was in a safe place, and despite the end of the Baath's power, was hesitant and I could see the fear in his eyes. With every question, he started his answer with "I do not know." For example: "I do not know what you mean by resistance because I am not a Baathist. The probability is I do not encourage many things of the Baathists, so you know, I do not know. I think it is based on nationalism. I expect, I expect so" (Al-Aamarrayi, PI, May 25, 2015). I noticed this kind of hesitation from other Sunni Arabs who were very powerful people in the era of the Baath's authority, but living in the UK, which in comparison is a safe haven. They were unwillingly complaining throughout three years of promising and procrastination; finally, they declined to meet me or even answer my calls.

Religion and Failure of the State Institution

Here, was the Baath ideology caused by the division that exists between the components, and did this cause the bloody conflict that led to the genocide, or at least to the failure of state institutions? Regarding this issue, Chinar linked the violence to some dimensions of Arabic culture, as she added: "Certainly, when they are embracing such ideology, they should and they will serve it. The complexity here is not the state but the culture. This kind of ideology is part of Arab culture. It has been proven that Arab regimes in other Arab countries, deal with their own people using violence and isolate culture" (PI, June 4, 2015). It could be that this generalization of the idea is not scientific, and all other participants have avoided this point. However, it is understandable that every participant will have had a specific and unique experience with the Baath authority. On the other hand, Sharif saw this ideology as the main cause of the conflict and the failure of the state institutions, as he stated that "those who hold the Baath ideology perform it as a religious duty" (PI, June 6, 2015).

Thus, from most of the interviews, the position of religion for Baathists is for it to be under the command of Arabs. Here, Karim goes back to Arab history to find the relevant answer, and he claimed:

First: I said Muslims were divided into Arabs and followers. Imagine Omer bin Khattab (the third Muslim khalifa) was not agreeing with followers staying in

Madina, the capital of Arab Muslims. If we are going back to the literature of Aflaq, his view is: who is in an Arab homeland resident, is Arab. Therefore, they accept you when you are serving them. In Baath ideology, national security is divided into two kinds: First: Those who came from the outside of the borders. Second: Ethnic minorities, who are causing the sabotage of the internal harmony. (PI, June 7, 2015)

Thus, the religious position, in the Baath's doctrine, is important on two hierarchical levels:

Cultural level: this is because they consider it to be part of Arab culture, as is naturally comes from the Arabian Peninsula. In this regard, Aflaq has stated that

> Islam is an Arabic movement and it means renewal of Arabizm and its perfection. The language of the message was the Arabic language, and its understanding of things was through the view of the Arab mind. The virtues which were reinforced were Arabic virtues including its overt and covert virtues, and the defects that have been fought were Arabic defects on the way to their demise. The Muslims at that time were only Arabs. (Aflaq, 1987: 145)

Thus, for Aflaq, Arabism is central to every movement and every silence. The spiritual level: here, Aflaq is considering religion as being the spirit of Arabs as he claimed: "In our past is an authentic spirit, in our past a free and Semitic life" (1987: 74).

The Correction of Nationality

The policy of correcting nationalism was considered one of the Baathists' main features, and it is characterized by abhorrent racism against the non-Arab element. "The Ba'athist government adopted . . . a narrow ethnic policy against non-Arab nationalities, which is the policy of 'correcting nationalism' he regime distributed 'correcting nationality' forms to the Kurds, Turkmen, and Assyrians, asking them to change their nationality and register themselves as Arabs" (Saeed, 2017). This racist policy was followed even after the uprising in 1991 in the city of Kirkuk and that policy was included in one of the United Nations reports under the "background of forced displacement and Arabization of Northern Iraq" (HRW, 2004). In this context, the participant Karim continued: "Look, for the general census of 1966—I was here. They (Baath authority) imposed the Arabic nationality upon all Christians, Shabaks and Ezidis. It was compulsory, whether they agreed or not. Baath's concern was how to create an Arabic homogeneous society from one nation, one party, one flag, one army, one media, one leader and one doctrine. It is totalitarianism" (PI, June 7, 2015). Hence, the Revolutionary Command Council, which is the highest Baath organization, decided on changing nationalities, and the totalitarian element was a daily phenomenon for all Iraqi residents. However, the Baath's totalitarian procedure in Kurdistan was exceptional and dependent on an emergency situation. Jambaz has revealed this element as being a Kurdish phobia, as previously been mentioned: "There was a phobia called the 'Kurdish phobia' and this led to the commencement of the Arabization of Kurdistan" (PI, May 27, 2015). Thus, there was a systematized policy for Arabization, as Jambaz claimed, "The Bathists, except the Arabs, considered all non-Arabs as guests. They would use every possible method to assimilate Kurds and the Amazigh in 'North Africa.' The best example is the correction of nationality forms, or changing the nationality of Kurds and Turkmens in Kirkuk city" (PI, May 27, 2015).

Al-zubaidi was asked whether these measures are legal, and if he considered them legal, "because the state forbids tampering with its institutions, and considered them steps towards the national trend. If the state were to merge the components as planned, Iraq would have been a glittering country in the Middle East. This is the mono view that wanted to assimilate everyone into the Arab crucible" (PI, June 28, 2015).

THE COUP AND TOTALITARIAN AUTHORITY

The majority of the participants interviewed, depending on their ethnic affiliation, differed on their view of Iraq as a country, but they were united when it came to the discussion of the Baathists. Legitimation is another dilemma which is important for any authority. A coup is one of the methods used to seize power, especially in the Middle East and Africa. Thus, Iraq is considered the second country in terms of military coups, after Turkey, if we only include the major coups. In addition, after examining nine coups, in the case of Iraq, seven of these coups occurred from 1958 to 1968 and all of them by the Sunni Arabs, except the movement headed by AbdulKarim Qasim on July 14, 1958, when he toppled the monarchy rule; note that he had Shi'a roots from an Arab Shi'a Father and a Kurdish Shi'a Mother. Here, these coups are considered one of the main causes of the failure of the state, and as a result, they led to the process of genocide. In addition, an MP for KRG and a Kurdish intellectual, Aso Karim, noted, "We cannot generalize it. Many coups have happened in Iraq even inside the Baath Party. It is true that it is a non-democratic method to seize power because in democratic countries nobody attempts to seize power through a coup. These coups are a phenomenon in countries that have no constitution, or they have weak institutions or are backward countries in the third world" (PI, June 7, 2015).

As a result of this kind of method being used to seize power, it caused an imbalance in the political culture, as well as instability in the psychogenesis. Based on the results of the regimes that came about through coups "any substantial increase in normal political tensions leads, with or without a military coup, to a more repressive government" (Leicht and Jenkins, 2011: 169). In this regard, according to al-Alusi, seizing power through a military coup causes instability, as he claimed: "It is true that the political and military coups have always been the reason for the absence of the institutional building of a civil state that respects the law, serves the people and guarantees the chances of its components" (PI, May 24, 2015). For this reason, al-Alusi has confirmed the possibility of genocide in such circumstances, as he continued: "It is not possible for the occurrence of crimes of genocide to take place under democratic conditions, and therefore the absence of democracy deprived the people from expressing their true position and the opportunity to respond to the crimes and the criminals" (PI, May 24, 2015).

This means there was a failure of society and a failure of its institutions. This kind of failure led to a lack of interdependency chains and interrelationships, which paved the way to totalitarian rule and unilateral domination. In this regard, Sharif also excluded the possibility of genocide if there is a democracy, but the problematic issue was that the Kurds were considered to be the enemy. This means they were close to the idea of enmity and there was a lack of interdependency chains, making them close to the circumstances of genocide, as Sharif confirmed: "In democratic circumstances, genocide is not a requirement and it is not considered as an option. The importance here is that the Baathists considered the Kurds to be enemies; therefore, there are no conditions that would have prevented what they have done. The only component that was not subordinate to the BP was the Kurds" (PI, June 6, 2015). Thus, the Baathists with their aggressive ideology, and the consideration of the Kurds as outsiders, meant the possibility of genocide was more of an option. Chinar is not far from this view as she confirmed that "without a shadow of a doubt, any military coup leads to a dictatorial regime and is inherently mentally active" (PI, June 4, 2015). However, Chinar is going back to the past and did not acknowledge any difference between the past and present because of their mentality. Here, as she previously mentioned, the dilemma is the culture and their mentality, as she claimed:

> If we want to understand it and to justify this coup of the BP, and its aggressive ideology, we should justify the previous rulers, but how? Why did the Arabs before the BP not behave with the Kurds in the right way? Even during the era of King Faisal and at the time of the establishment of Iraq. The behavior of the Arabs with Kurds was less aggressive in the past because of colonialism and

the existence of Britain and the interests of international policy in the region. Otherwise, the Kurds, under the hegemony of the successive regimes and their similar mentality, were always suppressed. Thus, I do not think that the coup of the BP is the only reason for such a mentality and their behavior. This is an existing mentality. (PI, June 4, 2015)

This kind of argument and feeling was apparent among the majority of the Kurdish participants, and it was noted that throughout more than ninety years of the establishment of the state of Iraq, the ruler's elite could not find an appropriate political, social, and economic solution to the issues between the Kurds and the Iraqi Arab authority. This long suppression led to one participant arguing that

> another aspect is the Arab Bedouin culture, which has its hegemony in their social life. Bedouin culture includes the raid, looting, self-esteem and a kind of social life through violence. This nature of the Bedouin has been transformed and become innate in the Arabic personality. Therefore, Arabic design through the religion and Bedouin persona is a feeling of greatness because always the Bedouin is the source of pride. He is oppressing but it is justifiable because of the evidence of power and force. This greatness proudly led him to a peculiar view of the surroundings. Therefore, he is not seeing himself as an occupier but considering himself to be an owner. (Saad Chinar., PI, June 4, 2015)

These ideas are from the theory of Ibn-Khaldun, which binds the Arab personality to the Bedouins, which includes being aggressive due to the dependency on "'Al-Asabiyya' (a type of virtuous solidarity)" (Ritzer and Stepnisky, 2017: 15). Ibn-Khaldun "is also convinced that when the Asabiyyah becomes absolutely ingrained in a nation, it turns aggressive by its inherent nature" (Ritter, 1948: 40). Al-Asabiyya is a concept which forms the central element of Ibn-Khaldun's sociological work. However, it was criticized by Prophet Muhammad, and "the Islamic Brotherhood" replaced Al-Asabiyya with Al-Qabaliyya, which means tribal solidarity. In addition, in raising the question "What is Asabiyya? It is pointed out that this concept is close to the idea of virtue proposed by Machiavelli" (Ritter, 1948: 2). Hence, the concept of "virtue" could have a positive feeling that is different to that of "Al-Asabiyya," which connotes a negative feeling. It has appeared in an article called "The Concept of Virtue in Machiavelli," which is considered "a skill, especially political ability: A virtuous man reaches his goals in political life" (Laino, 2008: 3). The Machiavellian concept of "virtue" is closer to Machiavelli's famous sentence "The end justifies the means," because he justified the use of virtue in terms of legitimacy. Moreover, Al-Asabiyya means "support one's own fellow tribal members when they are right or wrong." Thus, Chinar was drawing on Ibn-Khaldun's interpretation of Arab tribalism, which is inherently a very negative exploratory understanding of Arab communities.

Kadir, in this regard, has a different vision as he argued: "The coup is a group of army officers deciding to seize power. The dilemma is who has been excluded did not have legitimate authority because they also came via a military coup" (Kadir, J., PI, June 8, 2015). Here, Kadir binds authority with state legitimacy, as it is necessary for stable interdependency chains and interrelationships between the different components. However, Kadir links this coup to the defeat of Arab countries against Israel as he claims:

I, many times, have linked this coup to the Arabs defeat against Israel in 1967. If you imagine, the Baath manifesto of 17th July 1968, admitted the reaction to the Arabs' defeat in 1967. I think, they are, "as a defeated nation in a war," their dignity was offended because it was the defeat of many Arab countries against one small country. They were speaking about the end of Israel, but later they discovered that large Arab areas had been occupied. (PI, June 8, 2015)

Hence, the popularity of the Baathists may be seen as the result of a crisis; therefore, it has been examined whether the emergence of Baath's ideology was a result of different crises in the region. Thus, if the ideology itself is a by-product of a crisis, and the mentality has been shaped by successive endless crises, the creation of a future crisis could be a determinist consequence. According to many documents and interviews, when the Baathists seized power, they had a tendency to seek revenge for their defeat. They were looking for a target. They could not reach Israel for revenge. They also could not do anything with Iran. Yet they were continually looking to find a target.

IN ORDER TO FIND A TARGET

Thus, Iraqi society, with its unstable state institutions and tribal dimensions, including different suppressing components, formed the dominant ruling elite, who under the influence of an aggressive ideology, meant that violence was a forgone conclusion. These circumstances were accompanied by tensions in the relationship between the Kurds and the Iraqi government. Here, Karim highlights an important aspect of the situation, as he argued: "The ideology of many Arabic political organisations is built on hostility to other ethnic groups, nationalist arrogance, and some populist tendencies based on demagogue characters, to influence the lower social classes" (PI, June 7, 2015). This understanding means that such an environment is an appropriate haven for the growth of an ideology, and for finding a weak link in terms of a possible target; specifically, the Kurds were the determined target. Kadir elaborated on this point:

> The Kurds were the easiest target for two reasons: primarily, due to the accusation that they played a significant role in the defeat of the Arabs. Secondly, that they were an obstacle in the way of the Iraqi army, including the relations with Israel. Moreover, they are "a dagger in the Arabs' side." Thus, for these imagined reasons, the Kurds were a weak circle because all support had been disabled. All the states around them were against the Kurds. However, in the atmosphere of the cold war, the Kurds could not support any side, simply because all the other sides were against them. (PI, June 8, 2015)

This gloomy picture was painful and led to the disability of all aspects of life in Kurdish society. The creation of these circumstances was an outcome of the successive crises in the Arab countries, including Arabic Iraq and all its political parties and elites. According to Kadir, "What has occurred against the Kurds by the BP, generally, was part of the Arabs' defeat" (PI, June 8, 2015). Furthermore, when the major crusade of the Anfal Campaigns occurred, all Arabic and Islamic authorities, even the international community, were in complete silence.

SUMMARY

The essence of this chapter is an attempt to approach the most important causes of genocide in Iraq by focusing on state formation and the ideology of the Baathists through the explanations and opinions of the interviewees. The first indication of the formation of the state is its establishment and the subsequent instability. The participants insisted that the conduct of the Arabs before and after the Baath's rule remained the same, and the coup did not affect the process of the nation state, whereas the non-Arabs became the victims of a power conflict. However, despite the failure of the state institutions, Arab-centrism presented the strongest face of Arab ideology.

The annexation of Mosul province to Arab Iraq, according to one participant, can be compared to the Balfour promise, when Palestine was given to Israel, in that they gave something to someone, which was not their inherent right. It has been described as a continuous crime because it is worse in comparison to colonial rule. Thus, the dilemma is not only the annexation of Mosul province but the belief that this province is their property. Additionally, if there are some Arab participants who consider Mosul province to be undivided, all the Kurdish participants see it as an injustice that was imposed on the Kurdish people and that it should be terminated.

In addition to the issue of Mosul, which is inherently Arabized, the advent of the Baathists caused the annihilation of all hopes of peaceful coexistence between the components of Iraq, particularly for the Kurdish people. Here, the participants have shared their memories of the Baathists. The experiences of the interviewees affirm that the conduct of the Baathists toward the non-Arabs was similar to the racism observed in Nazi Germany, particularly the use of discriminatory procedures against the non-Arabs. These procedures consist of rewriting the history, the ideology of unification, and power. Moreover, the role of religion and the failure of state institutions have also been described. In addition, the correction of nationalities in order to Arabize the rest of the remaining Kurdish population has been noted.

The last point in this chapter focuses on how the Baath increased its power and the steps it took toward totalitarian authority, which is part of the systemic thinking of the Baath's ideology. If there are various visions of Iraq as a country, all participants were united regarding Baathism, except for those who were members of the Baath. One of the important points regarding the Iraqi authority under the rule of the Baathists is its lack of legitimacy. In such circumstances, particularly when a regime seizes power through a coup, it disables the society and its institutions. This kind of disability led to a lack of interdependency chains and interrelationships, which benefited the totalitarian rule and ensured unilateral domination. In contrast, according to one of the participants, in democratic environments, genocide is not a requirement and is not considered a choice. The final point is that the Kurds were a very easy target for the Baathists, in accordance with its ideology and the propaganda that Baathists were issuing among Iraqis. Thus, for these reasons, the ground for genocide was set for the Baathists.

NOTE

1. Contact areas is all areas adjacent to the Arab areas in Kirkuk, Diyala and Mosul. Mam Qadir rejected the word 'mixed' areas because as he said "these areas are not mixed but adjacent to the Arab areas and have been Arabized. Thus, it is mixed or cleansed from the Kurds because of the Arabization."

REFERENCES

Arab Baath Socialist Party (ABSP). The constitution of the Baath Arab socialist party. *BASP National Leadership*, August 31, 2015. https://bit.ly/2Wq2hYJ.

Davis, Eric. History suggests an Iraqi democracy is possible. *Global Citizen 2000: Building a New Iraq*, July 1, 2004. Accessed November 28, 2020. https://bit.ly/2JhT29X.

Davis, Eric. *Memories of state: Politics, history, and collective identity in modern Iraq*. University of California Press, 2005.

Eskander, Saad. Southern Kurdistan under Britain's Mesopotamian mandate: From separation to incorporation, 1920–23. *Middle Eastern Studies* 37, no. 2 (2001): 153–180.

Fattah, Hala Mundhir, and Frank Caso. *A brief history of Iraq*. United States: Infobase Publishing, 2009.

Fletcher, J. *Violence and civilization: An introduction to the work of Norbert Elias*. Cambridge: Polity, 1997.

Goodrick-Clarke, Nicholas. *The occult roots of Nazism: Secret Aryan cults and their influence on Nazi ideology*. New York University Press, 1992.

Habib, Kadhim. Said Qazaz Wa I'adat Kitabat Altarikh Fi Al-Iraq. *Al-Hiwar Al-Mutamaddin*, December 10, 2006. Accessed December 15, 2020. https://bit.ly/34jbAym.

Horowitz, Donald L. *Ethnic groups in conflict*. Berkeley, CA: University of California Press, 1985.

HRW. III. Background: Forced displacement and Arabization of Northern Iraq. *Claims in conflict: Reversing ethnic cleansing in northern Iraq: III. Background*, August 2004. Accessed December 28, 2020. http://bit.ly/2KFoa4f.

Husain, Saddam. *About writing history 2*. Baghdad: Dar Al-thawra, 1978.

Jones, Adam. *Genocide: A comprehensive introduction*. London & New York: Routledge, 2010.

Kibaroğlu, Mustafa, and Ayşegül Kibaroğlu. *Global security watch: Turkey: A reference handbook*. Greenwood Publishing Group, 2009.

Leicht, K. T., and J. C. Jenkins. *Handbook of politics*. USA: Springer, 2011.

Michel Aflaq. *Fi Sabeel al-Baath*. Beirut: al-Tali'a Publisher (V.1), 1987.

Rafaat, Aram. The 1926 annexation of Southern Kurdistan to Iraq: The Kurdish narrative. *American Research Journal of History and Culture* 3, no. 1 (2017).

Ritter, Hellmut. Irrational solidarity groups: A socio-psychological study in connection with Ibn Khaldun. *Oriens* (1948): 1–44.

Ritzer, George, and Jeffrey Stepnisky. *Modern sociological theory*. Washington DC: SAGE Publications, 2017.

Shields, Sarah. Mosul, the Ottoman legacy and the League of Nations. *International Journal of Contemporary Iraqi Studies* 3, no. 2 (2009): 217–230.

UNHCR. Iraq: Resolution no. 1096 of 1985 (nationality). *Refworld*, November 13, 1985. Accessed December 27, 2020. https://bit.ly/2M6ySRz.

Wilson, Wilson. "The fourteen points," USA: Documents to Accompany America's History, 1918.

Chapter 6

Personal Views and Experiences in the Process of Genocide

As demonstrated in chapter 5, the process of state formation in Iraq was based on pan-Arab-centrism, with an attempt to marginalize non-Arabs in order to establish a pure Arab state; its successive failings include dimensions of pan-Arabism. In addition, the role of Baath ideology in strengthening pan-Arab-centrism has been examined, including its influence in relation to the unilateral tendencies in Iraq. This chapter will analyze the inclination of the BP toward genocide in five main sections, chosen according to the concepts that the participant interviewees expounded upon. The concepts and titles in this chapter are structured according to the chronology of events. Thus, it starts with the policy of Arabization undertaken by the BP, which became an excuse for the behavior of the Baathists. In this regard, it will focus on the forced camps, the Faili Kurds, Barzani men, chemical attacks on Halabja city and its causes, as well as the procedure and the implementation of the Anfal Campaigns. Here, the causes of genocide and the utilization and exploitation of state institutions, and the economic wealth of Iraq, remain imperative in examining any de-civilizing activity. In addition to the theoretical description of pan-Arab-centrism, the so-called chauvinist behavior and the stages of the genocide process will be examined in this chapter, especially during the Anfal Campaigns. Before delving into the views of the participants, I will quote one of the standpoints which Saddam Hussein took: "It is imperative that in our view to history and in writing it, we should have a . . . Baathi way" (Baram, 1983: 426).

Thus, the Baath's path for Iraq, as envisioned by Saddam Hussein and various Baath leaders including Aflaq, was an endeavor at a de-civilized model. As a consequence, through the statements of the participants, the previous chapter explored how Arab-centrism or al-Uruba was one of the main goals that led to the eventual genocide process. This process was implemented in different stages and forms, supposedly in the name of "Allah."[1] Thus, if the mass killing of the Jews was carried out in the name of a nation (Lash and Featherstone, 2002: 266), in the case of Iraq, the erroneous claim was that they were being carried out in the name of Allah (God), as well as in the name of the nation.

THE ARABIZATION POLICY OF THE BP

The previous long quote from Mam Qadir reflects the causality of the harsh and total ideological violence meted out against the Kurdish people, who were deemed to be outcasts. The definition of ethnocentrism by Graham Kinloch was presented in chapter 1 as a road map to genocide, as well as Elias's theory of the establishment and the outcast group. In this regard, Elias explains "how a group of people can monopolize power hegemony and use them to exclude and stigmatize members of another very similar group" (Elias, 2000: 12).

Additionally, if this is the case regarding a "very similar group," depending on the groundwork of Elias, this book involves a "very different group." Article 11 of the Baath's constitution provided a permanent road map for the implementation of a pure Arab state in order to secure the "one Arab Nation, with an eternal message." Thus, in this section, via the ideology of Arabization, the Arab nationalist behavior toward the non-Arabs, particularly the Kurds, will be highlighted according to the real experiences of the participants.

Mam Qadir described the suffering of an elderly man through a long period of poor conduct by the Baath against the Kurds. In addition, there is a common perception among the Kurdish participants regarding the aggressive and prejudiced attitude of the Baathists against the Kurds. Senior academic lecturer at Baghdad University, Professor Nouri Talabani suffered from the Baath's policy, including deportation. He is the author of *The Policy of Arabization of Kirkuk* and in a detailed interview, he concluded that

> the first stage of genocide in my view was the Arabization of Kirkuk region, then the Anfal campaigns. The policy of Arabization before the AC started intensely during 1963. After the collapse of first the Baath's coup and the coming of both Arifs successively, the Arabization was continuous, but a little less operative. When the Baathists returned, the Arabization started again. (PI, July 1, 2015)

It seems that the process of Arabizing Kirkuk, according to Talabani, involved different procedures and stages. What caught my attention from

Talabani's book is the mentioning of a short conversation between one of his colleagues in the US and Hanna Batatu, the author of *The Old Social Classes and the Revolutionary Movements of Iraq*. Accordingly, in his visit to Kirkuk, Batatu was asked if he had met any communists or Kurds in terms of gaining more knowledge and understanding their vision. His answer was "no because the Iraqi regime did not let him do that" (Talabani Nuri, 2003: 46). Thus, from this conversation, it shows how the Iraqi regime had a single-minded attitude toward Kirkuk and the Kurds in order to expedite the completion of the process of Arabization. Murad Hakeem, another participant with family who were exposed to genocide, has a PhD[2] in sociology, hails the Barzani tribe, and works as a lecturer in Salahaddin University; he argued:

Arabizing the land was important for Bathists. They were ready to deport Faili Kurds to Iran. They were ready to exclude people from their places. They attempted to Arabize the Turkmen. But Arabizing the Kurds was not as important as land if the Kurds were leaving the land that they alleged to own. Arabizing meant discharging the land. However, the land was not important if it was not part of Arab land. (PI, July 4, 2015)

Thus, the first important stage concerning Arabization was the evacuation of the land from its indigenous Kurdish people and bringing Arabs in to replace them. The reason, according to Hakeem, is: "I think they understood that confronting the language and culture needs time and it is not necessary because when this region converts to an Arab region, the remaining Kurds will assimilate through a normal process" (PI, July 4, 2015). Thus, they were thinking to assimilate the non-Arabs into the contact areas through different procedures, which have been mentioned by Nouri Talabani in his book *The Policy of Arabization of Kirkuk*. Initially, the deportation was ongoing in a soft way and intermittently, to cover the operation and to prevent the occurrence of any public display. However, the writer and genocide activist Arif Qurbani,[3] from Kirkuk, was able to collect ample Anfal Campaign–related information and painful stories from the victims and some of the perpetrators in the campaigns. He is one of the interviewees who has accumulated a large and indispensable archive for researchers; he concluded that "the Arabization has a direct relation to the tribal Arab mentality in Iraq. History has shown that the Arabs could not live with diversity. They always attempted to eliminate disparity among themselves or aim for assimilation, whether religious doctrine or ethnic differences" (Qurbani, PI, July 10, 2015).

For this reason, according to Qurbani, the Kurds were the target of Arabization for no reason. This is because "the main reason was to change Iraq to a pure Arab country and to cleanse Iraq from the non-Arabs but with long term patience" (Mam Qadir, PI, June 25, 2015). Thus, it was a soft procedure as long as the process of assimilation was possible. In this regard, historian professor Jabar Kadir, who is from Kirkuk, provided a deeper interpretation of the Arabization phenomenon and Arab mentality, as he argued:

> In terms of the Kurds, in the Baath's vision, Iraq is an Arab country, the Kurds are part of the Arabs. They were interpreting it differently at different stages. They believed that as long as the Kurds are able to speak Arabic, and they have adopted the Arab culture because they are Muslims; in addition, the majority of Kurdish intellectuals speak the Arabic language. According to some of the Baath's vision they have to be counted as Arabs. This means cultural, not racial, integration. (PI, June 8, 2015)

This interpretation of Aflaq's view and other Baathists is precise. The Kurds and other components in the Arab homeland had a commitment to the Arab regime, which was the Baath Party. The most striking point is they obligated the Kurds to be educated in the Arabic language and to be exposed to other Arab cultural practices to change the culture of the citizens, as they argued that the intellectuals were speaking Arabic. However, although they were speaking Arabic, they maintained their language and culture.

Additionally, Ahmad Al-Darraji, as one of the Baathists who still believes in his ideology, concluded that

> "Iraq has been an Arab state since time immemorial. The unity of Iraq for us is part of our holy places. Iraq's affiliation with the Urubah is in good standing. Who wants to live with us, they will be respected and who does not want to, the doors are open."
>
> Question: "Does this mean Kurds are guests?"
>
> "I'm not saying the Kurds are guests, but they were part of the Arab people who are respected as long as they remain part of the Arab people. When they do not want to stay, so, this is their choice and they can live in any place they want." (PI, August 10, 2015)

This admission from Al-Darraji confirms what was said by Murad Hakim, as he concluded, "but Arabizing the Kurds was not so important as land if the Kurds were leaving the land that is alleged to be their land" (PI, July 4, 2015). Thus, in the Baath's vision, the land is Arab land, as has been identified in the constitution of the Baath. Consequently, the Arabization was centralized and became the preoccupation of all Arab rulers in Iraq. In this regard, Falakaddin Kakayi implied that Arabization precedes the Baath rule:

> The Arabization started before 1963 with the advent of Abdul Karim Qasim. We have learned to applaud Qasim and we thought he was a good man and friend

of the Kurds, but later we discovered that Qasim was worse because he had designed the policy of Arabization. Do not take my word for it, I can prove it:

For example, Kirkuk from its management formation and the establishing of its Provinciality from the 1920s until 1958, its Governor was Kurdish or sometimes a Turkman. There is a list of Governors and it does not include any Arabs. Thus, Qasim imposed an Arab governor without any previous agreement, despite his knowledge of the sensitivity of the equation. We did not know until later on that it was part of the Arabization procedure. The mayors of Makhmur town from 1937 until 1958 were successive Kurds but with the advent of Qasim, the successive mayors were Arabs, until the collapse of Saddam Hussein. Even Erbil, the capital of Kurdistan region, go and look at the official governor list until 1958, as per which, all of them were Kurds, including one or two Turkmen, but with the advent of Qasim and onwards, they became Arabs. (PI, May 27, 2015)

This elaborate explanation from a participant is a reflection of their awareness of the dimensions of Arabization as a central unchangeable policy of the Arab political elite. Moreover, it also shows the seriousness of the process of Arabization, with no essential distinction made between the parties of the political process since the establishment of the state, and through the rule of the BP with its Uruba unification. In addition, another neglected but important side of Arabization was discovered. It was raised by Chinar Saad, as she concluded:

I studied this subject for my Master's dissertation. Look at the history of Iraq; it does not refer to the Kurds as a nation specifically, it is as if they do not exist. They talk about many aspects of the state since the Caliphs, but without any reference to the Kurds. See, for example, the famous Shanidar Cave. The history is talking about the lives of Neanderthals at a place located in a mountainous area in the depth of the Kurdistan region. However, the history of Iraq considers it as part of the Arab homeland without referring from near or far that this cave is located in the Kurdish areas, even it does not mention the name of Kurdistan. This is a systematic distortion of history. This is an implied reference that there is an orderly process leading people into oblivion. Therefore, we believe the Baathists were acting based on a systematic program. There were many topics in the Kurdish or Arabic lessons, but they were totally focused on the Baath and Arabism as if it has nothing to do with the Kurds. (PI, June 4, 2015)

Here, we discover that the BP was working on the memory of citizens to ensure the future generations would forget their origins and cultural identity. Therefore, as Jeannette Marie Mageo in her book *Cultural Memory: Reconfiguring History and Identity in the Postcolonial Pacific* explains,

"This grounding in narration, in recapturing existence in the form of a story, suggests that memory is a point of transit of unparalleled import, most significantly perhaps between the social and the personal. What remains in memory for the long duration (long-term) is what has significance for us individually or collectively" (Mageo, 2001: 2). Thus, when the history or any other national literature has been changed or rewritten to benefit a specific ideology, it could form a dangerous issue for future generations. This is what Saddam Hussein emphasized originally—to rewrite history—and this is what they attempted to do to Arabize Iraq at heart.

Hence, whatever the means, the goal was to perpetuate Arabization as a first step to changing Iraqi identity to that of a pure Arab country. Here, I had a chance to meet one of the senior BP members in London to find out his perspective on different matters in relation to the Kurds on one side, and the Arabs and the Iraqi state on the other. In this regard, Abdul Razzaq al-Baathi described his views on the process of Arabization, stating:

> Look, I want to express my opinion downright. The country of Iraq is a sincere Arab country. The Kurds and other components that live in this country have to know the country's Arab identity and respect it. There is an overwhelming Arab majority in this country, thus the minority has its rights and duties according to the philosophy of the state, and also the majority has its rights and obligations.
>
> However, a few men wanted to distort the facts, but when the state did not listen to their irrational demands, which were colonial and Zionist demands to weaken Iraq, in this case these people should be hit with an iron fist. They should not provoke nor should they grieve. (PI, August 15, 2015)

In this extract, two points are significant, primarily, the only identification of Iraq is Arabism, the "we-identity," which contradicts a democratic system, and the commitment to the philosophy of the state is essential, which according to Saddam Hussein, is the "way of the Baath." This vision is inherently similar to that of Aflaq and the constitution of the BP. This is what Al-Husary emphasized as "he has refused the establishment of Uruba dependence on the diversity" (Ziyada, 2005).

Thus, the contradiction between different visions—the established group, the Arab nationalists including Baathists and the outsiders (in this context, the Kurds)—is conspicuous. Here, Baath's vision of a perfect Iraq is the only way of the Baath and it is single-minded and al-Uruba only. In this regard, we face the German model in its acceptance of Jews, as Fletcher describes: "In keeping with the relative instability of the we-identity and sense of self-worth encoded in the German national habitus, acceptance of outsiders such as the Jews proved not only extremely difficult, but tragically impossible" (Fletcher, 1997: 161). Thus, the Arabs as a dominant group did not build the

Iraqi state on a specific, collective, and coherent philosophy for all people, but contradictory, alongside the age of the Iraqi state, they proved that the non-Arabs in this country were unwelcome. Consequently, this policy led to the building of dozens of forced concentration camps in the Kurdistan region.

FORCED COMPLEXES

After the collapse of the armed movement of Gulan in 1975, the situation in the Kurdish region was one of disarray. The process of Arabization and the oppression by the BP increased. The process of the evacuation of villages and rural areas in 1976–1977 was the most dangerous stage for several reasons: first, the Kurds themselves were like birds with broken wings, and they could not defend themselves; they were arrested for trivial reasons or no reason. Second, the majority of these villagers and rural residents were farmers, and they were producing to meet the needs of the urban population. Third, these deportees were accumulated in forced camps, jobless, and living in a deadly vacuum without knowing what to do. In his description, Mam Qadir explains how the process began: "To discharge the village and rural areas in terms of creation, a security belt of a depth of 20-40 km, alongside of the borders of southern Kurdistan with Iran, Turkey and Syria was created. They deported the villager residents by throwing them in the coercive camps under very harsh conditions" (PI, June 25, 2015).

In the same direction, Qurbani reiterated this approach as he concluded: "A security belt around the borders of Iraq was built. This meant by 1976–1979 after the collapse of the Gulan revolution, a security belt from the beginning of the Iranian border to Syria through the Turkish border had been created. The villages in these targeted areas were destroyed up to a minimum depth of 15 km on the pretext of security conditions" (PI, July 10, 2015).

Adalat Omer who was displaced to Iran, and as a genocide activist, also confirmed this information, stating, "I was among those who were displaced to Iran after the setback in 1975 with my family. Then we discovered that the regime had discharged the border areas up to a depth of 20 km and no one could walk around these areas" (PI, May 23, 2015).

In accordance, tens of thousands of people, including children and the elderly, were displaced in a chaotic situation. They were "deliberately inflicting on the group conditions of life calculated to bring about its physical destruction in whole or in part" (UNGAS, 1951: 1). In this regard, the participant Fatih[4] (age seventy-nine), who identified himself as previously being an Imam, concluded: "These forced camps were lacking the most basic means of a dignified life. Many important social figures with social and political influence died from anxiety and depression. The BP did not kill them, but this was what they wanted. The Baathists were happy because those people were dying, but not in mass graves. They died in a 'modern complex'" (PI, April 23, 2015).

Thus, the residents who were mostly illiterate or nonprofessional in any industrial sectors in these areas were compelled together in forced camps. These forced camps were very similar to the Nazi concentration camps. The previous Iraqi environment minister AbdulRahman Siddiq, who studied civil engineering and lived in one of the forced camps for some time, described the circumstances inside the forced camps in Kurdistan. Siddiq explained:

To my knowledge, there was a kind of similarity between both models of camps in Kurdistan and Germany:

1. The movements of residents of these camps in Kurdistan were significantly restricted to a limited area inside the camps. We were under constant surveillance.
2. These camps were inside the Kurdish areas; therefore, residents were quickly accustomed to the situation. They started building houses, including attempting to engage in agriculture on small areas of land; for this reason, many of them were exposed to expulsion from these camps to another in order deprive them from new natural conditions of life.
3. Inside these camps, the BP built extensive military and intelligence security centers around the camps for the Baathification process.
4. Appropriate work for men was restricted, and also they were subjected to arrest if they attempted to work; therefore, the women had to work under bad circumstances. (PI, May 30, 2015)

This, along with Fatih's extract, illustrates many different themes that led to a dangerous psychological position for the deported people. The first important theme is the restriction of movement inside the camp for rural residents who were mostly from mountainous areas, and therefore accustomed to a free environment, which made it all the more traumatic. This situation could be an important reason for people engaging in some activities similar to their previous work. What we have discovered from this extract is that along with the displacement of the population, they were exposed to psychological and spiritual torture because of limited freedom and restricted movement, as well as being deprived from engaging in any kind of work, particularly agriculture, even on a small piece of land, due to Baathification. The other strange theme in this displacement of people is the work of women. This is not because people do not allow women to work. Culturally, men and women in the Kurdish rural areas were working together without any restrictions, but the movement limitations placed on men gave the Kurdish men a very bad feeling. However, the Baath Party, according to "Siddiq," pursued the policy of scorched earth to evacuate these areas from its residents as a process of ecocide. However, if we audit the percentage of farmers from Kurdish rural areas, we find that the majority of the Kurds were living outside the cities that were exposed to destruction. Here, Siddiq explains: "According to the census of 1965: 85% of Sulaymaniyah province was rural residents, 85% of Erbil province was rural residents, 76% of Duhok province was rural residents" (PI, May 30, 2015).

Thus, according to this census, 82 percent of Kurdish residents in these three provinces were living in rural areas, and the majority of this population was working in the agricultural sector, so at least they were not importing foreign products. Destroying the infrastructure of the area, and the displacement of the population in this way, led to a terrifying decline in production and the destruction of heritage and archaeology. Furthermore, draining wells is a reason for the displacement of animals, thus creating agonizing circumstances which were difficult to revert to their original state.

In a similar trend, the prominent Kurdish writer and political figure, Nawshirwan Mustafa,[5] who led "Komelei Rencderani Kurdistan,"[6] a national Marxist group in the 1970s and 1980s within the Kurdistan Patriotic Union against the Iraqi authorities, stated that "Baathists in 1963 had a program to seize the oil-rich areas. In addition, they attempted to capture areas that were considered the central strength for the Kurds" (PI, May 28, 2015). Hence, two paradigms are noticeable here, which are acquisition and deprivation. On the one hand, the Baath Party was attempting to control all oilfields in the Kurdish area, while at the same time implementing its policy of Arabization through deportation and new settlements. On the other hand, they were attempting to deport and assimilate the indigenous people from these evacuated areas in order to deprive them of a decent life.

In contrast to these Kurdish visions, with differentiable themes, it all led to one inevitable result, which is Arabization or Arab-centrism in the form of the establishment and outsiders; here, two different Arab visions need to be considered. The first participant is Al-Alusi, who describes Arabization as a crime and states that it must be acknowledged as a crime, as he explained: "This is not a hypothesis. Arabization actually has been implemented on the ground according to each definition of the crime. The crimes of Arabization have been committed throughout the period of Ba'athist rule. Everyone must revisit this crime based on an accurate historical and political minute. The details should be made available to everyone" (PI, May 24, 2015).

Thus, according to Al-Alusi, Arabization is a definitive act that was pursued without any hesitancy and should be admitted as being a crime. However, in front of this decisive vision, here is a participant figure that was involved in the BP's mission, and he still believes in what the BP implemented. He is just not sure of what the BP did, but he is also bold enough to defend what has been committed. He considers it to be a struggle and patriotism, as he added:

My dear, the state was responsible for the security of its citizens. The deportation
of families from an area A to another area B, since their lives were in danger,
or when the state's strategy for the economy or for any other reason to maintain
the stability of the state, the state has the right to move them to another place.
Thus, the cylinder of deportation and Arabization are concepts of colonialism.
Iraq was fine and people were living blissfully. So, it was the multiplication of
the enemy and the result was devastating. (AbdulRazaq PI, August 15, 2015)

Hence, the most important point here is that this participant is admitting
that the deportation happened, but he claims it was a procedure in terms
of pursuing a strategy by the government. The other important point is the
state as an actor has been sanctified, regardless of the quality of life under
the shade of this type of state. The third important point which is prominent
in this extract is that Baathists have considered an attempt or opposition to
the Baath's plan or ideology, which is based on the conspiracy theory of
subservience to Israel and the West and was an accusation against anybody
expressing their opinion or demanding their rights.

THE NEW ERA OF DESTRUCTION

When the first phase of the deportation had gradually terminated during the
years 1977 to1988, with the rural areas evacuated and termed prohibited areas,
the camps became the new inhabited crowded areas. As a consequence, the
Arab BP members who had absolute power became very active inside these
camps in terms of the process of Arabization and controlling the security situation. In addition to this new model of establishing forced camps, the deportation, Baathification, and Arabization processes were ongoing, as well as other
forms of oppression being undertaken. This continuation was dependent on the
possibility of a kind of action, as Kadir has implied: "The Iraqi government
was classifying Kurds into a few groups. The most concerning group for the
BP after the Faili Kurds were people who resided in rural areas because these
areas were appropriate for the guerrilla movement. They thought the cities
were under control. They could handle it as they wanted" (PI, June 8, 2015).
Here, two divisions are important in terms of controlling Kurdish society. On
the one hand is the classification of its components, and on the other hand,
gathering them in some areas in terms of the enforcement of Baath's purposes.

The Faili Kurds

Thus, the classification of the targeted population as a pursued culture of
genocide was an ongoing process. The most concerning group had been

gathered in camps and was being deprived of everything they owned to be an easy target for the purposes hypothesized by the Baathists. Hence, regarding the Faili Kurds, who were the first target of the BP, the participant, Khalil Ismail Faili, asserted:

> The project of Arabization started after the establishment of the Iraqi state. This project had three axes. The first axis of Arabization was Mosul province. The second axis was Kirkuk province, and the third axis was the province of the Faili Kurds, which started from Baghdad and extended through the borders of Iran-Iraq. Strategically, the axis of the Faili Kurds was very important because of its proximity to Baghdad. (PI, January 2, 2015)

Here, Ismail Faili argues that Arabization was a project, and as has been explored in the literature review, Arabization could be considered part of the Arab elite's morality, because most of the Arab political elites and army officers, including King Faisal, participated in the Arab revolt against the Ottoman Sultanate out of Arabism and Arab unification. In addition, the impulse of Arab rulers was organized for the long term to convert Iraq to a pure Arab country, and it claimed three axes of provinces. These three provinces separated the Arab areas from the rest of the Kurdish areas, on the one hand, and on the other hand, all three provinces are rich areas in terms of agriculture, energy, and tourism. The other important point, as has been reiterated, is the position of the Faili Kurds in terms of their proximity to the capital, Baghdad. Here, Mam Qadir as a participant and because of his close ties with the Faili Kurds sees it as a more complicated position regarding the psychological consequences of the Faili Kurds. In addition, he was more specific, as he claimed that

> the position of the Faili Kurds is difficult because the harm they suffered at the hands of the BP is irreversible; they can never return to a similar situation as they were in before. Now, as a reaction against Saddam as a Sunni Arab, they lost their sympathy with the Kurdish movement in order to strengthen the Shi'a sectarianism against the Sunnis, and because of their remoteness from Erbil the Kurdish capital, despite what had been done against them because of their Kurdishness, and Shi'a Arabs being prevented from this kind of procedure—why?
>
> Because the spirit of Arabization in Baathists was dominant in contrast to the pure religious doctrine, although some people used religion for their own interests. In addition, the number of Shi'a Arabs who used to implement the Baath's policy was not few. (Mam Qadir, PI, June 25, 2015)

Here, according to this extract, the central issue is the Faili survivors who returned to Iraq after the collapse of the Baath regime in 2003; they lost their

sympathy with the Kurdish movement as well as Kurdish society for two reasons: because of their distance from the Kurdish center and due to their proximity with adjoining areas of Arabs. The other reason is because the majority
of them joined the Shi'a movements as a reaction to the Baath's Sunni rule
that pursued ethnic cleansing against them. This change in behavior is a direct
consequence of the crimes perpetrated against them. It could be considered
as affection for Arabization, including the reduction in the huge numbers of
the Faili population. To understand the sorrow of the Faili Kurds, Sami Faili,
a political activist, asserted that

> the Baathists started the destruction of the Faili Kurds in 1963. Yes, it was
> genocide. Imagine, 12,000 Faili youth have been buried somewhere. We have
> attempted to find them without any result. Even those who participated in the
> Faili Kurds' genocide are in prison, like Mezban Khidir Hadi who was directly
> responsible, and Barzan the brother of Saddam Hussein, as well as a group of
> military intelligence officers that are still in prison. Unfortunately, even the
> Maliki government has not attempted to ask those accused Baathists in order
> to find out where these Kurdish Faili youth have been buried. (Sami Faili, PI,
> June 25, 2015)

Thus, they were exposed to the genocide process on a large-scale, and even
the trial of Baath leaders did not help to heal their wounds, not even in the
slightest. In this regard, Hiwa Afandi (age sixty-eight) one of the previous
BP members who was working at the Kurdish issue department of the Iraqi
Ministry of Interior, concluded: "I'm not specialized in the legal field, but I
know it has been confirmed that the Baath authority was attempting to end the
Faili existence using every force. Actually, in the early eighties, the existence
of the Faili was in limbo" (PI, August 5, 2015).

This extract is in line with the next point about the migration of Faili Kurds
to Iraq. Despite his denial that the Faili Kurds are a national Iraqi group,
AbdulRazaq Al-Baathi claimed that "there were no campaigns against anybody, specifically because they are a component, but the state implemented
what was necessary to maintain the prestige of the state, its independence and
unity. The so-called Failis, they were an Iranian minority living in Iraq, and
when we knew about their betrayal and loyalty to Iran, the authority sent them
back to their native land" (PI, August 15, 2015).

This understanding, and his insistence on it, comes from a mentality that
is difficult to understand. Although this person lives in Britain, he knows
that immigrants acquire British citizenship within six years, and if they are
granted residence, they enjoy the same rights as those born in Britain from
British parents (Khan, 2013: 235). If we were to accept the controversial
claim that the Faili Kurds came to Baghdad a hundred years ago, and the

third generation was born there, and do not know a homeland other than Iraq, should they not have the right to preserve their dignity and live safely as Iraqi citizens? Yet, in exchange for honoring those who rendered great services to Iraq, they have faced mass expulsion, and accordingly, many of them died or were killed on the way to Iran, immaterial of the causation and its consequences. For the progression of the BP, and in line with Arabization, they were mass murdered in Iraq.

Barzani Men (Gendercide)

Despite the indifference of the genocide process between Kurdish elements, the division and classification of them according to their documents and interviews have been confirmed. The second mass campaign against the Faili Kurds started in 1980, just after the initiation of the Iraq-Iran war. However, the pressure on people and the violence against them using different techniques, and for various purposes, continued. Thus, in 1983, another dangerous campaign on a large-scale, against Barzani men aged fourteen years and above, was implemented. In this regard, Mam Qadir stated:

> In the case of the Barzani tribe, who were dwelling in camps, generally they were ordinary people and were busy in their non-political lives, and the majority were not involved in the Kurdish political movement. It could be because Mustafa Barzani's family was leading a political party and the time of the Baath's authority was appropriate to take revenge and cleanse the Kurdish areas, even if there was only one Kurdish citizen. Therefore, Barzani men from 14 years old were arrested inside the complexes and they were exterminated and buried in mass graves under mysterious circumstances. (PI, June 25, 2015)

Hence, given the reason behind this campaign, according to this participant, the cleansing of Iraqi Kurdistan and the reduction in its Kurdish residents were one of the motives behind these campaigns. On the other hand, the majority of these people were not involved in any political action—they were children, and unaware of the ongoing circumstances. In addition, it fails to justify how a tribe can be made liable for their opposition to the present regime. Here, in terms of an answer to this question, the participant Hiwa Afandi claimed that

> Barzanis were taken to mass graves and it has been acknowledged by Saddam Hussein on a live TV programmed that "Barzanis have been taken to hell and they have got their punishment." However, in contrast to this acknowledgement, the whole picture is shown in the image of the long-term impact, because these

people were uprooted from their villages and taken to the camps and then onto the second stage, when they were taken to their fate. (PI, August 5, 2015)

In addition to this extract from the interview, and according to Taha Suleman, "8000 Barzani were arrested and shot in the desert of 'the southern bourse'" (2014: 37).

In contrast to Hiwa Afandi's extract, Abdulrazaq al-Baathi expressed the views of the regime and underestimated the entire process. This means that they continue to deny the recognition of the genocide they committed, as he claimed that

some Barzanis were clear agents of Iran and they were helping Iran to control the capabilities of the Iraqi people. The state could not stand idle and the authority should deal with the issue from a legal perspective. So, a couple of hundred who plotted against Iraq, were arrested and as our martyred president has acknowledged, "they have gone to the hell" and this is an appropriate penalty for the traitors. (PI, August 15, 2015)

Thus, this confession comes from insisting on confusion because the Barzanis who were arrested were civilians and resided in the compounds under the observation of the Iraqi security forces, as mentioned previously. In addition, they were arrested because they belonged to a specific tribal national component while their neighbors were not arrested because they belonged to another Kurdish tribe.

Halabja Chemical Attack

The devastating war between Iraq and Iran was exploited at the highest level to cover the success of the process of genocide. In 1987, many villages and towns were attacked with chemical weapons, including Halabja city. Regarding this issue, Hiwa Afandi has claimed that "chemical attacks on Halabja included a series of chemical attacks on many Kurdish villages and towns as a supplement to what they had started—to ensure any possible chance in terms of the end of the Kurdish presence or at least the Kurdish opposition to the BP's plans" (PI, August 5, 2015).

Chemical weapons are the fiercest weapons in existence due to the extent of their reach beyond any barrier or wall. The thematic aspects are analogous to Holocaust mechanisms and the only difference lies in its bureaucracy, yet both were forms of genocide. In contrast to this view, Abdulrazaq al-Baathi argued that "Halabja is an excellent Iranian scenario. It was attacked by Iran but they declared that Iraq had launched a chemical attack on the city of Halabja to discredit Iraq" (PI, August 15, 2015).

Here, we have a unanimous view between the participants about the theme of the chemical attack on Halabja, despite the vision of the Baathists that Iran was behind this tragedy. However, the Iraqi Supreme Criminal Court has confirmed the responsibility of Iraq, and it has been recognized as genocide (Suleman, 2014: 166). In addition to the use of chemical weapons in Halabja, they were also used in many rural areas in Kurdistan, and I remember when Balisan valley and other villages in the area were hit. I personally saw the wounded people when they were brought to the main hospital in Erbil. All these wounded people disappeared at night in order not to use them as evidence against the regime.

ANFAL CAMPAIGNS (FINAL SOLUTION)

The Anfal Campaigns are considered the main operation and took place over seven months in 1988. Despite some possible macro-causes of the Anfal Campaigns, the questions around causality, or the retreat of nation building as a micro-cause, were directed to the interviewees in terms of exploring their feelings and beliefs. These feelings and beliefs are important because of the direct experiences of the interviewees, who were involved or not involved in the genocidal activities of the Iraqi authority. This section further inspects the Baath's behavior, or the position of the Iraqi authority toward the Kurds based on interrelationship or interdependency chains, in order to highlight the prejudice of the state authority regarding the process of de-civilization.

The Causes of the Anfal Campaigns

Due to it being the main issue being addressed in this book, the participants were asked to consider which common theme spurred on the Anfal Campaigns. The aim of asking the participants a general question was to discover whether there is a common theme regarding the involvement of people. Here, one of the senior lecturers who is living with the feelings and circumstances of his students, and has come directly under the radar of the security forces, Nuri Talabani, argued:

> It is not necessary to ask about causation. Look at the Baath's cadre, except for the Arab homeland, they do not see anything else. They have extended the Arab homeland borders to the city of Wan[7] in the North and to the city of Kermanshah[8] in the East. This is totally Kurdistan territory, but they consider it as part of Arab land. The Arab wise men are saying the Kurds are living here and we should care about them until they become Arabs. (PI, July 1, 2015)

Thus, the indirect yet specific theme here is Arabization, whether the Arabs are concerned with expanding the Arab homeland or assimilating the non-Arabs into Arab society. What draws my attention in this extract is the vision of the Arabian wise men. This common vision is not surprising because of the other extreme themes. Nuri Talabani's vision is a consequence of his very long experience as a legal expert, lecturer, and writer who was involved and lived among Arab society in Baghdad and Basra. Thus, if the wise men hoped for the assimilation of the Kurds, it means that Arab-centrism became innate and they cannot see the difference, and all different characters should be eliminated. In this regard, Arif Qurbani, as a Kirkuk city resident, stated that "what we have seen from this new state (Iraq) and what has been implemented by the BP in a very bloody destructive manner, I think it was a strategy to refuse difference, or to refuse those who were considered as outcasts. The Kurds as an ethnic and religious or sectarian component, simply were not acceptable to the state of Iraq" (PI, July 10, 2015).

Thus, the majority of the participants have confirmed the refusal of the idea of difference at the level of the state and within the Arab population. Examining this theme requires a focal point due to various reasons, which have previously been explained. As a consequence, the established culture of Arabism took place over a long period and accompanied the state's formation. The Kurds, whether invisible because of their geographical position, or in the context of Baath propaganda, had their image tarnished and this reputation has been the subject of controversy as the main reason for the division of the state. This highlighting of the division is not something that came out of nowhere. The difference was well known to both sides, but the authority was unable to find an appropriate way for them to live together. As a consequence, a participant, who has had direct involvement in the state authority, also has raised the theme of difference. Muhammad Sharif, a previous deputy Iraqi minister of Kurdish background, argued:

> Of course, the difference caused the Anfal Campaigns. There is a distinction between a difference and a difference. The difference between the Kurds and the Arabs is a profound difference because the difference lies in the language and the foundations, including interests, history and background in all its dimensions. For example, there is a difference between Jordan and Iraq, but the commonalities between them are much more. Here, humanity is the only common factor between the Kurds and the Arabs. We also share the same religion, but the values were not being respected, and they did not make any account for it—it remains zero on paper. (PI, June 6, 2015)

Muhammad Sharif stresses the importance for a common life between Kurds and Arabs. He worked for the Iraqi army as a religious Imam for a few years, and then joined the authorities as deputy minister of endowments and religious affairs. Thus, the limitation in the commonalities between two different national components still leaves one factor, which is humanity. This suggests a sense of the impossibility of coexistence between the two traditions because of the scarcity of common factors between them. This traditional mentality lacks knowledge and broadmindedness, which is reflected in the interrelationship and interdependency chains.

When difference becomes a dilemma, and ideology becomes the main principle for the interrelationship, and as an alternative to the interdependency chains, the way to the de-civilizing process is clearly paved. Here, Falakaddin Kakayi expressed his feelings regarding the causes of genocide:

I attribute it to the structure of the state and to the policy of Arab nationalist ideology. Basically, who dragged us to Iraq was the British colonial power. When Britain announced the existence of oil in Kirkuk, Kirkuk became an Iraqi-machine. Thus, they tied Kurdistan to Iraq to form a state. However, the policy of the Arabs towards the Kurds is very old and rooted. I have to say it is the Arab war against the Kurds. If there was resistance in 1988, then what about the previous attempts? The proof is the policy of Abdul-Karim Qasim and his motivation for Arabization.

The primary reason is Arab nationalism or Arab ideology in Iraq. The state of Iraq was built on the basis of the ideology of Arab-centrism. It is a chauvinist ideology. The successive regimes in Iraq were similar, from the Kingdom, to the republic, from Abdul Karim Al-Qasim to the communists. After the collapse of Saddam Hussein in 2003, a similar policy has been implemented. Nouri Al-Maliki has a similar approach, and he has willingly called his people to an ethnic war against the Kurds. Sunni Arab Islamists include Tariq al-Hashemi as an example of someone with a similar policy. Thus, the state was built to eliminate the Kurds. Kurds are not part of this state. (PI, May 27, 2015)

In this long extract, two themes are important, and both themes have subthemes. The most important theme is the state or the system of the state. Here, the Arabs as an ethnic entity do not believe in sharing power for two reasons; the first reason is because the system of the state was unilateral—it was formed for one ethnicity. They are monopolizing the means of violence and all other constitutions of the state, including taxation. The other part of the dilemma is the ideology, including the religious aspects. On the one hand, they are the majority in Iraq, and in particular the capital is seen as an Arab city and far from the Kurdish areas. On the other hand, they think Kurdistan has always been part of Iraq and any decentralizing of the state means the wavering of their rights. Thus, the ideology of Arab-centrism is the main dilemma, which is creating a strong difference based on an outsider. As a consequence, this kind of Arab-centrism has become a culture and is rooted in the memory of the Arab population. Therefore, if they theoretically believe in sharing the power, practically it is impossible. In addition, it seems that all the other participants emphasized similar themes. Mam Qadir, in a very short extract, concluded that "the main reason was to change Iraq to a pure Arab country and to cleanse Iraq from non-Arabs, but with long-term patience" (PI, June 25, 2015).

Thus, in order to strengthen the hegemony of the Arabs in Iraq, they planned to evacuate at least some areas from non-Arabs, depending on economic or strategic grounds. As Jabar Kadir and others emphasized, the Kurds throughout the age of Iraq could not be assimilated into the crucible of the Arabs, and according to their analysis, they were always endangering the unity of Iraq. Here a new theme has emerged, which is the opposition. The Kurds from the beginning could not accept marginalization and the process of Arabization. They were considered to be outsiders and their existence was at risk. This is a simple consequence of the ideology of pan-Arab-centrism. Interestingly, the Arabization policy has its roots in pre-Baathist rule, and pan-Arab-centrism seems to be solid and nonnegotiable. This type of causation was voiced by the previous Iraqi environmental minister, AbdulRahman Siddiq, who stated that "the first cause is ideology. The ideology has priority. The ideology was a filter and the consequence was something else. These causes became the foundation for the same goals: Primarily, a Pan-Arab nation. Secondary is the process of poorness" (PI, May 30, 2015).

The theme of poverty here could be important as it carries different consequences. One of the penalties of the forced camps was that citizens were stripped of their crafts and industries, which they originally owned. When they were isolated inside the camps, they became physically disabled and slowly become emotionally disabled. This disability extended to all dimensions of life, and even relationships and the stability of personality were affected, including interdependency chains.

In addition to all of these extracts from the interviews, the vision of Khalil Ismail al-Faili is more concentrated on logistical factors, as he stated: "Why were the Anfal Campaigns delayed to the eighties? Why did they not occur in the seventies, with the exception of displacement? It is because the situation in the eighties was suitable. This means Saddam Hussein and the Baath authorities knew that the situation for the process was now convenient. But unfortunately, the situation continues" (PI, January 2, 2015).

Thus, despite the ideology, there has always been the question of why the Anfal Campaigns were delayed to 1988. This is another aspect of the strategy of the process of genocide. It means the genocide was planned, but it had to be postponed until a convenient period. However, the participant is concerned about the continuity of the process because of the current tensions between the Kurds and the Iraqi authority. On the other side, for the Kurdish participants, what drew my attention was the Arab participants who are more severe than the Kurds themselves when supporting the Kurdish question. Al-Alusi, as one of those Arabs, confirmed that "the annihilation was based on a political, fascistic and chauvinistic decision" (PI, May 24, 2015). Thus, he is claiming that the annihilation is an important theme. The other different themes could in essence be a second aspect of pan-Arab-centrism, but more specifically it is a reference to the BP. In contrast to figures like Al-Alusi, here is one of the Baathists who still believes in the BP's policy regarding the Kurdish position in Iraq. The participant is AbdulRazaq al-Baathi stated: "It is not true. Iraq did not want to destroy our Kurdish brothers, but the Iraqi government, due to its duty, was required to end the insurgency of separatists who wanted to split Iraq, in the service of global Zionism, and it was a major conspiracy against the Arab nation" (PI, August 15, 2015).

This extract includes many themes, which are a reflection of, or similar to, the vision of Aflaq or Saddam Hussein, or any other Baath figure. The themes of unity of Iraqis, conspiracy, separatists, Zionism, the wise leadership of Saddam Hussein, and so on, have been reiterated without any critical vision of the relationship between the Kurds and the Iraqi authority. However, the extract shows what happened to the targeted people, and how it is considered a successful campaign against the Kurds as outsiders.

The Anfal Campaigns as Genocide

Despite the reasons for genocide, or whether the Anfal Campaigns were a consequence of internal or external factors, the participants did not conceal their belief in describing whether the Anfal Campaigns were genocide or not. Thus, in this part, some of these beliefs are highlighted.

The circumstances of war, for any perpetrator, are an opportunity for the implementation of an intended act. The participants, in different ways, have reiterated the theme of genocide and its subthemes. In this regard, Jabar Kadir claimed: "Yes, what has happened was an act of genocide. It was an act according to all genocide definitions, like the measures of the Holocaust or the Armenian genocide and all acts of the 20th century genocides from Rwanda to Bosnia and Herzegovina. Yes, what happened was an act of genocide" (PI, June 8, 2015). Thus, the theme of genocide as an act is one of the main themes, and the participants are aware of their views. In the same direction, Newshirwan Mustafa claimed: "Of course, it was genocide. What the BP did, particularly in the years of the 1980s under the name of the series of Anfal 1, Anfal 2 and until the 9th Anfal or the terminated Anfal, during which thousands of people were killed" (PI, May 28, 2015).

Thus, the Anfal Campaigns are substantially confirmed as being genocide. In addition to that, there is a strong agreement between the Kurdish and Arab participants in terms of the adjectival genocide of the Anfal Campaigns. Here the paradigm of the Sunni-Arab participant, Tayseer Al-Alusi, argued that "the annihilation or genocide was based on a political, fascistic and chauvinistic decision" (PI, May 24, 2015). Hence, the choice of the Baath's authority to commit genocide, according to Al-Alusi, was based on its fascist and chauvinistic nature. Al-Mutallibi also did not hesitate to describe the campaigns as genocide as he concluded: "Yes, the Anfal Campaigns were a systematized process against a particular race. It was not based on a political or ideological factor. The Kurds are a particular race or a specific nationality, and they have been exposed to mass destruction because of their ethnic affiliation" (PI, June 24, 2015).

Thus, here we have four figures, as well as all the other participants who agree that the Anfal Campaigns were based on the crime of genocide. However, it is important to include two other participants who were members of the Baath Party. The first one does not believe in the ideology of the BP anymore, whereas the second one still believes in the Baath ideology. Regarding Hiwa Afandi who has left the Baath ideology, they explained: "Finally, the Anfal Campaigns were aimed at putting an end to the Kurdish issue. A lot of people during the period of the war returned to their places, but the Baath authority took advantage of the war situation to carry out the final elimination of all the Kurdish presence in these areas and others" (PI, August 5, 2015).

Thus, this is an admission that the Baath's authority exploited the war to put an end to the Kurdish existence in the prohibited areas, or other areas, specifically in Kirkuk province. At the very least, this is an admission that the intention of the Baath authority was to reduce the Kurdish influence both physically and emotionally. He has not mentioned the concept of genocide, but "to carry out a final elimination" is a reference to genocide. In contrast to this statement, AbdulRazaq al-Baathi claims that

the Republic of the quack Khomeini has exposed Iraq to a criminal campaign and a brutal aggression. There were some villagers in the north who harbored greedy motives and turned their back on the country that sheltered them, approached and served them, but nevertheless they were helping our enemy; therefore, the state decided to deal with those malefactors, so, they received their just punishment. (PI, August 15, 2015)

Here, regardless of underestimating the lives of tens of thousands of rural citizens, he has admitted that those people were punished. The subtheme in this, and other extracts, refers to an intentional act, regardless of the causes of the existence of these people in these areas. The other important theme is the involvement of the state in these acts of genocide. All participants, regardless of their background, have referred to the involvement of the state directly or indirectly in these inhumane acts.

THE PREPARATION FOR THE ANFAL CAMPAIGNS

The preparation for this process was mainly on two levels: the first level is its dimensions and historical roots. The second level is the relationship with the quality of the implementation through an accurate process. The next section mainly relates to the first level because, strategically, it is associated with the ideological dimensions and the intentions of the Baath authority. The second level is mainly correlated to the logistic and bureaucratic implementation of the process.

The First Level of the Dimensions and Historical Roots

In this part of the book, the participants are seen to highlight the historical roots of the Anfal Campaigns, whether directly or indirectly. The information provided here is partly associated with their experience and the eyewitness accounts of the interviewees. The other information is considered to be as a consequence of their direct or indirect involvement in the events of that period. Nuri Talabani, who was indirectly involved, argued: "I think the policy of Arabization in the regions of Kirkuk, was the beginning, and the Anfal Campaigns were supposed to be the last stage. According to the plan, which had been exposed and was to Arabize the targeted areas, they were able to implement it in a highly professional way. So, the policy of Arabization was a clear face of genocide" (PI, July 1, 2015).

Here, the theme of Arabization has been reiterated as a dangerous prior level in association with the process of genocide. The roots of this danger-ous level could be considered a strategic level in relation to the nation state's dimensions. A state, according to the Baath's vision, should be intellectually stable and take on the Urube characters as a pan-Arab-centric model. Thus, the most important targeted areas had been Arabized on a previous level prior to the evacuation of the large areas along the borders as a security belt. According to another participant who is one of the 1983 Barzani sur-vivors, he claimed that for the Iraqi Baath authority, the land was the most important aspect, as he stated: "First: the Arabization of the land. Second, the Arabization of the people. Third, they were rather indifferent to the language, because they were only targeting the land" (Hakeem, PI, July 4, 2015).

Thus, Arabization of the land was imperative, as opposed to its people; therefore, could this point be interpreted as an argument for the entire destruction of the population specifically in the targeted areas? However, the targeted areas at the time of evacuation were smashed to smithereens. This was in order not to leave a mark of human life or even something beneficial for the wildlife, including water sources. The area actually became barren like a desert. This is what Abdul Rahman Siddiq meant when he concluded:

> The implementation of a scorched-earth policy, after discharging it from its residents at the border areas, includes the areas in Kirkuk province that were also evacuated, and the Arabs were brought to those places for the purpose of Arabization. Finally, they started a race in carrying out the annihilation of the unsuspecting people from the so-called Forbidden areas, in addition to many other regions outside these areas in the Anfal Campaigns. (PI, May 30, 2015)

Thus, we are facing two kinds of evacuated areas; on the one hand, the areas in Kirkuk, Diyala, and Mosul were evacuated from the Kurds and then inhabited by the recruited Arabs. On the other hand, the areas adjacent to the Iraqi-Iranian, Turkish, and Syrian borders and all the border gateways were considered as purely Kurdish areas. These evictions formed a challenge for the Kurdish citizens on two levels: on the first level, there was progress in forming a security belt, in addition to the possibility of Arabization of these areas in the coming stages. Second, the creation of a block between Kurdish citizens on both sides of the border, where there are mixed families on both sides in terms of familial relations, or affinity, or cultural commonalities. This factor in itself makes it possible to form an understanding of the aim of the Iraqi Baath authority, because of the mutual emotions and the interdependency chains, the interrelationships between Kurdish political parties on both sides, and the cooperation between them, which was increasing. Moreover, the cultural interrelations include historical dimensions—the Kurdish language and literature knows no borders between the four sections of Kurdistan. Thus, regarding the theme of Arabization, Sami Faili concludes: "Believe me, the stages of annihilation are clear. They start with the Arabization of the land and then the Arabization of the people. When they failed to Arabize the people, they started with the stage of genocide to end the Kurdish presence in some places and to humiliate them in other places" (PI, June 25, 2015). This extract emphasizes the similar trend of the pan-Arab policy, and it shows the importance of land above people. Here, another participant who is a genocide activist stated: "I have about 5,000 documents in my hands. Since 1983-1987, the destruction of villages and regrouping people in camps was on-going. Elimination of the Kurdish people by the state varied from period to period. According to some archives, many people were executed because of cultural, language and clothing issues. But the acts overall show that the process was systematically planned" (Omer, PI, May 23, 2015).

This participant did not mention the theme of Arabization, but the extract shows that the destruction of the villages during 1980s was ongoing. This is consistent with the previous extracts and confirms that the deportation was for the purpose of Arabization, and the Arabs were brought to the Kurdish areas in the city of Kirkuk and its subsidiaries, in addition to Khanaqin and large areas in Mosul. Thus, it could be that Arabization was the most important reason behind these executions. In the same trend as the theme of Arabization, Muhammad Sharif claimed that

> the Arabs' acceptance, initially, to bind the Kurds to the state of Iraq, is an inhumane way to address the issue of the Kurdish people. Primarily, just thinking about the Arabization of the Kurdish areas and the Kurdish personality is enough to consider the inhumanity of the successive authorities in Iraq. If they had the chance to stay, they would have attempted to exterminate the last Kurdish man. (PI, June 6, 2015)

In addition to the theme of Arabization, some other themes have been reiterated such as inhumanity, humiliation, and destruction. In addition to the theme of inhumanity, specifically regarding the extract, "Arabs should not accept the annexation of the Kurds to Iraq," it is due to fraternal feelings, which stems from an over-confidence in others based on religion. Thus, the emphasis on such overconfident feelings within the religious brotherhood is a prominent feature of Kurdish political ideology, forgetting that the interests overcame the emotional aspects. In addition to this disappointment, which represents the dominant feature of the Kurdish figures, the bitter answer was the Arabization of the entire region using the theme of destruction. In this regard, Falakaddin Kakayi claimed that

First: They began to create distrust amongst Kurds themselves and they became afraid of taking any initiative in general, due to insults and the ongoing humiliation, including the stripping of human sense.

Second: They strangely began to lay-off the Kurds from administrative, social and political aspects.

Third: The beginning of the phases of displacement and deportation to make these people dependent on the authority. In addition, the Baathists exploited the dire situation of these people to buy their receivables and then forced them to take up arms as mercenaries of the state.

Fourth: These mercenaries were used and exploited in a very bad way during the Anfal Campaigns, because without these mercenaries the success of the campaigns was impossible.

Fifth: The Baathists took advantage of modern instruments, from weapons
to the modern military system, through the building of isolated camps
to control its residents, and finally the completion of the process through
starvation and terrorism, to carry out its objectives.

Sixth: The denial of genocide widely, and until this moment, it continues. (PI,
May 27, 2015)

Here, the new themes in these extracts are striking. The psychological
impact on the lives of those people who were expelled from their hometown
and gave their lives to it, suddenly, after the destruction of everything that
was built and invested in, were banished and exported to another place, which
is entirely different from the previous place; the psychological morbidity is an
expected consequence and generated serious results. Thus, as a consequence,
the theme of dehumanization is applicable to such social, economic, political,
and psychological circumstances. In this regard, throughout collecting these
people in these camps, the Baath Party could approach several targets.

On the one hand, the emptying of rural areas was a major attempt to isolate the sources of funding from the Peshmerga. This influential procedure
included social and moral aspects in addition to the economic aspects. On
the other hand, the residents of these camps were easily controlled because
they were crammed into surrounding camps by the Iraqi army, the Popular
Army (Al Jaysh ash-Sha'bi), the security and intelligence services, and
Baath's circles. These camps were mobilized to create mercenary groups, or
in Kurdish, "Jash," and in English "Jackass," as another theme mentioned
by the participants. In addition, the Baathists aimed to force these people to
comply with joining the armed mercenary organizations, through the Baath
authority's "Light regiments," which were attractive units since their part-
time obligations included a good salary.

Moreover, the Baath authority attempted to evacuate the areas adjacent to
the international border between Iraq-Iran, Turkey, and Syria, to enable the
creation of a security belt of more than 15 kilometers in depth. This security
belt led to the isolation of the other three parts from the Iraqi portion of
Kurdistan, since the Kurds from across the border were related to each other
on a variety of levels, inclusive of political interdependence between the
Kurdish parties, who were sometimes cooperating with each other. The interrelationship included cultural aspects, particularly at the level of literature,
intellectual, historical, and linguistic commonalities. They were also socially
related across both sides of the border, mingling through birth or marriage
and kinship, or even emotionally, they were united by a common background
and sense of Kurdish brotherhood. The other theme is the modern instrument
in all its dimensions and its subsidiaries. Primarily, the idea of gathering
people in the camps could be a modern idea which may have been derived

from the Nazis, because they were similar to the Nazi camps in some aspects. They were comparatively easier to manage and control, preventing people from joining the armed opposition or running away, and it was possible to arrest any person they wanted, as they did with the Barzani community. This was accompanied by a modern army, and a huge military arsenal of heavy and light arms, equipment and military vehicles, in addition to a bureaucratic structural management. The other theme, which has been emphasized, is denial. This is one of the essential concepts in all genocide processes. However, although the crime of genocide in Iraq has been recognized by the Iraqi High tribunal court and Iraqi parliament, the Baathists, including the current Iraqi presidency system, has not apologized for the implementation of these heinous crimes.

This extract, although it comes from a Sunni Arab, brings together the most important previous themes. Here, regarding the preparation, Al-Alusi, with his rich background as an academic expert in political sciences and long experience as a left-wing activist, explained: "Primarily, there was a socio/political preparation, via two kinds of discourse, through the media and social direction. Campaigns of cleansing, Arabization and the division of administration in a way that facilitated the crime from the border villages to the contact areas between the Kurds and Arab sections, within the Kurdish area, were underway" (PI, May 24, 2015).

Thus, the preparation exceeded a lot of expectations. The political and media preparation required enough time and was accompanied by the pre-conditioned intention for the implementation of the supposed plan, using all available means of media and social platforms, which belonged to the Baathists; inclusive of television channels, newspapers, and the party's platforms—even some religious platforms. Hence, the preparation underwent several dimensions in order to implement their plan accurately and without any errors. Thus, among the themes contained in the extract, the practical numbers confirm the campaigns were brutal, ruthless, and lacked discrimination between adults and children, men or women, or senior citizens; they included an economic siege and other forms of collective punishment. Hence, cleansing and Arabization was the ultimate goal of the Bathists, which was passing through the means of bureaucracy, of administrative divisions, such as the administrative procedures in Kirkuk, Diyala, and Mosul, and also the social measures of ethnic division, such as the correction of nationality among other procedures. All of this was passed through the enormous possibilities of the state and its institutions, which were recruiting members of society by exploiting the legitimacy of the state and the national economy. The exploitation did not stop at this, but skipped the international border and violated international law and the possibility of neighboring countries assisting to end the Kurdish movement. Thus, they resorted to the Algerian

Agreement, which was signed between Iraq and Iran, under the supervision of the Algerian state and the knowledge of the United States and possibly other countries.

Here, regarding the international community, Arif Qurbani has also referred to the international factor: "I think in case of the Iran-Iraq war, the bipolar system between the Eastern and Western powers, the foreign interests and the fear of the victory of the Islamic Republic of Iran caused the silence from the international community. I do not think that the world did not know what was happening in Southern Kurdistan" (PI, July 10, 2015). Hence, this extract is further confirmation of the exploitation of international circumstances, including the national capabilities of ensuring the success of the operations. Therefore, Fatih, in terms of the international bystander position, stated: "It is a crisis of ethics, sir. The wickedness of these nations reached the bone. I was always worried about this level of abjection" (PI, April 23, 2015). Thus, both participants believe that the international community did know about the process, but they did not interrupt for several reasons. However, according to Fatih, this was a crisis of morality in the international community at large.

The Bureaucratic Level

The second level has been considered a process of large magnitude, which must have been prepared previously and with accuracy. The process needed funding and equipment, both militarily and civilian. Much of this equipment was monopolized by the state, especially the army inventory. This process demanded a large military force to be able to carry out the campaigns according to an accurate process. In this regard, Gregory Stanton argues, "Preparation for genocide includes identification. Lists of victims are drawn up. Houses are marked. Maps are made" (Gregory Stanton, 2013). For these reasons, Jabar Kadir has referred to some important points as he claimed: "I guess the Baathists were benefiting from the previous genocide acts with all three main stages: the identification of the target, regrouping them and then eliminating them in silence. Moreover, they gave the confidentiality aspect of this ethnic cleansing great priority. All this demonstrates that the process was highly organized and systematically orchestrated, and had been previously planned" (personal interview (PI), June 8, 2015). Thus, according to this extract, the hierarchy of the steps of genocide and the structure of the plan ensured that the decision was made collectively, and no national institutions were excluded from participating in the process of genocide. Furthermore, Hiwa Afandi, as a previous Baathist, experienced this issue and concluded:

For me the picture is very clear because I was behind the camera. I remember when I saw the decision for the deportation and it was on the table, but I do not remember when this decision was made. I also remember prejudiced decisions such as forbidding the Kurds from taking certain kinds of jobs and specific kinds of studies related to security or anything in relation to secrets concerning the Baath or the State.

The Kurds were always the subject of contempt and they attempted to dehumanize them. They were always insulted, perceived as violent and uncivilized. They were deliberately attempting to make them hopeless in order to expedite surrender.

The 11th March agreement was just a game, not just for inside, but also it was a message to the international community, primarily in order to leave a positive image, then nobody would believe anything about the atrocities. The campaigns were implemented according to a plan in advance. The areas had been identified previously. The areas had been named as forbidden areas. These areas had accurately been identified to include the most crowded and sensitive areas, specifically, the areas of the 3rd Anfal Campaign. (PI, August 5, 2015)

Thus, according to the knowledge of this participant, who was aware of much of the events that were taking place in Kurdistan because of his membership of the North branch of the interior ministry, what was happening was not spontaneous or reactionary. Hence, the themes in this extract have great importance. The process of dehumanization that has been reiterated includes many subthemes, psychologically and pragmatically, leaving its influence on the Kurdish personality. This extract shows that al-Uruba or Arabization is the unchanged factor that formed the core of the state's strategy, and it is a constant point in the Baath's agenda; all tactics revolve around this agenda. In this regard, al-Uruba as Arab-centrism is at the core of the process of the Anfal Campaigns, and it was a way of addressing an ethnic state—not a nation state.

The following two extracts are totally different in their expression compared to those previously discussed. The first participant considers himself as not having any involvement, even indirectly, although he has admitted that he was in opposition to the regime. In contrast to his admission, he has rejected any stages or anything else because everything was under the control of Saddam Hussein and no one owned his word. Thus, sarcastically, he answered: "Stages? I am not aware of the stages. I know Saddam Hussein was issuing his orders and nobody would oppose his orders. This is the problem. This is what I know. There are no stages and sub-stages. He was saying a word and the subject is finished" (Samarrayi, PI, May 25, 2015).

This statement is bordering slightly on ignorance because if he was a political activist in the ranks of the opposition, he should know the ideology of the opposing party. This line of response does not exceed two possibilities—it could be that he was not part of the opposition, but actually does not want to reveal any recognition because it falls within those who deny the genocide, particularly because of his belonging to the Arab-Sunnis, or he is still living in fear of the BP and he is escaping from any potential liability in the future.

In contrast to this or other extracts, here are two different Baath participants: the first one claimed: "There were neither steps nor genocide, nor shall they grieve. The state was working hard to create a safe space for all citizens. Enemies besieged Iraq, and traitors inside were working for the collapse of the state. The state began to cut-off the road from the traitors aiming to hand over Iraq. Is this what you call stages? Yes, some pocket clients were planning openly to divide Iraq and we cut-off the road'" (AbdulRazzaq, PI, August 15, 2015). This participant is not denying the atrocities, but here he is augmenting the events and calling the Kurdish movement pocket clients in terms of dehumanization of the outsiders. In the same trend, the second participant argued that

> there was no extermination process, but what happened was a process of returning the prestige and sovereignty of the state over its territory, which was occupied by Iran. Thus, the Iranians were expelled with some Iraqi traitors. As a consequence, the Iraqis celebrated the victory in all parts of Iraq and it was indescribable. The steps evident in this case, were the state and the institutions concerned about developing plans to address the crisis. (Al-Darraji, PI, August 10, 2015)

Here, both statements concur as one ideology in two different contexts. Both of them consider the Kurdish insurgency to be traitorous in order to justify the military campaigns against the Kurdish population. Both of them are using the war as a pretext to cover the operations and consider the atrocities as part of the war. They highlight the similar mentality of the BP's pan-Arab ideology, which is the fear of the division of the country and considering the Kurdish opposition as the pocket client of an imagined enemy.

This attitude of the two previous participants can be compared to the position of an opposition participant on hearing such an admission. In this regard, Fatih explained:

> I left my job as an Imam in a mosque, because I do not like hearing the word Anfal any more when someone was reading Quran or praising the behavior of Saddam. Simply, they were mere spectators. If someone told you nobody could say a word against the regime, I am saying what about during the post-fall of the regime? Arabs, especially Sunni-Arabs, do not consider Saddam or his team to be criminal, but rather they consider him to be a martyr. Thus, they are worse than the Nazis. And ask me why?

Because the Germans, after the fall of Nazism, they followed a strict procedure against the Nazis, and they even prevented Hitler's name and his book from being shared. However, the Arabs call their president a martyr. The Germans apologized and offered compensation, but what did the Arabs in Iraq do? There is a massive difference. (PI, April 23, 2015)

Finally, this contrast between the victims and perpetrators or supporters of the perpetrator, in one way or another, highlights the contrast between two we-differences. This contrast is confirmation of the strength and inflexibility of ethno-Arab-centrism.

SUMMARY

The aggressive policy of the Baath Party, and its authority as an established group opposing the Kurds, who were considered as outsiders, is highlighted by the real experiences of the participants quoted in this book. Some of these participants are survivors or eyewitnesses, even if they were the followers of the Baath Party. Arabization was the first and foremost ideology of the Baathists in order to secure the Arabic identity of Iraq. This extreme focus on Arabization is confined within the theoretical term ethnocentrism. It means that the Baathists inherited this policy from pan-Arab-ethno-nationalism. Thus, Iraq was built upon the philosophy of Arabism without giving any space to non-Arabs. Additionally, as a consequence of this policy of Arabization, hundreds of thousands of Kurdish people were resettled in forced concentration camps. This process entered the implementation phase after the Algiers Convention between Iraq and Iran. In addition to the campaigns of the BP against the Faili Kurds in 1980, in 1983, Barzani people were taken to five concentration camps in a large-scale campaign, and all Barzani men were taken to an unknown place in South Iraq. As a consequence, Saddam Hussein has admitted that these Barzani men "have been taken to hell and they have got their punishment."

The aforementioned events continued successively, and the pressure on the Kurdish factions was increasing with and without cause until the preparations were underway for the Anfal Campaigns, with the appointing of Al-Majid as commander of the northern district. In this regard, the participants have indicated the causes of the Anfal military campaigns and see Arabization as the main motivation behind the BP confining the Kurds to these narrow spaces as a prelude to psychological and spiritual surrender; or alternatively, they were to be subjected to genocide. Additionally, many factors have been mentioned by the interviewees, including the illusion of the Arab homeland borders; the rejection of ethnic diversity; the economical motivation; the origins of state formation and pure Arab-centrism; the preference of Arabs over others in residing in limited areas and the expulsion of the indigenous population of Kurds; dehumanization and the humiliation of the Kurds in a range of ways, and the BP's ideology, which according to one participant, included political, fascist and chauvinistic decisions.

Clearly, the events that occurred were an act of genocide, and the preparation for the Anfal Campaigns took place on two different levels: the historical and the bureaucratic. Thus, the origins of the historical dimensions vary, and the policy of Arabization of the land and people remain the most problematic dilemma in this issue. Here, in order to Arabize the land, different atrocities were perpetrated. In addition to the deportation of the Faili Kurds and the gendercide of the Barzani men, it includes the destruction and the genocide and finally, the lasting solution, named the Anfal Campaigns, confirmed the genocide process. However, all of these elements in the genocide process were not implemented without a clear plan and bureaucratic approval. Additionally, the state institutions and its means of violence were mobilized in order to execute the process successfully.

NOTES

1. Allah (الله) is the Arabic name for God. All the official documents and decisions from the BP and the Iraqi government and its institutes were liberated in the name of Allah and the laws in the name of Allah and the nation, even the documents of Anfals and the aggressive policy of Baathists.

2. Murad Hakim's thesis is "The Social Consequences of the Policy of Deportation of the Kurds in Iraq during the Baath's Period."

3. Arif Qurbani has been able to write eighteen books: four books about the witnesses of AC; five books about survivors from mass graves; one book about the children of Anfal; and three books about Halabja and its victims who were deported to Nuqra Salman; one book about the driver of the Bulldozer; three books on ethnic cleansing in Kirkuk; and one book about Timor—the most prominent survivor.

4. Fatih claimed that he was working as imam at one of the mosques of the Ministry of Endowments (Awqaf), but he left the mosque when the BP launched the AC because "he could not bear to hear one more word in the Arabic language, particularly the term Anfal."

5. Nawshirwan Mustafa (December 22, 1944–May 19, 2017) has been a prominent political, intellectual, and Kurdish struggler since 1960. He joined the ranks of the Patriotic Union of Kurdistan (PUK) and became deputy party secretary of Jalal Talabani, the previous Iraqi president, until late 2006, when he announced his resignation from the party and opened the center of Wisha "Word," including the issuing of a weekly newspaper in the Kurdish language, as well as a website titled Sibei "Tomorrow." Finally, he was the founder of the "Change Movement" in 2009, and his

party became the second winner in the last election in the Kurdistan region (Danly, 2009: 5). He has written dozens of books and articles.

6. Kurdistan's Labour League.

7. Van or (Wan) is a Kurdish city located in the eastern Anatolia region on the eastern shore of Lake Van in Northern Kurdistan. It has an area of 19,069 kilometer square and has a population of 1,035,418 inhabitants (2010).

8. Kermanshah in Kurdish (Kermashan) is a Kurdish city and the capital of Kermanshah Province, located in Eastern Kurdistan (Western Iran) close to the Iraqi Kurdistan borders. According to the 2011 census, its population was 851,405. The people mostly speak Southern Kurdish.

REFERENCES

Baram, Amatzia. Mesopotamian identity in Ba'thi Iraq. *Middle Eastern Studies* 19, no. 4 (1983): 426–455.

Elias, Norbert. *The civilising process: Sociogenetic and psychogenetic investigations.* London: Wiley Blackwell, 2000.

Fletcher, J. *Violence and civilization: An introduction to the work of Norbert Elias.* Cambridge: Polity, 1997.

Lash, Scott, and Mike Featherstone, eds. *Recognition and difference: Politics, identity, multiculture* (vol. 2). United Kingdom: SAGE, 2002.

Mageo, Jeannette Marie, ed. *Cultural memory: Reconfiguring history and identity in the postcolonial Pacific.* University of Hawaii Press, 2001.

Stanton, Gregory. *The ten stages of genocide.* Genocide Watch, 2013.

Suliman, Taha. *Al-Ibada al-Jamaiya Lil-Alsha'b al-Kurdi; al-Buhuth wal-Ihsa'at wa-lma'lumat wa-lwathaiq.* Erbil: Jin Publisher, 2014.

Talabani, Nuri. *Siyasat al-Taarib fi Karkuk.* Kurdish Academi. Ebil, 2003.

UNGAS. *The convention on the prevention and punishment of the crime of genocide.* UN, 1951. Accessed December 27, 2020. https://bit.ly/2WOEy4P.

Ziyada, Ridwan. al-Usul al-Falsafiya Li-Nadzariya al-Qawmiya al-Arabiya. Beirut, 2005. Accessed March25, 2021, https://bit.ly/3lSz70l.

Conclusion

The process of genocide, as has been theoretically addressed under the discipline of sociology, is never an accident or a spontaneous event; rather, it is connected directly or indirectly to the state as the perpetrator, particularly in the case of Iraq. For this reason, nation building in Iraq, as an important element in the theory of the civilizing process, has been examined in this book in connection with the process of genocide and the reasons behind the genocide in Iraq as part of the de-civilizing process. Two main processes that occurred in Iraq have been presented in terms of causality and its effects. The first process, as the main cause of the genocide, concerns how Iraq was created and the subsequent nation building that led to such a critical imbalance in power relations between the main ethnic groups inside the country, particularly between the Kurds and the Arabs. The second process, as an outcome of the first, focuses on how successive Iraqi authorities, particularly the Baath authority from 1963, pursued the policy of Arabization of the country in various ways, including evacuation, deportation, and the destruction of land and people in a clear process of genocide.

The aim has been to illustrate how nation building in Iraq caused the process of the destruction of the infrastructure of the land, and the physical and psychological destruction of the Kurdish people, through a systematic process using all possible governmental instruments and the legitimacy of the state. Furthermore, various theoretical approaches have been used to analyze the framework of ultra-nationalism in Iraq, including the policy of the BP's ideology, and how its instrument of violence has been confined. In this regard, Graham Kinloch strove to examine genocide as a sociological discipline because of the collectivity of the concept. He has attempted to provide a general framework for the early stages of the division of society and its consequences by borrowing the concept of ethnocentrism. Having examined the concept of ethnocentrism, it became clear that it was possible to approach the origins of the tendency toward genocide. Moreover, it is important to consider this tendency in the prevention of the process of genocide. Two key elements are important for recognizing the tendency toward genocide, which are official and traditional ethnocentrism. In this case, it includes the Baath's ideology of ethnocentrism, or Arabization, and the governmental procedures put in place against the targeted component. Thus, I believe that the roots of genocide are based on multiple sources, and these sources participate in the creation of ethnocentrism.

The main characteristic of social division, according to Kinloch's view, is ethnocentrism as the central phenomenon within a dominant group, and its consequences include the dehumanization of the subordinated or less important group. In association with this issue, Kinloch complements Sumner's definition and claims: "This kind of ubiquitous normative prejudice represents the basis of in-group harmony and out-group hostility and the perception of out-group members as non-human, often expressed in extreme forms of nationalism, patriotism and chauvinism under stressful circumstances" (Kinloch, 2005: 29).

Here, the best reflection of the ethnocentric behavior of Arab nationalists during the period of the Baath's rule appears in the Iraqi state's implementation of "national correction," in that the Kurds should change their nationality, particularly in Kirkuk province, Khanaqin city, and the rest of the contact areas. Ezidi Kurds and Shabaks in Mosul province were forced to change their nationality from Kurdish to Arab, and this was enforced on a large scale. This policy even led to the imposition of Arabic clothes and the wearing of the Arabic black iqaal headdress (al-Iqaal al_Arabi), which still remains.

It is worth mentioning that this view of one's own group's centrality converges with that of Euro-centrism in the framework of civilization, which has been used by Elias to describe the Western expression in terms of explicit self-consciousness. In this regard, Elias argues: "The West believes itself superior to earlier societies" (Elias, 2000: 5). This kind of vision existed among Arab nationalists during the establishment of the Kingdom of Iraq throughout the period of republican authorities, and after the overthrowing of the king, ending with the Baathists in Iraq as the main principle ideology.

Chapter 1 presented the theory of the civilizing process and nation building and illustrated how the civilizing process as a general framework shaped an important approach to recognize the most significant elements of nation building in Iraq and the power relations involved. The concept of the civilizing process has been linked to different factors. Primarily, a comparison between society and culture has been considered, which uses the habitus of people of the UK, France, and Germany as examples. These ideas have been explained via elements of culture and altering habitus, and Elias explains that the civilizing procedure is a change in human behavior and emotion that follows a quite specific course. Moreover, this has been backed up by clarification of the essence of aggression and the formation of the state as a significant part of the civilizing process. Therefore, the de-civilizing process, as the reversal of the civilizing process, is a noteworthy basis for the genocide process.

Numerous characteristics are involved in the process of state formation. The most vibrant characteristic, following Elias, is the fiercely competitive process of "conflictual affairs" between numerous groups of people. The most predictable consequence of this rivalry is a persistent unit and consecutive states, starting with a primitive state, via many dissimilar forms to reach the nation state. These forms in the state process follow the control of means of aggression and taxation. Therefore, Elias has focused on the founding of the control of one group and the ultimate creation of a country within his analysis of European history, particularly the UK, France, and Germany, which is referred to as the civilizing process. Furthermore, vital to the civilizing process is the snowballing division of functions. Utilities could be one of the central developments of the human structure at both micro and macro levels. The most significant purpose of the state, as per Elias, is the shared defense of its populace's own lives, the existence of their individual group in the face of attack, and a willingness to launch an all-out attack on other groups. These three overall functions form the system of the modern construction of present societies, where in the past, precisely in the case of feudal states, these functions were prominent in the hierarchy of the state.

The main question addressed in this book is: Why was the genocide, as a de-civilizing process, carried out against the Kurds in Iraq? In order to understand the whole process of genocide as a de-civilizing process, it was initially necessary to discuss the state of Iraq, and how it has been formed and structured. Hence, through state formation, all of the characteristics involved in the process of Iraqi nation building have been explored in order to discover the causality between the process of nation building in Iraq and the process of genocide.

In this regard, Iraqi state formation, as described in chapter 2, has been investigated according to the civilizing process and its elements, and how three Ottoman provinces were deliberately annexed in favor of colonialism and its allies—the Sunni Arabs, in the region. This compulsory formation facilitated the way to an imagined nation, built in favor of the Sunni Arabs who were courting British colonialism against the Ottomans, although previously they were the essence of the Ottoman Sultanate. This kind of facilitation led to placing all the ingredients in one pot under an artificial monarchy with the support of hundreds of the previous Arab, Sunni Ottoman officers.

This kind of artificial monarchy, under the surveillance of the colonial powers, led the Sunni Arabs in Iraq to strengthen and defend their domination over the country, along with the desire to Arabize the land and its people and to suppress those considered as outcasts in order to destroy them. These new circumstances led to the emergence of Baath ideology, which has been examined in detail in chapter 2. Thus, with the pan-Arab-ethnocentric ideology, the process of genocide took on dangerous dimensions. The ideology of ethno-pan-Arabism, and later on the Baath's ideology, may be considered to be the result of around fifty years of attempts to build a pure Arab nation in Iraq, and as a direct second main cause of the genocide.

Another question that had to be addressed is: To what extent was genocide a result of the state failing or a matter of the illegitimacy of the state? In order to understand the process of nation building and its retreat, it has been necessary to examine two main stages of the formation of the state of Iraq. The first stage is the formation of the Kingdom of Iraq under the surveillance of the colonial power in the Middle East after the First World War ended and the Ottoman Sultanate was defeated, including the annexation of Mosul province. The second stage started when the BP began to dominate Iraqi state institutions, starting in 1963, including the Iraqi army and the security forces.

Although the BP's authority and its ideology as a roadmap to genocide has been discussed, a brief investigation has revealed the process of state formation, including how and why King Faisal was chosen to lead Iraq; the ideological tendencies of the Arab Ottoman officers who supported the king and shaped the core of the Iraqi army, including pan-Arab nationalist theorists who interred Iraq accompanied by King Faisal, and how ethno-Arab-centrism evolved in Iraq. From these different macro and micro points, "the relationship between civilizing and de-civilizing processes are here clearly conceived in terms of a balance between dominant and less dominant processes" (Fletcher, 1997: 83). Thus, according to historical documentation, the only concern of the dominant group in Iraq was not the democratic state or state citizenship, but the absolute domination of King Faisal and his ideologist administration team, Sati' al-Husri as an example, over Iraqi institutions and their strategy of assimilating non-Arabs, in order to convert the country into a purely Arab nation state.

Here, I will refer to some points in order to determine the causes of the retreat of nation building in Iraq as a civilizing process and the lack of legitimacy of the state. In a brief description by the historian Hanna Batatu, one could imagine the situation of the region before creating the state of Iraq or "the annexation of three Ottoman Vilayats," as he explains: "Iraq was composed of plural, relatively isolated, and often virtually autonomous city-states and tribal confederations, urban 'class' ties tended to be in essence local ties rather than ties on the scale of the whole country" (Batatu, 1978: 7–8).

In addition, when Iraq was created, there was no civil strategy on economic, social, or political integration, as Dobbins, Lesser, and Chalk argue: "In the case of Iraq, the political structures created by British after World War I did nothing to resolve these questions" (Dobbins et al., 2003: 169).

This means the leadership was effectively handed over to the previously planned group in order to serve the colonial powers, which has been explained in chapter 2, under the title "The Interests of Colonialism." The other important point concerning the imagined Iraq is the recruitment of a foreign individual from a religious family of Al-Hijaz (Saudi Arabia). Here, as a starting point to Iraqi state formation, King Faisal and his elite followers, from the beginning, struggled to become the identity of Iraq. This kind of nation building, while not pursued as outwardly as the Al Saud in Saudi Arabia, was inwardly pursued in order to have a pure Sunni ethnic Arab kingdom. Therefore, King Faisal wanted to build Iraq based on two important criteria, which are Arab nationalism and religion. In this regard, Elie Podeh explains that "the Hashemite rulers in Baghdad, whose source of legitimacy sprang from their religious ancestry and their prominent role in the Arab Revolt against the Ottoman Empire during World War I, regarded themselves as the natural standard-bearers of pan-Arabism" (Podeh, 1995: 2).

Thus, pan-Arab nationalism and religion as two criteria have been utilized to dominate the country. Additionally, pan-Arab nationalism was the most prominent element of identity for the imagined Iraq, and religion was the second; the main element of it, as Sylvia Kedourie discovered from the nature of Faisal's discourse, is: "We are Arabs, he used to say, before being Muslims and Muhammad is an Arab before being a prophet" (Kedourie, 1962: 35). Thus, this kind of national policy as the de-civilizing process throughout more than seven decades of attempting to build a nation in Iraq as a civilizing process caused total failure of the state, which also led to genocide.

Thus, the retreat of the state institutions and the lack of legitimacy were the principal causes of failed nation building in Iraq. There is another related point concerning an imagined Iraq, which was that the Sunni Arab Ottoman officers were elected to have a vital role in the future of the country. This vital role has been described by Simon Reeva, who explains, "the officers, educated in Istanbul and returning to Iraq to play a leading role in the new state, were first and foremost Sunni pan-Arab nationalists, dreaming of the unity of an Arab nation encompassing the Fertile Crescent and Arabia" (Simon and Tejirian, 2004: vi). Thus, the imagined Iraq was created through the annexation of three different vilayats (provinces) under the leadership of a foreign Sunni Arab king with the assistance of Sunni Arab Ottoman officers. These and other characteristics pushed the Sunni Arabs together to defend their domination over the country, along with a desire to Arabize the land and its people and to suppress those considered as outcasts in order to remove or integrate them. This situation affected the legitimacy of the state, and with the emergence of the BP, this legitimacy decreased to its lowest levels.

Hence, an imagined Iraq was created under the leadership of an elite who was carrying a prejudiced ethno-pan-Arab-nationalist ideology, along with Sunni Arab religious sectarianism. This ideology paved the way for the emergence of Baath ideology and the new stage in the interrelationship with non-Arabs in Iraq. However, the only characteristic of this interrelationship with the Kurds was the genocidal relationship in its different forms, from Arabization to the highest degree of destruction.

A further issue is: What was the role of religion in its interdependence with state organizations? If we look back to the Iraqi elite's attitude and its media from the early days of this state, religion always has been the second face of Arab ideology and has been widely adapted in the process of Arabization. Hence, for the reasons previously mentioned, the religious and sectarian background of King Faisal provides one answer to the question concerning the influence of religion, due to its interdependence with state organizations. Moreover, this background of the king had a vital impression on building a specific relationship inside the Sunni community and for the future identity of Iraq.

Here, the influence of King Faisal spread across the Sunni Arab community, and it had a fateful impact on the political elite in Iraq. In addition to these kinds of dimensions, although the BP was a secular party in its rule of the state and its administration, it claimed religious dimensions, and they could be mobilized internally and externally for various purposes. These dimensions have been indicated in the interpretation of the Baathi's ideology and the vision of Michel Aflaq. These dimensions quickly emerged and were mobilized against Iran, as a Shia Muslim state, during the war with Iran. In this regard, the Baath Party in its genocidal campaigns against the Kurds also adopted the religious language and its symbols. In order to gain support for the military campaigns under the guise of religion, several Islamic names and symbols, including the term Al-Anfal and the names of some other military offensives, were adopted in the war against the Kurdish areas. This included a broad change in the names of schools, streets, towns, complexes, and cities from Kurdish to Arab/Islamic names, and this was considered to be part of the Baath's religious policy against the Kurdish existence. Thus, relying on sectarianism and religious mobilization as a weapon, this led to a lack of interdependency and interrelationships between components, which could be a major reason for the decline of the state's legitimacy.

The fourth point concerns the civilizing process, and the questions that beg to be answered: Was pan-Arab nationalism, including the Baathist ideology, a consequence of the nation building that led to the process of genocide? The emergence of the BP as a new era in the history of Iraq meant the continuation

of the policy of Arabization against non-Arabs, and Arabizing the state institutions more aggressively. Hence, all the mechanisms of the civilizing process were turned into the de-civilizing process. The signs of the de-civilizing
process in Iraq under the leadership of the BP have been addressed often,
particularly the BP's relationship with the non-Arabs in Iraq. The main Baath
ideology, displayed from different angles, includes Arab-centrism as the first
ethnic structure of self-image. This self-image appeared in the phrase "one
Arab Nation with an eternal message." This motto is defined in the institution
of the ABSP as "the Arab Resurrection Socialist Party, a popular national
revolutionary movement striving for Arab unity, freedom and socialism"
(ABSP, 2015). Thus, the motto refers to the Arabs as a nation—one that owns
an eternal message. According to this motto and all the articles of the Baath's
institution, there is no autonomous space for non-Arabs in Iraq, as it is the
eastern gate of the Arab homeland.

Michel Aflaq and other Baathists have interpreted the eternal message in
different ways and forms. This idea was derived from German philosophy,
as he argues, "Aflaq historical studies and his acquaintanceship with 19th-
century German philosophy are brought out in the program's section on the
'immortal mission' of the Arab Nation" (Torrey, 1969: 447). Thus, there
is more than an indication that Baathizm developed its theory based on the
ideas of the Nazis. Additionally, the Baath ideas were influenced by German
philosophy, as he confirms that "although 'Aflaq and Bitar emphasize the
'uniqueness' of the Baathist message, the influence of Western concepts is
found throughout their teaching" (Torrey, 1969: 447).

Moreover, various issues of culture in the Baath's ideology, particularly
regarding the non-Arabs, cannot be ignored. The only social tie for Baathists
is Arabism—not citizenship—and the "others" had to be assimilated, as the
BP's constitution states: "It will guarantee their fusion in the crucible of a
single nationality" (ABSP, 2015: 198). However, the Kurdish struggle in
the view of the Baathists was always the subject of concern; therefore, they
utilized a different kind of discourse to tame the Kurds. In this regard, Aflaq
has described the Kurdish existence in Iraq as a racial minority, as he stated,
"Let us take a racial minority such as the Kurds, for example; we ask why the
Kurds or some of them are afraid from the Arabism 'Uruba'" (Aflaq, 1987:
181). Aflaq here is simplifying the interrelations between Kurds and Arabs
and wonders why the Kurds are afraid of Arab culture. This contradiction is
an expression of the dominant mentality, as they denied the recognition of
the rights of the Kurds to have an autonomous existence. Thus, Aflaq here
is admitting that fear is the essence of the interrelationship between both
groups, which, as has been explained, is a genocidal relationship.

Thus, as the process of genocide was a product of pan-Arab nationalism,
including the Baath's ideology, the process of Iraqi nation building facilitated

suitable ground for the emergence and spread of pan-Arab-centric national-ism in Iraq, which led to the process of genocide. It has been explained that Iraq as a country was created under specific circumstances under the surveil-lance of colonialism. The interrelationship between all components of the new state of Iraq was unbalanced from the beginning. This is because the authority had been handed to a minority with a specific desire to build an ethnocentric nation state. The dilemma in this case is that the state with all its authority, including military weapons, was handed to a minority, and the rest of the population was marginalized. Thus, from the beginning, we face a serious problem of legitimacy, and the oppressed groups would not surrender to the dominant authority, particularly when the policy of the new state was based on an ethno-sectarian-centric ideology. In this regard, James Dobbin argues, "Nation building in Iraq faces a number of challenges. Iraq has no tradition of pluralist democracy; politics has always been about authoritarian rule and the settlement of disputes by force" (Dobbins, 2003: 169). Here, in the case of Iraq, as long as the state was losing its emotional control, the dominant authority instead of developing the interdependency chains and building a balanced interrelationship developed a policy of ethno-sectarian-centrism and moved toward authoritarian rule.

In addition, regarding the process of nation building in Iraq, when we study the power relations, we realize a kind of a convulsive psychological attitude was dominating Iraqi Arab politicians. This means that the delega-tors of the power resources still did not leave their tribal attitude and culture in the form of ethno-Arab centrism. Therefore, the creation of an imaginary internal or external enemy always existed. This is because as long as the state is weak, the ideas of the imagined enemy become stronger and start to appear in nationalist discourses. Thus, after four or five decades, particularly after the Second World War and the establishment of Israel, Iraq, and the other Arab countries drowned in their ultranationalist ideology, as Barrett points out, "By 1939, Syria and Iraq had become hot-beds of Arab nationalist sentiment" (Barrett, 2015: 31). This is an indication that the ultranationalist ideology accompanied the crisis of the country, and the apparent cause was the internal or external enemy. Therefore, in the case of Iraq, after the mili-tary coup in 1958, which caused the overthrow of the Iraqi monarchy, during the following five years two armed militias were established outside of the national army. The first one belonged to the Iraqi Communist Party, which was close to the new authority of the military coup of Abdulkarim Qasim, but it was annulled after one year. The second militia, which belonged to the Baathists and was established in 1963, is the "Nationalist guards," and it is these "guards" who perpetrated several atrocities. These consequences could be considered a dynamic result of the state failing, which led to the genocide process.

Thus, regarding these atrocities, for the establishment of ethno-Arab-centrism in an attempt to Arabize Iraq, a series of procedures were applied to begin the process of genocide. In this context, the BP began adopting violence in order to execute its philosophy. This stage could be thought of as the beginning of the de-civilizing process. Therefore, when the Baathists assumed power in 1963, they launched the first task of violence by creating paramilitaries in order to fortify their authority. In this regard, for the first time, they utilized the legitimacy of the state institutions to build a national guard under Article 2 of the Act. From this situation, it can be understood that the Baathists were bent on imposing their philosophy by force, as they propagated it openly through their rhetoric and discussions. Henceforth, it is clear that the national guard was an instrument used to further Arabization in the form of protecting the Arab presence in Iraq.

Principally, the Baath Party, through its discourse from 1968 and onwards, was working in two directions: on the one hand, to transform the state into a protectorate of its dominance and, on the other hand, to militarize society through the creation of enemies in order for it to find its feet and strengthen its population. This kind of discourse succeeded in transforming the state into an instrument against non-Arabs in Iraq, and the non-Arabs were targeted as enemies of the Arabs and the state of Iraq.

Thus, it can be concluded that the Baath's struggle to build a nation paved the way to legitimizing the extermination of its enemies through different methods. This attempt initiated the establishment of several armed militias outside the national army, and their names are mentioned in chapter 2. This phenomenon caused several atrocities and the process of genocide, which has been carefully analyzed in the documentary parts of chapters 3 and 4, as well as the experimental work presented in chapters 5 and 6.

In more detail, the framework of the Baath's ideology of the national ideal is mentioned throughout the policy of "the country is part of the Arab home-land," which is contained in the Iraqi constitution. The BP developed the idea of disintegration through the pathway of purging the country from all those who did not have loyalty to the regime's policies. These policies were depen-dent on some pillars that the BP was pursuing. One of these pillars, which has been studied carefully, is violence. Thus, dependent on "the development of the monopoly over the means of violence by a centralized state authority" (Fletcher, 1997: 32), the BP was struggling to seize power, regardless of the method used to access that power, in order to implement its policy. Therefore, the BP, during its rule from 1968 to 1988, established several armed militias outside the national army. These armed militias were used everywhere as a hammer against the Iraqi people, and particularly against the Kurds.

The Baathists, in order to subjugate the Kurds, pursued a prejudiced policy. One of these methods was the partition of the Kurds (Divide and Rule);

therefore, the process of domination was ongoing during the BP's power until April 2003. The first Kurdish group that was targeted from the first day of taking power was the Faili Kurds: "Under the Ba'ath regime, they (Faili Kurds) were specifically targeted and killed, or stripped of their Iraqi citizenship, under suspicion of having links with Iran, traditionally considered an enemy by Iraq" (Taneja, 2011: 8).

The Faili Kurds were dramatically targeted for ethnic, sectarian, political, and economic reasons. The majority of them were expelled twice, in 1970 and 1980, to Iran, and many of them, particularly Faili youths, disappeared. Coinciding with what happened to the Faili Kurds, all Kurdish components, including all cities, towns, and villages, were under the threat of the Baath's authority. During the 1970s and 1980s, thousands of Kurdish rural areas were evacuated and destroyed. The population was transferred to south Iraq or was gathered in forced complexes. This kind of transformation is confined to the framework of the civilizing offensive. The civilizing offensive is a theoretical framework that has been derived from Elias's work. Ryan Powell describes it as follows:

> The term "civilizing offensive" is used by Dutch sociologists and historians to refer to a wide range of phenomena, from nineteenth-century bourgeois efforts to elevate the lower classes out of their poverty and ignorance and convince them of the importance of domesticity and a life of virtue, to the oppression of popular culture in early modern times and, in general, "the attack on behavior presumed to be immoral or un civilized." (Powell, 2013)

Additionally, if any community is forced to move to a different place other than their own, under any kind of circumstances, it is considered a civilizing offensive. This kind of deportation was imposed upon the Kurdish rural population who were forced into complexes. In this regard, Human Rights Watch argues: "In their propaganda, the Iraqis commonly refer to them as 'modern villages'; in this report, they are generally described as 'complexes'" (HRW/Middle East, 1995: 22). In addition to this displacement of the Kurds, the Kurdish suffering from the Iraqi authority's policies continued. Several other atrocities against the Kurds were committed, including due to the impact of the Iran-Iraq war between 1979 and 1980; the second mass deportation of the Faili Kurds in 1980 and the gendercide of Barzani men in 1983, which have been explained in chapter 3, along with the case of Halabja and the Anfal Campaigns.

In chapter 4, the Anfal Campaigns have been approached independently. The name Anfal Campaign carries in its essence several dimensions, and these have been explained. Terminologically, this name was chosen very carefully and was very effective. Primarily, the BP, based on figurational sociology, has always been inspired by its past. It connects the past with the present, mobilizing its religious and cultural dimensions as instruments for the purpose of its ideology. Anfal Campaigns in its meaning send a dangerous message to the targeted people that they are considered nonbelievers, traitors, and spoils of war. This assisted with the task of dehumanization and humiliation. Along with the religious interpretation, the term Anfal, and the mood of the Iran-Iraq war and its direct effect on the Kurds have been explained. Thus, there is no causal relationship between the Anfal Campaigns and the Iran-Iraq war, as Stuart Adam Miller in his book *Iraqi Kurds: Road to genocide* has argued: "After eight years of fighting, the Iran-Iraq War had finally come to a halt, but the fight continued for the Kurds" (Miller, 2014: 60).

Furthermore, the initial stages of the Anfal Campaigns involved legalization, identification, a census of the population, the advent of prohibited areas, and the issue of Resolution Nr. 4008 of the campaigns. The second stage was the concentration camps. Thus, according to Raul Hilberg, the deportation (or seizure) and concentration camps are the fourth stage of the procedure in order to annihilate an out-group. Additionally, the whole process was conducted with the intention of the de-Kurdification of the region, which is how it appears in the General Assembly Resolution 961: "Genocide is 'a denial of the right of existence of entire human groups'" (Smith, 2013: 228). In addition to examining the stages of the Anfal Campaigns, the phases of their implementation throughout eight campaigns, and how those people were annihilated, have been analyzed, along with the characteristics of the Anfal Campaigns.

The interviews with different participants made up of Kurds and Arabs from different ideological backgrounds, including both innocent people and those who were active in opposition within an organization, as well as active members of the BP, show that there are some differences in perspective. The Kurdish participants unanimously accused the Iraqi authority of prejudice and bias toward the Kurds. They stated that there was national racism on both an official and a popular level, including the personation of the policy of Arabization.

Thus, the process of nation building or the process of a nation under the name of the Iraqi nation, according to J. Kadar, has completely failed. Primarily, what King Faisal and his followers strived to achieve continued when the Arab nationalist movement in Iraq, in the form of its fascist and Nazi organization, modeled on 1930s Germany, emerged. As a result, the non-Arabs' reaction led to greater affiliation with their language and ethnic culture. This kind of state policy compelled the Kurds to hate the country that had become a big prison for them and full of suffering. The trouble is that around thirty years after the Anfal Campaigns, some Arab participants, who were also Baathists, still do not believe that these atrocities occurred, and their view is totally in contradiction to what the Kurdish, and some Arab, participants believe.

Additionally, it is imperative to examine the root causes of genocide in the Iraqi domain by concentrating on the spirit of the age, as well as the ideology of the BP. The first indication of the formation of the state is its formation and then its deformation. The interviewees emphasized how the Arab ultra nationalist behavior with the Kurds was standard prior to the BP's rule. It changed after the BP came to power, as the coup was ineffective in destabilizing the nation state process, and the non-Arabs were the ultimate victims of the power struggle. However, despite the failure of the state institutions, Arab-centrism was the focal point of Arab ideology, which could be termed an elitist ideology.

Apart from the issue of Mosul, which was fundamentally Arabized, the arrival of the BP instigated the obliteration of any hopes of nonviolent existence between the Iraqi elements, mainly the Kurdish population. The participants described their recollections of the BP, and these have confirmed that the conduct of the BP toward non-Arab groups was similar to the racism recorded in German schools, as largely discriminatory practices were perpetrated on the non-Arabs. These processes consisted of redrafting the history books and the philosophy of union and power, in addition to the role played by religion and the failure of the state institutions. Apart from that, the alteration of citizens' nationality in an attempt to Arabize the remainder of the Kurdish population was also undertaken.

The dynamics through which the BP increased its power, and the steps it took to establish its totalitarian authority, are an integral component of Baath ideology. There existed various visions regarding Iraq as a nation; entire members were cohesive about the BP, except those known as die-hard members. One of the significant points concerning the Iraqi authority during the tenure of the BP is its alarming legitimacy. Under such conditions, chiefly when an administration seizes power through an overthrow, it dismantles the society as well as its organizations. This kind of disability led to a lack of interdependency chains and interrelationships, which benefits totalitarian rule and unilateral domination. In contrast, according to one of the participants, in democratic circumstances, genocide is not a requirement and is not considered an option. It can be reasonably assumed that the Kurds were an easy target for the BP, since it was vulnerable to its own ultra nationalist ideology, and it spread propaganda against the Kurds to further its agenda. Therefore, due to these reasons, the grounds for genocide became possible for the Baathists.

This book has revealed key insights into the essence of the civilizing process, including through research into the BP literature, and relating this and the theory to the causes of the genocide process, in particular in Iraq. In terms of its contribution to theory, the essence of the civilizing process is the main issue addressed in this book. In the framework of the philosophy of the civilizing process, the knowledge of the process of nation building in Iraq, and the position of the existing components within the state have been analyzed. In addition, the state institution's relationship with its components, on the one hand, and the levels of the interrelationship between the components themselves, on the other, and the interdependency chains, are necessary to discover the roots of genocide. In this regard, the investigation of the governmental documents and historical literature, as well as the interviews, has revealed that Iraq has been built on the denial of the existence of the Kurds, who have been considered outsiders or an out-group. This denial, along with the rise of the BP's power, has been systematic.

Arabo-centrism in the framework of ethnocentrism is a new concept in Arabic literature. Yet, it has been revealed in several ways that a section of Sunni Arabs in Iraq, from the establishment of the state until the end, emphasized the denial of the rights of the Kurds through the policy of Arabization. The roots of the policy of Arabization include religious motivations, either by utilizing religion or by believing in it as part of their history, and as a way of assisting the march toward the "Arab renaissance."

In the process of building a pure Arab nation state, along with excluding non-Arabs from power, the state authority insisted on denial and marginalization. The evolving of traditional Arabo-centrism against the Kurds, and the pursuit of the policy of Arabization throughout the various decades of successive powers, especially during the period of Ba'athist rule, was an indication that the state of Iraq, under the BP's authority, would commit massacres against the Kurdish people. Thus, it has been revealed that genocide in Iraq was not an accident, and it was not a consequence of the Iran-Iraq war. Hence, this means that the hegemony of the unilateral state, of the political authority and the influential official and traditional Arabo-centrism led to the genocide.

Moreover, all of this history of denial and prejudice toward the rights of an important component of the state should have been enough for the international community to intervene to prevent these massacres against the Kurds.

During the formation of the Kingdom of Iraq, a form of Sunnism with its aim of Uruba (Arabism), as a hidden element between the Ottomans and the new kingdom, suddenly dominated the political, economic, and social reality in Iraq. This element has been revealed through the investigation of the integration of hundreds of Arab Sunni officers in the Iraqi army, and as a consequence, an army mentality dominated the powers in Iraq. This kind of domination over the power in the country led to various military coups during the successive governments—from the period of the kingdom until the BP seized power through a bloody military coup. This issue is one of the most important dimensions in genocidal relations.

The unilateral attempts of nation building in Iraq as part of the civilizing and de-civilizing process have also been investigated, and through this approach to the civilizing process, the violent behavior that occurred in Iraq has been analyzed. Thus, as has been illustrated in chapter 1, according to Elias's interpretation, we are facing a changing society, and violence, as a phenomenon, has its causes and circumstances. Therefore, the violent behavior was an element used to impose one style of nation building on Iraq through state genocide because the interrelations between the state and the Kurds had been built on the policy of assimilation and Arabization.

REFERENCES

ABSP. The constitution of the Baath Arab socialist party. *BASP National Leadership*, August 31, 2015. https://bit.ly/2Wq2hYJ.

Barrett, Roby C. The collapse of Iraq and Syria: The end of the colonial construct in the greater Levant. Joint Special Operations University MacDill AFB United States, 2015.

Dobbins, James F. America's role in nation-building: From Germany to Iraq. *Survival* 45, no. 4 (2003): 87–110.

Elias, Norbert. *The civilising process: Sociogenetic and psychogenetic investigations*. London: Wiley Blackwell, 2000.

Fletcher, J. *Violence and civilization: An introduction to the work of Norbert Elias*. Cambridge, MA: Polity, 1997.

Hanna, Batatu. The old social classes and the revolutionary movements of Iraq: A study of Iraq's old landed and commercial classes and its communists, bathists and free officers (1978).

HRW/Middle East Watch. Iraq's crime of genocide: The Anfal Campaign against the kurds. *Human Rights Watch*, 1995.

Kedourie, Sylvia. *Arab nationalism: An anthology*. Berkeley, CA: University of California Press, 1962.

Kinloch, Graham Charles, and Raj P. Mohan, eds. *Genocide: Approaches, case studies, and responses*. New York: Algora Publishing, 2005.

Michel, Aflaq. *Fi Sabeel al-Baath*. Beirut, al-Tali'a Publisher (V.1), 1987.

Miller, Judith, and Susan Meiselas. Iraq accused: A case of genocide. *New York Times Magazine* 3 (2014): 12–17.

Podeh, Elie. *The quest for hegemony in the Arab world: The struggle over the Baghdad Pact* (vol. 52). Leiden, MA: Brill, 1995.

Powell, Ryan. The theoretical concept of the "civilising offensive" (Beschavings offensief): Notes on its origins and uses. *Human Figurations*, July 1, 2013. Accessed December 28, 2020. http://bit.ly/2TADaD7.

Simon, Reeva Spector, Eleanor H. Tejirian, Gary Sick, and Gary G. Sick. *The creation of Iraq, 1914–1921*. New York: Columbia University Press, 2004.

Smith, Rhona K. M. *Textbook on international human rights*. New York: Oxford University Press, 2013.

Taneja, Preti. *Iraq's minorities: Participation in public life*. UK: Minority Rights Group International, 2011.

Torrey, Gordon H. The Ba'th: Ideology and practice. *Middle East Journal* 23, no. 4 (1969): 445–470.

Index

About the Author

Ibrahim Sadiq was born and raised in Erbil. He is a Kurdish sociopolitical researcher and writer. He has obtained a PhD in Sociology from Brunel University London (2016). He is a research associate at the Research Department of iReMMO, Paris, and is a visiting research fellow at CTPSR, Coventry University, based on a postdoctorate from Soran University, in the Iraqi Kurdistan Region, where he is also a sociology lecturer since 2013. He is a fellow of the Norbert Elias foundation in Amsterdam and is on the editorial board of the *Journal of Middle Eastern Research* (JMER). He also served as a member of the International Advisory Board of the International Panel on Exiting Violence (IPEV) from 2016 to 2018. Currently, he is working on the politics, ethnic conflict, and state-building process in the Middle East, including the Arab Gulf.

He is specialized in the study of genocide and nation building, and his main research interests include genocide and human rights, state and nation building, religion and political Islam, culture and identity, and terrorism and extremism.